THE VIOLENCE

- What is the 'remainder' that linguistic theory leaves out of its account of language?
- What can linguistics learn from poetry?
- How are all speakers violently constrained in their use of language?

Any theory of language constructs its 'object' by separating 'relevant' from 'irrelevant' phenomena, and excluding the latter. As a result, all theories of language leave out a 'remainder'. This remainder is the odd, untidy, awkward, creative part of how all of us use language all the time. It is the essence of poetry, and of metaphor. Jean-Jacques Lecercle argues that, although the remainder can never be completely formalized, it must be fully recognized by any true account of language. He thus here attempts, for the first time, a theory of the remainder – which has to face the hard contradiction: who speaks? Language, or the speaker? And this leads to a discussion of the *violence of language*: the fact that all speakers are 'violently' constrained in their use of language by quite particular social and psychological realities.

Jean-Jacques Lecercle is Professor of English at the University of Paris, Nanterre.

THE VIOLENCE
OF LANGUAGE

Jean-Jacques Lecercle

London and New York

First published 1990
by Routledge
11 New Fetter Lane, London EC4P 4EE

Simultaneously published in the USA and Canada
by Routledge
a division of Routledge, Chapman and Hall, Inc.
29 West 35th Street, New York, NY 10001

©1990 Jean-Jacques Lecercle

Typeset by J&L Composition Ltd, Filey, North Yorkshire
Printed and bound in Great Britain by
Biddles Ltd, Guildford and King's Lynn

British Library Cataloguing in Publication Data
Lecercle, Jean-Jacques,
The violence of language.
1. Linguistics. Theories
I. Title
410.1

Library of Congress Cataloging in Publication Data
Lecercle, Jean-Jacques.
The violence of language / J. J. Lecercle.
p.   cm.
Includes bibliographical references.
1. Pragmatics. 2. Linguistics. 3. Languages – Philosophy.
I. Title.
P99.4.P72L4 1990
410-dc20   90–8343

ISBN 0 415 03430 2 (hbk)
ISBN 0 415 03431 0 (pbk)

CONTENTS

v

CONTENTS

ACKNOWLEDGEMENTS

I would like to thank the following publishers for permission to include copyright material: Faber & Faber and Harcourt, Brace, Jovanovich for a quotation from T. S. Eliot's *Collected Poems, 1909–1962*; the *Times Literary Supplement* for Alison Neville's poem, 'The Masochist's Week', which appeared in *TLS*, 4 September 1987; Oxford University Press for 'Slate', by David Gascoyne, in his *Collected Poems* (OUP, 1965); Éditions Ramsay, for the first stanza of G. Perec's poem, 'Ulcérations', which appeared in *La Bibliothèque Oulipienne*, vol. 1.

I would also like to thank the students in my *maitrise* seminar for their patience.

Lastly, I wish to thank Andrew Benjamin and Alex Callinicos for their comments on the manuscript. The mistakes that remain are, of course, mine.

INTRODUCTION

After all, there is nothing like dead silence. My one dread was lest our conversation of last night should resume us where it had left us off.

(Samuel Beckett)

A LETTER

In the winter of 1862, Edward Lear wrote the following letter to his friend Evelyn Baring:

> Thrippsy pillivinx,
>   Inky tinky pobblebockle abblesquabs? – Flosky! beebul trimble flosky! – Okul scratchabibblebongibo, viddle squibble tog-a-tog, ferrymoyassity amsky flamsky ramsky damsky crocklefether squiggs.
> Flinkywisty pomm,
Slushypipp.[1]

This appears to be a hoax. There is nothing to wonder about, nothing to understand. The only surprise is that a man of 50 should still indulge in such childish games. We are faced with an instance of pure linguistic chaos, where language has utterly dissolved.

THE LINGUIST TRIES

But has it? A linguist will not confess impotence that easily. Since this is undoubtedly a text, complete with punctuation, capital letters, and signature, the linguist can approach it with his analytical tools. Accordingly, I shall attempt to conduct a linguistic analysis at the four levels that make up the structure of Saussure's *langue*: phonology, morphology, syntax, and semantics. To our surprise, we shall discover that the results are far from null.

One of the most striking features of the text is that, although I fail to understand what it means, I know that it is written in English, at least as far as sounds are concerned. Not only can I read it, but if I pronounced it in my best Maurice Chevalier accent, I would be conscious of letting the text down. There is such a thing as the Englishness of English phonemes. It takes centuries of cultural development, and a lifetime of pronouncing 'th' sounds, to utter 'crocklefether squiggs' in the correct fashion. In other words, our text abides by the rules of English phonotactics. All the words are coined, but all are possible. 'Abblesquabs' happens not to be an English word as yet; it fully deserves to become one. However, there are limits to this analysis – some of the sequences, although they can easily be pronounced, do not seem to form presentable English words, either because they are too long, or because they sound alien, or both. 'Scratchabibblebongibo' is a good instance of this.

I have crossed into morphology. Here, too, the analysis will yield results. The text is indeed composed of words, the first and essential condition for it to be analysed at this level. No doubt the fact that it is a *written* text, with spacing and punctuation, is the determining factor – our analysis is provided for us ready-made. But again, there is more to it than this. For instance, we find at least one complex word, with its hyphens: 'tog-a-tog'. Some of the words or their subparts actually have independent existence in English: 'ferry-', 'scratch-', 'inky'. Some of the subparts look strangely like common suffixes for adjectives or adverbs, as in 'tink-y' or 'flosk-y'. There are limits to this attempt. Not all words are analysable into morphemes, and an analysis that fails to account for the whole of the corpus is of little help.

Perhaps syntax will fare better. The coherent use of punctuation isolates the basic units of syntax: sentences. There are four sentences in this letter. Furthermore, I can ascribe a sentence type to each of them. The first is interrogative. The second and third are exclamative and probably elliptic (for the second, this is a certainty). The fourth is declarative. We may add that the third sentence, grammatically speaking, is an expansion of the second. Again, there are obvious limits to this analysis. With the partial exception of the third sentence, I am unable to give the internal structure of the sentences, in the guise of an immediate constituent analysis or Chomskyan trees.

So far, in spite of the limits of his analysis, the linguist has not remained speechless. Tentative forms seem to emerge out of chaos. No such thing happens, however, when we reach the level of semantics. Here, the linguist's impotence is complete. I am not even sure that the existing English words that I have recognized in the text have their usual meaning. But perhaps I am looking for the wrong meaning. If I forget denotation and look for connotation, in other words if I go from semantics to pragmatics, the text as a whole acquires meaning. This is a letter, with a signature, and the usual conventional phrases for addressing one's correspondent and taking leave of him. The only uncertainty is that I do not quite know whether 'Flinkywisty pomm' means 'Best wishes' or 'Go to Hell!'. Perhaps I may even go a little further. We all have to write official letters, full of the expression of high-flown but empty feeling, of conventional phrases and clichés. We congratulate a colleague on his promotion, we thank a distant acquaintance for a lovely dinner party. Hollowness, sometimes even hypocrisy, are the order of the day. Would not a semantically empty text, keeping only the pragmatic skeleton of a conventional letter, aptly embody the artificiality of such letters? Lear's meaning, if my hypothesis is correct, is satirical, but it is a full meaning, and our task is completed. There is no longer a limit to this analysis, as the contradiction between the global meaning of the text and the lack of meaning of its constituent parts is essential to the satirical effect.

THE LINGUIST FAILS

This global interpretation, however, is not entirely satisfactory. It reaches its climax in the discovery of pragmatic meaning, calculated through Grician implicature, and therefore postulates an intention of meaning in the author.[2] The reasoning that leads to this conclusion might develop along the following lines: the letter is unintelligible; however, it is presented as a letter, and the author was neither mad nor drunk when he wrote it; *ergo*, such blatant flouting of the conventions of letter-writing (the main feature of which is that a letter is supposed to make sense) must be deliberate; the simplest explanation is that the author meant to be satirical. Clearly, such reasoning requires a certain amount of background knowledge. Had I been the recipient of the letter and Lear's friend, I could have made such a calculus. Grice's maxims are meant to apply to conversations, i.e. situations where the speakers are either actually present or available for response. But I am not Evelyn Baring, and my calculus leads to shaky conclusions drawn from a single, and variously ambiguous, fact – that the text is meaningless. It would appear that the semantic emptiness of the text, its nonsensicality, ruins any attempt at discovering coherence.

Yet this lack of meaning that obtrudes is no dissolution of language. Beneath the apparent chaos, another, irregular and partial, attempt at order emerges. The failure of the linguist's account makes the sheer resilience of language even more apparent. The lack of meaning turns out to be a kind of excess; the floundering of any global meaning, or global structure, reveals a proliferation of partial meanings and structures, as if the failure of analysis did not put a stop to it but on the contrary prevented it from stopping.

If we go back to the sounds the text is made up of, we must note that the language of possible English words is not the only imaginary language present in the text. E. Souriau makes a distinction between three types of imaginary languages: *charabia*, or the coinage of possible words, *baragouin*, or the imitation of foreign words, and *lanternois*, in which the speaker's obsessional phonemes compulsively proliferate.[3] *Charabia*, we have seen, characterizes the text. But we can also find instances of *baragouin* in 'amsky flamsky, ramsky' which sounds like Russian (rather, like the conventional idea an English speaker has of Russian). And we find Lear's own *lanternois* in a word like 'scratchabibblebongibo', which reminds us of that celebrated Learesque character, the Yonghy-Bonghy-Bò. The sound shape of the letter is determined by the compulsive repetition of a few phonemes, like the consonant cluster 'bl'. The passage from *charabia* to *lanternois* is important. It means that, if no sense is conveyed by the text, a certain quantity of affect is.

By letting our linguistic attention wander, and our eyes roam freely over the text, we note incipient series and partial structures. The text has rhythm. This is due to the presence of prosodic units (like the pleasant symmetry of 'flínkywísty pómm'), to the incremental repetition of 'inky tinky' or 'Flosky! beebul trimble flosky!', or the series of *baragouin* words – a series that, if we cancel the pseudo-Russian endings, reveals English words: 'am', 'flam(e)', 'ram', 'dam(e)'. Meaning creeps into the text.

It is not the coherent meaning of information and communication but the partially (in)coherent meaning of emotions. Lear's compulsive phonemes, like the *fort/da* of Freud's grandson, are loaded with affect.[4] The quality of this affect is not hard to discover. We can imagine that Lear, who was a homosexual, became emotionally involved with his handsome young friend, and that, for various reasons (age may have been a factor: Baring was thirty years younger than him), he found it impossible to make his feelings explicit. They may not even have been entirely conscious, in which case Lear would have been in the situation of Judge Schreber, whose paranoid symptoms, if we adopt Freud's theory, were the surface translation of an unsayable unconscious sentence, 'I, a man, love him, a man.'[5] It is striking that the other letters to Baring that have been published are full of visual and verbal nonsense.[6] One is reminded of Freud's claim that coined words are made up of fragments of private sexual words. We understand the function of the textual excess that both ruins the coherence of the text and compensates for its lack. The excess of *délire* is the expression of the excess of desire.

THE REMAINDER

In the passage from the linguist's attempt to his failure a crucial change has occurred. In the linguist's account, the text was the *expression* of a meaning, which the original speaker *intended* to *communicate*. There appear to have been problems with the *instrument*, but the recourse to implicatures set them right – the text turned out to contain a conscious and deliberate implicit content. From this point of view, there is no doubt that 'the speaker speaks his language' that he is fully in control.

But the linguist's failure has cast a doubt on the speaker's mastery. Emotional meaning may not be conscious; its transmission is hardly deliberate. We are closer to obsession or possession. Seen in this light, the text is the paradoxical utterance of the unutterable – it is written in Lear's *Ursprache*.[7] Language is no longer a mere instrument, it seems to have acquired a life of its own. Language speaks, it follows its own rhythm, its own partial coherence, it proliferates in apparent, and sometimes violent, chaos.

It is the object of this book to treat Lear's letter as an emblem of language. I shall treat every utterance as an instance of Freudian compromise between the two extreme positions: 'I speak language' and 'language speaks'. As a consequence, I shall no longer treat language as a scientific object, susceptible of a comprehensive description in terms of system and coherence, i.e. in terms of Saussure's concept of *langue*. There is another side to language, one that escapes the linguist's attention, not because of his temporary failure or failings, but for necessary reasons. This dark side emerges in nonsensical and poetic texts, in the illuminations of mystics and the delirium of logophiliacs or mental patients. It is the object of this book to provide a description and a theory of this other side. For reasons that will soon be clear, I have called it 'the remainder'.

NOTES

1 Quoted in V. Noakes, *Edward Lear*, London, Fontana, 1979, p. 197 (first published 1968).
2 H. P. Grice, 'Logic and conversation', in P. Cole and J. L. Morgan (eds), *Syntax and Semantics 3: Speech Acts*, New York, Academic Press, 1975.
3 E. Souriau, 'Sur l'esthétique des mots et des langages forgés', *Revue d'esthétique*, 18, Paris, 1965, pp. 19–48.
4 See Freud's 'Beyond the Pleasure Principle', in S. Freud, *On Metapsychology: the Theory of Psychoanalysis*, The Pelican Freud Library, vol. 11, Harmondsworth, Penguin, 1984.
5 See Freud's analysis of Schreber, in S. Freud, *Case Histories II*, The Pelican Freud Library, vol. 9, Harmondsworth, Penguin, 1977.
6 E. Lear, *Selected Letters*, Oxford, Clarendon Press, 1988, pp. 191–5.
7 This is the name Schreber gave to the language spoken by his voices.

1

LINGUISTICS AND THE REMAINDER

Something about scouring, or scourging, he can't remember, and a teacher he once had who called his lectures 'lechers'.

(Robert Coover)

A CORPUS OF TEXTS

In Somerset Maugham's *Cakes and Ale*, a Cockney landlady utters the following sentence:

'I'm not so young as I used to was!'[1]

Were I to read this in a student's paper, I would underline the last word in petulant red. As a reader of fiction, I enjoy the sentence. But what exactly is it that I enjoy in it? The elaborate narrative setting that enables Maugham to commit a solecism and yet get away with it? The picturesque character of the Cockney dialect at the turn of the century, and the accuracy with which the author of *Liza of Lambeth*, that notorious slum novel, adds a touch of local colour to enliven his otherwise blameless style? A first answer would be: a little of both.

It is clear that the sentence blatantly breaks an elementary rule of English syntax. Infinitives, not finite verbs, are immediately preceded by 'to', and the phrase 'used to' is therefore followed by an infinitive. The error is all the more enjoyable as it is obvious, a kind of syntactic malapropism. The Cockney landlady allows herself to do what I, as an 'educated' speaker of English, do not dare to do, and I secretly envy her. (Perhaps there is such a thing as sinning against language, which produces the same mixture of guilt and excitement as the common and garden variety.) Like all errors,

7

this solecism requires an explanation – and it is easy enough to find one. You cannot expect an illiterate Cockney to speak like a young gentleman just down from Oxford, or, to put it more kindly, they speak different dialects, of unequal value in social intercourse but of equal interest to the student of language.

This explanation is superficial. It fails to stress what the dialects have in common: the narrator – and the reader – treat it as an *English* sentence, which is entirely meaningful for all English speakers. It may not be acceptable, but it is understandable. It receives an unambiguous semantic interpretation, and is therefore less problematic than many 'correct' complex sentences. No doubt this is due to the fact that its deviance from the equivalent correct sentence is minimal: merely a matter of substituting 'be' for 'was'. But this raises interesting questions. The flouting of a major syntactic constraint has turned out to be semantically negligible. If we operate within the Chomskyan tradition of the centrality of syntax, this is not what we would expect. For this rogue 'was' does breach a principle of syntax: there is only one verb inflected for tense per clause.

We can try to save the rules of syntax, and avoid the dilemma, by treating the so-called error as rational. The sentence is in fact perfectly acceptable if we consider that here, although not in our usage, 'used to' is not a verb but an adverb. If this is the case, the as-clause has only one finite verb, 'was', and everything is as it should be. We could explain the passage in terms of a portmanteau phrase, produced by the coalescence of 'as I used to be' and 'as I was'. Or we could treat it diachronically, as a case of conversion, where 'used to' has changed, or is changing, its grammatical category. In fact, there is every reason for it to do so. First, from the semantic point of view, suffixes of tense are close to time adverbials, all the more so if the verb that bears them has intrinsic temporal meaning (here the equivalent of a habitual aspect). The sentence might indeed have taken the form:

'I'm not so young as I was before (in the old days).'

It is irrelevant to point out that here the adverbial is placed after, not before, the verb, for it is easy to produce a sentence where it is in the right position:

'He wasn't so chirpy as he generally (usually) was.'

No doubt the existence of 'usually', an adverb phonetically similar to 'used to', has encouraged the conversion.

Second, there are grammatical reasons for the conversion. 'Used to' is a strange verb, which has always caused a good deal of uncertainty in grammarians. It is usually claimed that it behaves like a marginal modal auxiliary, although its meaning is aspectual. Mostly, however, it is a defective verb: there is no present form, even if there is no reason why we should not wish to refer to a habitual event in the present – indeed, this is one of the values of the present tense in English. Because of this semantic gap, the past suffix has tended to be neutralized, and is no longer always perceived as such, or even pronounced: /juːzd tə/ has become /juːstə/. The uncertain state of the suffix appears in the hesitation over the negative form: 'he used not to smoke' is now often replaced, so my grammar assures me,[2] by 'he didn't use to smoke' (where the non-existent root form, on which the present tense is based, makes its appearance) and even, more significantly, by 'he didn't used to smoke', in which the same 'error' as the Cockney landlady's seems to have crept into the language. But all is well in the end, since my grammar adds that this last form is 'non-standard'. It also notes, nevertheless, that this uncertainty over the negative form of 'used to' impels the more astute speaker to avoid the problem by saying 'he never used to smoke'. But we can understand how a marginal and defective verb, which causes problems for everyday users of the language, is likely to turn into a more manageable word, an adverb.

This makes our explanation of this 'error' in terms of a different dialect untenable. This is no longer a case of another dialect of English having its own rationality and its own structures – one is reminded of Labov's description of the English of Harlem, and of his analysis of 'done' (in 'he done gone') as an auxiliary verb.[3] Not only do we understand the sentence, we also understand the rationality of the so-called error. This is a case of language changing. Today's terrorist leader is tomorrow's prime minister: today's solecism is tomorrow's rule of grammar. What we first perceived as corruption has turned out to be conversion, a perfectly respectable device, one that every language resorts to. The difference with the more frequent case of nominalization is that this adverbialization is not available to the speaker as an expressive choice, but belongs to the diachronic movement of the system. Who can tell that this sentence will not be standard usage in three generations? Language, in its evolution, is opening up a new path. Maugham, who has the ear of the stylist, is one of the first to venture on it – he is certainly not the last. The reader, even if he perceives the sentence as a malapropism or a Cockneyism, enjoys the experiment. Is not its *memorable* character the most striking aspect of this sentence? We enjoy sinning against language because the violence we impose on its structure is what makes it alive. A solecism is not so much an aberration from the rules of universal grammar or the grammar of English as a (potential) anticipation of the evolution of structures, the 'universality' of which is strictly historical.

The following sentence belongs to a rare but entirely respectable syntactic pattern - there is no question of solecism:

A poem is a poem is a poem.

The pattern seems to have two uses: emphatic tautology, as is the case here, or equality, as in the sentence 'Crime is money is consideration', where the copula is the linguistic equivalent of the mathematical 'equals' sign.

The sentence is acceptable, and yet it violates a fundamental rule of English (and perhaps universal) syntax, embodied in the first rule of phrase structure in most syntactic theories: S → NP VP. This means not only that a sentence is composed of a subject noun phrase and a predicate verb phrase, but also that it is made up of *only one* of each. No one would think of writing down a rule of the type: S → NP VP VP. Yet this seems to be the structure of our sentence.

Of course, there are traditional ways out of this quandary. The obvious one is to distinguish the surface from the deep structure of the sentence. Surface structures can have the wildest appearance, but their very wildness can be shown to derive from perfectly simple and regular deep structures. For our sentence, the most obvious candidate is coordination. If the structure 'NP VP VP' is bizarre, the surface structure 'NP VP and VP' is normal. I can paraphrase my second sentence as 'Crime is money; it is also consideration.' The trouble is that this will not do the trick. Our pattern is *not* a case of coordination. The coordinated sentence is tame and banal, the equality sentence emphatic and striking. This appears even more strongly if I try to paraphrase the first sentence, for 'a poem is a poem and a poem' is totally meaningless. There is no comma or pause between the two verb phrases – it is a case of emphatic repetition, not coordination.

The detour through coordination, however, is perhaps not entirely useless. Coordinated tautologies can produce interesting expressive effects. Suppose I say: 'My butcher is a butcher. And he is also a butcher. But most of all, he is a butcher.' The utterance is no longer meaningless. It cries out for the computation of pragmatic meaning through Grician implicature. Am I not saying that my butcher lives exclusively for his profession, that a more dedicated butcher is hard to find, that for him butchering is no mere avocation but a true calling? Or perhaps the slightest hint of disapproval creeps in, and I am insinuating that he is as narrow- as he is single-minded (if you allow me this German turn of phrase). In other words, if my utterance violates certain pragmatic rules (embodied in the grammar of 'and', 'also', 'but', and 'most of all'), this is only an instance of exploitation that, far from disallowing any interpretation, creates new meaning.

I would like to suggest that the original sentence is an instance of the flouting of syntactic rules, exactly as the utterance about my butcher exploits pragmatic maxims. What we have in 'A poem is a poem is a poem' is not elliptic coordination (a new pattern within the existing rules) but the flouting of basic syntax, a case not of rule-governed, but of rule-breaking creativity – perhaps a case of playing what the French linguist L. J. Calvet calls rhythmic competence against syntactic competence.[4] Indeed, the simple (and grammatical) tautology 'A poem is a poem' is a strange mixture of symmetry and asymmetry. For the naive user of the language, who follows his ear or his eye, the sentence is symmetrical: (a poem) is (a poem). But for the linguist it is deeply asymmetrical. The pattern NP VP, i.e. NP V NP, whether V is a transitive verb or the copula, has the following structure: (NP (V NP)), not a ternary but a binary, subject-predicate, structure. In the case of our sentence, it would have the form: (a poem (is a poem)). If we add another occurrence of 'is a poem', we only expand the illicit symmetry of our naive reading:

(A poem) [is (a poem)] [is a poem].

This is in the best style of the incremental repetition of Border Ballads. 'Incremental' is the right word, for the repetition threatens to become compulsive. There is no reason why we should not add another VP, as we do in 'a rose is a rose is a rose is a rose'. Only boredom will set a limit to the free-wheeling of this illegal syntax.

The allusion to Border Ballads is relevant in another sense. Repetition not only introduces symmetry – it creates rhythm, a tripodic rhythm (as one talks of the dipodic rhythm of ballads and nursery rhymes): 'A poém is a poém is a poém.' The sentence sounds like a jingle or a slogan and this is undoubtedly one of the sources of its force. Emphatic or playful repetition plays an important part in what Jakobson calls the 'emotive' function of language:[5]: 'No, no, no!', or 'his heart was going pit-a-pat, pit-a-pat'.

With this sentence, therefore, there is no question of an explanation in terms of solecism, local colour, or social dialect. Nor is it a case of language change or individual creative use. Since the pattern is conventional and productive (I can substitute any noun for 'poem'), it is a case of the English language tampering with its own rules. We might be tempted to interpret this in terms of modularity. There is a prosodic module in the grammar, which cooperates (and in this case interferes) with other modules to produce this apparently erratic pattern. The trouble is that in doing this we would stretch the concept of a module to breaking point. The crux is in the passage from 'cooperation' to 'interference'. For the cooperation of modules, rather like the combination of different forces, produces sentences within the acceptable structures favoured by the grammar of a language. Ours is a case of interference: the prosodic component plays with and against the phrase structure. From which we may draw two conclusions: (1) there is a phrase structure component (our pattern, by forgetting that there is one, reminds us of its existence, exactly as jokes about language locally and temporarily break syntactic rules); (2) structures can be violated for expressive purposes without producing gibberish or even solecism. In other words, the syntax of English, if I dare personify this august abstraction, is perfectly capable of treating its own rules as defeasible. Contrary to expectations, rules of syntax can be breached, like pragmatic rules and maxims.

The first sentence of *Pride and Prejudice* is, quite deservedly, one of the most memorable in the English language:

It is a truth universally acknowledged, that a single man in possession of a good fortune, must be in want of a wife.[6]

This first sentence is also the first paragraph, a motto inscribed on the threshold of the novel, a gnomic pronouncement which, in customary anticipation, spells out the moral of the tale and announces its ending. Except that, as a maxim, there is something wrong with it. At first, the reader is hardly aware of this; it requires the distance of a second reading to realize that there is a certain excess in the sentence, and this is where uneasiness is felt. Certainly, 'a truth universally acknowledged' is not an instance of pleonasm.

Not all truths are acknowledged, fewer still universally acknowledged. Yet we may wonder at this insistence, in the first sentence of a novel, not of a treatise of logic or epistemology. This sense of excess is confirmed by the occurrence of the modal 'must', which, it seems, we must take in its acceptation of 'it is logically necessary that'. One might think that the presence of 'must' reinforces the meaning of the first words of the sentence. But such is not the case: this 'must' is not even redundant, it is counterproductive. A sentence reading 'It is a truth universally acknowledged that a man ... *is* in want of a wife' would have the required meaning of logical necessity. Substituting 'must' for 'is' implies falling into verbal excess, thus inducing the reader to reinterpret 'must' according to another of its values, obligation. The single man in possession of a good fortune is under the moral obligation of marrying a wife.

The reader is now even more uneasy, for this reinterpretation of 'must' makes the sentence incoherent on two counts. It is hard to see how a universally acknowledged truth can be an obligation, and the sentence is grammatically dubious. Most English modal auxiliaries possess two sharply distinguished meanings, often called epistemic and radical – in the case of 'must', logical necessity on the one hand, obligation on the other. In certain contexts, the modal is ambiguous, as in 'your brother must work very hard'. But not here. For there are constraints on the use of radical modals. They do not normally combine with aspects, because they behave like performatives, and perform speech acts (obligation, for instance), which cannot have retroactive effect. You cannot impose an obligation in the past, and 'your brother must have worked very hard' can only have the epistemic meaning of 'it is highly probable that ...'. Furthermore, radical modals, for the same reason, do not normally combine with stative verbs and adjectives. In this, they behave like imperatives, which also exert force on the addressee. You cannot say to your child: 'You are being tall', 'Be tall!', or 'You must be tall' (with the 'must' of obligation). But 'being in want of a wife', as opposed to 'looking for a wife', is a stative phrase. Therefore, the modal *cannot* be interpreted as radical. You cannot say 'Be in want of a wife!' to an eligible bachelor, as opposed to 'start looking for a wife!'

If a meaning of obligation has, as I claim, crept into the sentence, it can only have done so at the cost of distorting the syntax of the language. The author's strategy is to ambiguize an unambiguous modal. Such things are of course possible, if, as we have seen, syntactic rules are defeasible. 'You must be tall!', as the bobby said to his small son who would not eat his porridge. Here the context takes over and changes the meaning of 'be' to that of 'become'.

I am faced with a paradox. On the one hand, a certain redundancy, a certain excess in the sentence (methinks the lady doth assert too much), impels me to interpret the modal as radical. On the other hand, the grammar of English compels me to understand it in its epistemic sense. There is an easy way out: perhaps my intuition is mistaken, and the ambiguity of the modal lies in my imagination. Alas, the second paragraph of the novel confirms it:

> However little known the feelings or views of such a man may be on his first entering a neighbourhood, this truth is so well fixed in the minds of the surrounding families, that he is considered as the rightful property of some or other of their daughters.
>
> 'My dear Mr Bennet,' said his lady to him one day, 'have you heard that Netherfield Park is let at last?'

'This truth is so well fixed in the minds of the surrounding families': it appears that the proposition is no longer *universally* acknowledged (except within the 3-mile radius of a Jane Austen setting, and even then only in the minds of young ladies of marriageable age), and that the name 'truth' that is given to it must be understood ironically. Far from being a universal truth, the proposition expresses Mrs Bennet's desire that such should be the case – not an analytic necessity, but the hope of a foolish woman. In this context of course, the radical sense of 'must' is much more adequate; nor is the logical or linguistic incoherence that it introduces a liability – it is rather an asset, for it gives us a hint of the illogical workings of Mrs Bennet's mind, of which countless comic instances will be given later in the novel. What appeared to be a solecism is the extraordinarily skilful handling of language by an ironic author. It would seem that the rules of grammar have been formulated for the express purpose of allowing authors, i.e. creative users of language, to interfere with them.

In Chapter 3 of *Alice's Adventures in Wonderland*, the Mouse is telling Alice and the assembled animals a story, the driest he knows, in order to help them get dry more quickly (they have all been swimming in the pool of tears). This gives rise to the following dialogue:

'Edwin and Morcar, the earls of Mercia and Northumbria, declared for him; and even Stigand, the patriotic archbishop of Canterbury, found it advisable –'
'Found *what*?' said the Duck.
'Found *it*,' the Mouse replied rather crossly: 'of course you know what "it" means.'
'I know what "it" means well enough, when *I* find a thing' said the Duck: 'it's generally a frog or a worm. The question is, what did the archbishop find?'
The Mouse did not notice this question but hurriedly went on ...[7]

The Mouse, who has all the characteristics of a bad pedagogue (the 'story' he is telling is actually borrowed from a history textbook), behaves like a schoolteacher who feels cornered by an awkward question from a bright but troublesome pupil. He tries verbal aggression ('of course you know what "it" means') and evasion ('but hurriedly went on'), which is an admission of defeat. It is left for us to try and answer the Duck's question. At first sight, this Duck holds a naive conception of meaning as reference. The meaning of 'it' is the object it designates, and since the word can refer to all sorts of different objects, it must be a kind of deictic, a linguistic accompaniment to an ostensive definition. Not only is the Duck a referentialist, he is also – this is where the cat is let out of Carroll's satirical bag – a gross materialist, since the referent of 'it' is 'generally' edible, 'a frog or a worm'. Naturally, it is easy to dismiss this theory of meaning as inadequate. But if we shift the meaning of the question slightly, we may realize that, although the Duck is not aware of the work of Frege, he is raising a non-trivial linguistic question. For behind the referentialist statement, there is a question about the linguistic status of the word 'it', in terms not of deixis but of anaphora. What the Duck is actually asking is, what is 'it' anaphoric of? And his answer is that generally, but apparently not in this case, it is anaphoric of a noun or noun phrase. This is the question the Mouse avoids, because he has no answer.
The dialogue is an excellent example of Carroll's acute linguistic intuitions. By making the Duck ask the question, he shows that he is aware of the problem, which is more than we can say of contemporary grammarians. The following is quoted from a Victorian grammar: 'When the infinitive is the nominative to a verb, it is often placed after it, and "it is" or some similar form introduces

15

the sentence.'[8] The example given is: 'It is impossible to make people understand their ignorance.' In the case when the infinitive is an object, and not a subject (a 'nominative'), it is analysed as 'an apposition to "it"', as in 'he thought it best to go.'

It is easy to understand the failings of this analysis. It acknowledges the fact that this 'it' is not strictly anaphoric, but (a) it restricts its occurrence to infinitives (whereas this 'it' also occurs with that-clauses: 'it is surprising that he should have come'), and (b) it gives two different explanations ('insertion' and 'apposition') according to the syntactic function of the infinitive, whereas nowadays we would like to think that there is only one grammatical phenomenon, susceptible of a single analysis. Besides, the analysis that merely inserts 'it is' (this is not even a constituent in sentence structure) is obviously an ad hoc attempt at concealing an unresolved difficulty.

For the modern linguist, this 'it' is interesting because it is one of the (fairly rare) cases where he has the impression that undeniable progress has been achieved in grammatical explanation. Indeed, in the 1965 version of the Chomskyan model,[9] we find a theory of extraposition that accounts for this in a unified and rather elegant manner. The Duck's 'it' has no (external) referent because it is the cataphor of an extraposed infinitive clause, which the Mouse spells out when he hurriedly goes on: '... found it advisable *to go with Edward Atheling to meet William*' (my italics). The constituent structure of the sentence can be simplified thus:

$$s_1 \text{ [Stigand } _{VP} \text{ [found } s_2 \text{ [for Stigand to go]}_{s_2} \text{ advisable]}_{VP}]_{s_1}$$

The embedded infinitive clause is extraposed after 'advisable', its original place being marked by 'it':

$$s_1 \text{ [Stigand } _{VP} \text{ [found } s_2 \text{ [it] } s_2 \text{ advisable } s_2 \text{ [for Stigand to go] } s_2] \text{ } _{VP}] s_1$$

The subject of the infinitive, being the same as the subject of the main clause, is then erased, yielding the surface sentence (again, the process is simplified). This type of 'it' is not an anaphor or a cataphor in the strict sense. It is purely contextual; it refers not to a noun but to a clause. More importantly, it is the end product of a movement transformation, the trace (the term is not used in the technical sense it has acquired in more modern versions of Chomsky's doctrine) of a grammatical operation.

This appears to be progress. The theory gives a single account of all extraposed 'it's, in the case of infinitives, gerunds, and that-clauses. When the extraposed clause is the nominalized subject of the sentence, the necessity of it-insertion (of the so-called trace being realized in the surface structure) becomes apparent, for the extraposed clause leaves the position of sentential subject empty, which is impossible with a finite verb. Thus,

s_1 [VP [is surprising s_2 [that he should have come] s_2] VP] s_1

is not acceptable, hence apparition of 'it':

s_1 [NP [it] NP VP [is surprising s_2 [that he should have come] s_2] VP] s_1.

There are few counter-examples to this analysis, essentially verb phrases with an 'it' but without extraposition, as in 'I must see to it that he does his homework.' Yet this appearance of progress may be questioned for two reasons. First, the model itself has been deeply modified, and a more recent exponent of 'modular grammar' confesses that extraposition is one of the fields that have been abandoned by the new theory as less fruitful than others.[10] Second, the analysis, elegant as it is, introduces a difference between the 'it' of extraposition and the truly anaphoric 'it', a separation that is deeply unsatisfactory for the linguist, who is lumbered with two 'it's instead of one. The shadow of an ad hoc explanation rises again. Consequently, there have been attempts to show that the 'it' of extraposition is in fact anaphoric in the normal sense. Thus, Bolinger explains the unacceptability of the first of the following sentences and the acceptability of the second in terms of anaphor:

[3] I understand it that the election hurt them.
[4] I can understand it that the election hurt them.

'In [4], *can understand* is obviously a comment on a prior topic.'[11] Anaphoric 'it' refers to this prior topic. This would account, incidentally, for the fact that in this case our 'extraposed' 'it' appears although there is no need to extrapose the that-clause, since, as an object clause, it is already placed at the end of the sentence.

The moral of our text is that, even where progress in linguistics seems most obvious, it is never assured. As in philosophy, but not as in the exact sciences, development often means going back to an older theory and re-exploring its potentialities. It is a story of gain and loss, rather than linear progress and cumulative increase of knowledge. The Victorian account of our word, although it raised the ghost of an expletive 'it' (so called because it explained nothing), at least did not suggest that it had a different function from the rest of its tribe. The transformational analysis accounts for the apparition of 'it' in nominalized clauses, and postulates the grammatical unity of these clauses, whether or not they have an 'it'. But what it gains on this count, it loses by isolating the extraposed 'it' from its anaphoric counterpart. Bolinger's analysis goes back to the grammatical unity of 'it'. In so doing, it loses the insights into syntactic structure that the theory of extraposition affords. Chomsky's modular grammar appears to follow the same path. Opening up new ground for our grammatical understanding, it leaves older fields fallow. (It would be rewarding, from this point of view, to chart the evolution of the account of passive sentences in the various stages of Chomsky's theory.) This, of course, raises questions not only as to the progress but as to the truth of linguistic analysis. What exactly do we mean when we claim that a linguistic analysis is correct?

INFERENCES FROM THE CORPUS

The starting point of a theory is generally the choice of the relevant metaphors, in terms of which it will proceed to construct its object. The four sentences or texts I have analysed were chosen because they suggest a metaphor different from the customary one: the rules of grammar are to be thought of not in terms of the laws of the physical universe, but rather in terms of frontiers. This metaphor will turn out to be complex, but we can begin with the simple image of a map. The linguist is a cartographer; the language he studies is the territory he maps out. And as the only truly exact map would be on a scale of 1:1, and would cover the territory it represented, the only comprehensive grammar of a language would be coextensive with the language itself. This makes grammar a frustrating business. If the metaphor is apt, there are parts of language that no grammar can ever reach. The fond hope of the linguist who thought that a finite number of rules would cover the essential features of a language has turned out to be mistaken. We have all shared the early optimism of the Chomskyan model, which projected onto syntax the advances made in phonology. If a score of phonemes can account for the sounds produced by English speakers, a score of phrase-structure rules, plus a limited number of transformations, ought to account for the syntax of the language. One must recognize a certain single-minded grandeur in Chomsky, who has never abandoned this programme, but has merely transferred it to the constraints and principles of universal grammar and the 'switches' or parameters that adapt them to a given language. The view of grammar I am suggesting runs contrary to this. The adequacy of a grammar strictly depends on its size. Not that the rules mentioned in a thin school grammar are 'false'. They just leave out more, under the uncharitable name of exceptions, exactly as a cardboard outline of Great Britain, meant to help schoolchildren reproduce the shape of the fatherland in their exercise-books, leaves out more than a set of Ordnance Survey maps. The details that any grammatical map necessarily leaves out constitute what I call the remainder. The four texts I have commented on are thus instances of the remainder. The Cockney landlady's utterance shows that when we have crossed a frontier we do not find ourselves in outer darkness, but still reside in language, in fact even in the same language. But cartographers know that their task is endless, that every peace treaty threatens to force them to start their work anew. The second sentence also shows that the difference between the two sides of the frontier is not as marked as we would expect. In the middle of the map, there remain uncharted territories, like the blank space that so fascinated Conrad in the middle of the map of Africa. And, as any reader of *Heart of Darkness* knows, once we have reached the heart of the unknown, what we find there conforms, if at all, to different rules. The beginning of *Pride and Prejudice* shows that a creative author can modify a frontier. She is not only an explorer, venturing into orderless and unruly territory, but also a ruler, who may decide to annex, temporarily or permanently, a small portion of the remainder. And Lewis Carroll was shown to be a practising cartographer, pointing his finger at a fuzzy spot on the existing map and expressing a need for clearer boundaries in that sector, a disputed piece of no grammar's land.

Scientific linguists do not use the map-making metaphor. Their favourite metaphors are borrowed from architecture. One *constructs* a *model* of the language faculty or the syntax of English: a THEORY is a BUILDING, as Lakoff and Johnson state.[12] Indeed, an important part of grammatical theory is the architecture of the various components. From the 1957 to the 1965 model, and then on to the Extended Standard Theory, to the Revised Extended Standard Theory, and finally to Modular Grammar, the complex history of Chomskyan linguistics can be told in terms of the

THE VIOLENCE OF LANGUAGE

architecture of the different models.[13] And the architectural metaphor also holds for his conception of constituent structure, in terms of a hierarchy of nodes and branchings-off, in other words in terms of tree structure. The narrative of progress in linguistics is basically a tale of the invention of ever more symmetrical, smoothly functional model architecture. Such a narrative is undergoing a deep crisis, of which the shift in metaphor I have illustrated is a symptom. Nor is it the only one to have met that fate. Linguistics is no exception. It is caught, like other sciences – like other scientific narratives – in what is now commonly called the 'post-modern crisis'.

If we follow the account of the crisis that Lyotard gives in his *La Condition postmoderne*[14] (similar strictures may be found, in the Anglo-Saxon world, in Feyerabend's epistemological anarchism), we shall concede that we no longer find it easy to believe in the City of God, the classless Utopia of Marxian socialism, or even the ordered cosmos of Galilean science. The main device that all these narratives use is the optimistic trope of progress: such optimism appears ever more questionable. But even if we provisionally concede all this, we must realize that the situation of linguistics among other varieties of scientific or non-scientific beliefs is both typical and untypical.

On the one hand, it does belong to the paradigm of science, which is alleged to be exhausted, and it shares all the characteristics of Galilean science. It has been argued that Saussure's founding concepts constitute an epistemological break, opening up the continent of language for science. His *langue* is constructed, through exclusion and separation, from the formless reality of language, by applying the typical scientific operations of abstraction and generalization. And we shall see that its conceptual structure can be reduced to a limited number of postulates characteristic of Galilean science. Even if linguists are modest in their claims; even if they conceive their task as descriptive rather than prescriptive; even if they restrict their pretensions to the lowest level of adequacy (one remembers Chomsky's distinction between observational, descriptive, and explanatory adequacy, and his claim to mere observational adequacy); even if they refuse to take themselves for profound philosophers or sound psychologists – they find themselves right in the centre of the paradigm of truth, the hubristic character of which the post-modernist critique denounces. There is no doubt that Saussure's *langue* purports to state the truth about language.

Like other sciences, linguistics fits within what Lyotard calls the pragmatics of scientific knowledge; like them, it is 'legitimized through its performativity'.[15] It does exert influence: it has provided and still, up to a point, provides a model for other sciences. It does wield power: there is a politics of linguistic funding, and a whole academic subject, complete with hierarchy and struggle for power, has cropped up. Not to mention the strictly political linguistic decisions that young nation states constantly have to take.[16] Lastly, and perhaps more importantly, linguistics has technological implications: to see a computer scientist, concerned with machine translation or speech-synthesizing or speech-interpreting machines, rediscovering the basic concepts of structural linguistics is a touching sight. In fact, if the 'post-modern revolution' is an effect of the explosion of communication techniques, it is only natural that linguistics should be plunged in the midst of it.

But this is where the picture is reversed, where the situation of linguistics appears to be untypical. If post-modernism is a shift from truth to fiction or narrative, from the world of experience to language, from the great narratives of truth to local language-games, in short if post-modernism is characterized by a *linguistic turn*, the science of linguistics cannot be in the same predicament as other sciences, precisely because it takes language-games as its objects. Linguistics is with us to stay, even if it must abandon its claims to be a 'science', even if pragmatics may supplant syntax as the core of the subject. This untypical situation is in fact no news. It has always been known under the name of 'the paradox of metalanguage'. A science of language is unavoidably reflexive, for it cannot easily distinguish between theoretical language and object language. A rule of grammar is written in the same language as the sentences it governs; it is itself a fit example for another rule of grammar, perhaps even for itself. There is no escaping not only the words of a natural language but also its syntax. The distance various linguists seek to take in complicated technical notations (like, for instance, Katz's 'semantic markerese') always proves to be illusory, and the so-called metalanguage a degenerate form of English. Linguistic metalanguage there cannot be. And yet there must be – for what else does a linguist do, if not talk about language from a point of view sufficiently distant to allow what he hopes will be an objective account? The philosopher's usual escape from this quandary is into some kind of *caracteristica universalis*, some artificial language, rid of the ambiguities and difficulties of natural language. The linguist, at least, does not share this dream. He knows there is no way out, no 'outside language', where problems are all the more easily solved as they no longer arise (this lets ordinary language, in its opaque dimness, persist in betraying its users, among whom not least the philosopher who constructs his artificial language). He thus attempts to draw a line, within language, between object language and instrument language (i.e. a set of concepts). The necessary failure of this operation appears in the jargonophasia with which linguists are chronically afflicted: a large proportion of a linguist's working life is spent in translating X's conceptual terms into the language of Y. But this is also where the linguist becomes a poet – in the inventiveness of his jargon. The French grammarians Damourette and Pichon have remained famous for this, and the Saussure of the anagram notebooks is also a poet in this sense: anagram, paragram, anaphony ... – only the silence of failure put an end to this terminological proliferation. In this paradoxical necessity and failure of metalanguage, I see another proof of the constitutive existence of the remainder. One cannot escape one's mother tongue, the tongue of one's memories and desires, a tongue that possesses the subject to such an extent that it is always in excess of any attempt to force it within the boundaries of rules.

Scientific grammar does not ignore the existence of a remainder. It denies it – which is a kind of avowal – under the collective name of 'exceptions'. In this sense, exceptions are temporary aberrations, not yet accounted for by the present state of the theory or the present collocation of modules, but certainly accountable for by the construction of module $n + 1$, or a novel combination of principles and constraints already formulated within the existing modules. Thus, in an older version of the generative-transformational model, Lakoff constructed a whole machinery of sub-rules and meta-rules to account for exceptions, Take, for instance, what Bolinger treats as counter-examples to the 'it' of extraposition, sentences of the type 'I hate it for John to do that'. According to the theory of extraposition, no 'it' should appear here.[17] Its presence is therefore explained as an optional exception to an obligatory rule blocking it-insertion in certain contexts. The lexical item 'hate' is ascribed a feature stating that in this case the rule indifferently does or does not apply (for an optional exception means that the rule *may* apply: 'I hate for John to do that' is an acceptable sentence). In Lakoff's text, exceptions are dealt with through partial rules or lexical features. They are thus reduced, and the general force of the rules is preserved. This tactic is still used in modular grammar, where a principle called RES(NIC), or the residue of the Nominative Island Constraint, was for a while adopted to cover the data the constraint in question failed to explain. In turn, this residue rule (obviously, not a very satisfactory name) was renamed the Empty Category Principle, when it was possible to restate it not as an ad hoc rule, but as a general principle.[18] The movement of the theory is the same in both cases. It is the scientific movement of generalization and abstraction: a certain rule is shown not to account for all the data, and thus leaves a residue; an exception rule is then produced in order to reduce this residue (a scientific grammar aims at being comprehensive as much as coherent); eventually, this exception rule is discarded in favour of a more general rule, at a higher level of abstraction, that covers the whole field, at which final stage no residue is left. The acknowledgement of exceptions is thus merely a confession of temporary failure.

The texts I have discussed are, I believe, not susceptible to this type of treatment. They are instances, not of a temporary residue, but of a constitutive remainder. I cannot conceive of a more general syntactic principle that would cover both the SN SV structure and the SN SV SV of 'a poem is a poem is a poem'. Banfield's attempt to introduce a component E within the phrase structure rules to account for 'exclamatives' ('your money or your life!') only renders the whole system of rules incoherent.[19] An 'exception' does not make the rule it breaks invalid, it just breaches the frontier it marks. And beyond the frontier, as we have seen, there lies not the outer darkness of linguistic chaos, but language that is still intelligible. Perhaps one could use a new metaphor for the frontier: not a map but a barrier, the barrier of censorship. In that case, the remainder would be the linguistic equivalent of the Freudian unconscious, excluded or repressed by the rules of grammar, but trying to return in jokes, slips of the tongue, solecisms, and poetry. Rather than postulating an innate faculty of language, containing syntactic rules that often turn out to be deciduous, we might adopt Freud's more light-hearted description of language learning, in his *Jokes and their Relation to the Unconscious*. First, there is a free playing with language, an experimenting with words without regard to their meanings. Little by little this enjoyable activity becomes forbidden, as 'the power of criticism' and logical thinking come to dominate. Presumably, the environment plays a crucial role in this evolution, the outcome of which is that the repressed tendency to absurdity only reappears in the displaced form of jokes, and even then, Freud adds, a little alcohol is often necessary to free the adult from the constraints of grammar.[20] The Cockney landlady's solecism is one instance of this re-emergence of what Freud calls 'liberating nonsense'. With it, the constraint appears as what it is, an imposition. A frontier is mapped, and the so-called chaos outside is made to return within English.

The concept of frontier has become more complex. I have borrowed it from the work of Judith Milner.[21] Frontiers in her sense have two characteristics. First, they are negative. The set of grammatical utterances is not constructed positively according to underlying or innate principles; it is simply the set of utterances that are not rejected as ungrammatical. Of course, one could argue that the native speaker's judgement of acceptability or unacceptability relies on his possession of a language faculty that contains the said principles. But to me this reversal, which treats grammatical sentences as a negative picture, strongly suggests that they form an arbitrary collection, not an ordered set. This is why the grammarian's task has to be descriptive. Why on earth is there a frontier in this place? Because language is as it is, 'parce que c'est comme ça': there lies the reality of language. The second characteristic is that frontiers are linked to the speaker's experience of his own body. Judith Milner argues that language is not the only field in which two sets of elements are articulated by a disjunction, each set *not* being the other. This is also how man experiences his body as a sexual body, as the body of a man and *not* of a woman, or vice versa. Perhaps this relation between the experience of language and that of the ascription of sexual roles is at the bottom of the parallelism I have suggested between the remainder in language and the Freudian unconscious. Perhaps there is a 'remainder-work' as there is a joke-work, which is in turn similar to dream-work. This is why frontiers are at the same time so entrenched and compulsively breached (even if in jokes, according to Milner, they are only temporarily forgotten). Nor are they immovable: expressive attempts not only manage to cross them but also, perhaps, to move them. A coined word that becomes established in a language is a good instance of this. It is, of course, much more difficult to prove that the same process exists in the case of syntax, and yet syntax itself does evolve. Crossing a linguistic frontier or attempting to displace it has roughly the same outcome as Freudian analysis, which brings the repressed material back to consciousness across the bar of censorship. This accounts for the strategic position of *délire*, as a form of literature that specializes in crossing frontiers, and that is also an expression of symptoms and attempts at bypassing censorship. In *délire*, the remainder is at work.

The analysis of my four texts inspires the following provisional conclusions. First, rules of grammar are comparable not to the laws of physics, but rather to frontiers. Second, what lies on the other side of the frontier is not beyond the pale. There is no chaos out there, only parts of language that are no longer or not yet acceptable – but that are potentially acceptable. Third, frontiers, although they are perceived by the speaker as forming a system, are in fact arbitrary and changeable; not the imposing architecture of the Greek orders, but rather the crumbling castles of Victor Hugo's Gothic sketches. Fourth, the paradox of metalanguage indicates that a remainder is not a sign of temporary shortcomings in the theory, but a constitutive part of language. Fifth, learning a language is not a Platonist cum Cartesian recalling and activating of innate ideas; rather, it is like exploring a territory. Sixth, the remainder is as constitutive as the Freudian unconscious; like it, it is always threatening to return in various guises. Lastly, we shall have to explore the parallelism between language and what Milner calls 'sexuation'. This is where language is material and becomes violent. This is also where it is social: what appears to the individual subject as a system, against the constraints of which his meaning attempts to break through, is a social and historical aggregate, a treasury of words, rules, and customs, not a piece of software in the mind-brain.

A constitutive remainder, nomadic frontiers, a view of language as governed by a tension between rules (language remains a rule-governed activity) and rule-breaking (this type of creativity is as important as rule-governed creativity): this does not look at all like a Chomskyan construction. In fact, it is hardly a building at all, rather a vision of Chaos. Does this mean that we have gone a century back, to a point before the foundation of linguistics as a science? At first sight, it appears that my conception of the remainder is incompatible with the celebrated dichotomies, and with the Saussurean axiom of the arbitrary character of signs. How can we think the remainder and still contrast *langue* and *parole*, synchrony and diachrony?

25

NON-SAUSSUREAN LINGUISTICS?

I shall argue that the remainder cannot be conceived within the Saussurean myth, but that many elements of its description are present in Saussure's text.

Linguists, like all primitive tribes, have their myths of origins and eponymous hero. The myth narrates the heroic construction of a scientific object, *langue*, out of the primitive chaos of philology – the famous Copernican revolution attributed to Saussure. It is a myth of exclusion, of the parting of the waters and the emergence of a new science. *Langue*, not *parole*, synchrony, not diachrony, value, not signification; everywhere the relevant phenomena are separated from the irrelevant. The result is a non-historical, non-social system, where communication is reduced to an abstract schema, and does not involve interaction between actual speaking subjects.

The myth does not ignore the existence of a remainder, which is located in the discarded elements of the dichotomies, in *parole*, diachrony, or signification. No doubt, my Freudian analogy between the remainder and the unconscious is already part of this myth. The excluded parts of language return within *langue*, but only in devious and indirect ways: in the anagrams – the very emblem of the remainder – that haunted the other Saussure, but that of course he never published. For even there the remainder is subject to exclusion.

But the remainder has another function – and here we recognize that the myth is a retroactive reading of the actual history of linguistics: its gradual disappearance, its reduction have provided a locus for the subsequent development of science. Because the exclusion of certain parts of language – syntax, for instance – raised obvious problems, or because of the natural urge to extend the field of science, linguistics has moved forward by occupying regions of the remainder, opening them up for scientific enquiry. The history of the subject is the history of its moves, into syntax, semantics, pragmatics, and discourse analysis. We understand the optimism of the Chomskyans: it is justified by this version of the history of the subject.

The problem with such a myth is that it is mythical. It grossly simplifies a rather complex situation. For a start, there are three Saussures, not two, each overshadowing his predecessor. The traditional but extraordinarily gifted philologist, whose masterpiece was the *Mémoire* on the vowel system of Indo-European (incidentally, the only Saussure known to his contemporaries), has been eclipsed by the revolutionary but rather staid social scientist, who was afflicted with a bad case of writer's block. He in turn was superseded by the forerunner of post-structuralist hermeneutics, who never wrote down his theories in coherent form. In Saussure, the Copernican revolution seems to have become compulsive, for it propelled him up the one-way street of the anagram notebooks. The historical character is, as usual, rather less straightforward than the founding hero.

Our own attitude to the sacred text – again, there is nothing unusual in this – is one of gross simplification. We no longer read the philological works that Saussure wrote – most of us no longer possess the specialized knowledge necessary to read the *Mémoire*, and there is even no easily accessible edition of the text. But we read the linguistic work that he never wrote, the *Cours de linguistique générale* (*CLG*).[22] As we are now aware, some of the best-known passages of that text were invented by the editors, without the least Saussurean pretext. Thus, the last sentence of the book, a worthy conclusion, printed in italics in case our attention should flag, '*La linguistique a pour unique et véritable objet la langue envisagée en elle-même et par elle-même*' ('The only true object of linguistics is *langue* considered in itself and for itself'), has no origin in the manuscript sources. The only justification for its insertion, as Roy Harris shows,[23] is that it echoes the first sentence of the text, and is thus an instance of textual *bouclé*, the stylistic device whereby the last line or page of a text repeats the first, with suitable variations. To compensate for this, we also read what he scribbled but never intented to publish, and discarded when his hypothesis was falsified: the anagram notebooks. Lastly, our reading of the *CLG* is notoriously selective. We concentrate on a few purple passages, which introduce the founding dichotomies: the Vulgate has been reduced to a catechism. This is the fate of most sacred texts. Saussure finds himself in the same position as those pre-Socratic philosophers whose ideas have survived only in textual fragments, more often than not quotations lifted from the works of their competitors, summaries borrowed from late compilers, or positions reconstructed from scant evidence.

Reading Saussure, to borrow the title of Harris's commentary, is therefore a necessity. The picture of language that a careful re-reading of the *CLG* gives is less clear-cut than the myth would have it. The text does not exclude the remainder from consideration in such a straightforward manner. Thus, a glance at the table of contents will show that as many pages are devoted to 'la linguistique diachronique' as to 'La linguistique synchronique'. The study of diachrony remains an integral and important part of general linguistics, even if, of course, it remains true that Saussure's new (and revolutionary) contribution is his focus on synchrony. Nor is the synchronic *'état de langue'* an ahistorical non-social object. The modern editor of the *CLG*, Tullio de Mauro, convincingly maintains that the arbitrary character of *langue* implies that it must be radically historical and radically social: the arbitrariness is that of determination not by rational norms or biologically innate tendencies, but by the social-historical conjuncture. (*CLG*, p. xiv). This is based on a new reading of Chapter 2 of Part One, which is entitled 'Immutabilité et mutabilité du signe'. As the title announces, it is a brilliant exercise in dialectics. The tension between variability and invariability, which are neatly balanced in the composition of the chapter, has impelled the editors to introduce one of their rare footnotes: 'one should not reproach F. de Saussure with being illogical or paradoxical because he ascribes two contradictory qualities to *langue* ...' (*CLG*, p. 109). But paradoxical is what he is being, even if the chain of reasoning that leads from invariability to variability is impressive. *Langue* is not the outcome of a contract. Unlike contractual institutions, language is not susceptible of sudden and general change. *Langue* is imposed on its users; it lies beyond their reach. This independence is due to the arbitrariness of signs. Where there is no rational norm, there is no reason to change anything. Or, rather, a change would mean only another arbitrary connection, with nothing to recommend it in preference to the connection it would replace. The result, of course, is that we feel no need to modify the language we inherit from our fathers. On the contrary, we feel attached to it, we are naturally linguistic conservatives, willing to militate for language conservancy and against linguistic decline (often to be found among those horrid people, the young). *Langue* is therefore the object of a tradition. But here a dialectic reversal occurs, for this introduces the time factor, which has another, contradictory effect – this is what worried the editors. If there is no reason to change *langue*, there is no other reason than our innate conservatism to keep it as it is. And the sad fact is that, like fish, *langue* does not keep. Time alters the signs, corrupts the signifier, the signified, or their relation. This alteration is of course also a mark of continuity: the sign that alters is the sign that persists. But in the long run, again because of the arbitrariness of signs, *langue* turns out to be radically impotent against change. Far from being an abstract system, neither social nor historical, Saussure's *langue* is *radically* social and historical, a situation registered in a diagram that the myth has forgotten:[24]

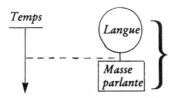

Arrows, dotted lines, brackets: the indications of the non-autonomy of *langue* are not lacking. But this is precisely what I wish to argue about the remainder. The mythical opposition between synchrony and diachrony is a mere windmill for subsequent linguistic Quixotes to tilt at. Saussure's *langue* has nothing to do with Chomsky's linguistic faculty. The same would apply to the conception of laws that we find in the *CLG*. Laws of language are certainly not physical laws, since *langue* is a social institution. They are not even laws in the legal sense, since they are not imperative and general. Synchronic laws, Saussure says, are general but not imperative, while diachronic laws are imperative but not general. Synchronic laws are not imperative not so much because individual speakers may break them – yet we have seen that the remainder is also about that – as because they are subject to change: 'in the language, there is nothing which guarantees the maintenance of regularity at any given point' (*CLG*, p. 131).[25] Diachronic laws are not general because diachronic events are accidental and particular in nature. *Langue* is the arbitrary and temporary offspring of historical accident. In other words, these laws are close to what I have described under the name of 'frontiers': their definition is negative, their exact shape arbitrary.

Of course, as we have seen, the myth does not claim that Saussure ignores the remainder. It describes the exclusion of the remainder, its restriction to *parole*, prior to its absorption into *langue*. *Parole* is the field where laws no longer apply and the freedom of the user is maximal. Thus, for Saussure, there is within *langue* such a thing as syntax (he even devoted his thesis to it) but it does not apply to sentences. There is a scale of freedom in the collocation of linguistic units. Rules constrain the combination of phonetic features into phonemes (There is no freedom for the speaker here); of phonemes into morphemes (the speaker's freedoms limited by the phonotactics of the language); of morphemes into words and phrases. This is the field of morphology and syntax, the latter being restricted to phrases or syntagmata. If my syntagma begins with 'in the nick ...' it must end with '... of time'. The archaic or technical meaning of 'nick' being lost on the ordinary speaker, this is a clear case where the meaning of the word is its contribution to the global meaning of the phrase. When we come to sentences, syntax ceases, and freedom is total. Of course, nobody would agree with this today. Sentences are definitely within the domain of linguistic rules, and for most grammatical theories the syntax of sentences is the core of *langue*. Rather than interpreting this evolution according to the customary narrative of progress, could we not sense in Sausure's position an intuition of the limits of linguistic rules, of their essentially defeasible character? The main interest of my concept of the remainder is that it stresses the fact that, when a rule of syntax is broken, the result is still linguistically coherent, i.e. intelligible, and that, therefore, the sentence is a locus for the exercise of the subject's expressive freedom.

Thus, the other Saussure, the demented seeker of anagrams, who was only too aware of the remainder, is already present in the *CLG* (we must remember that both undertakings were pursued at the same time). I suggest that we shall find elements for the description of the remainder if we look away from the founding dichotomies at other concepts and contrasts between concepts. For instance, Saussure makes much of analogy, as a system-building tendency. Yet, because analogy induces changes in the system, by reducing real or apparent anomalies, it is an ambiguous force. For it always threatens to become *false* analogy, like folk-etymology, to which the *CLG* devotes an often disregarded but nevertheless fascinating chapter. The tendency to prop up the system also contributes to is destabilization. And if analogy works for the system by analysing forms according to real or false regularities, the opposite tendency, anomaly, is also present. In the *CLG*, it is embodied in the syntactic operation of agglutination. Where analogy is paradigmatic, establishing regular series through analysis, agglutination operates syntheses according to physical proximity, thus producing monsters that analogy will then attempt to reduce. These operations are not rational in any way. Saussure shows that there is no choosing between objective analysis (the analysis of the linguist or etymologist, which is, etymologically, true) and subjective analysis (the analysis of the language user, which is more often than not false, as is apparent in folk-etymology). Both make the same contribution to linguistic change. I shall argue that this process of analogy-agglutination, or analysis-synthesis, pushed to excess, is characteristic of remainder-work.

One could argue that, although reality is more complicated than myth, the core of the Saussure myth, namely the arbitrary character of signs, remains valid. Since I shall try to show that the remainder has no respect for this arbitrariness, to that extent at least the concept falls outside the scope of Saussurean linguistics. But even here the situation is more complex than appears at first sight. Anagrams are not the only threat to the arbitrariness of signs: already in the *CLG*, the concept must be envisaged in a dialectical manner. Although folk-etymology is described by Saussure as pernicious and limited in scope (where analogy is general), its very existence, which the linguist duly acknowledges, raises questions about the absence of motivation in signs, for it is an attempt to motivate un- or de-motivated signs. From this point onwards, the question of the motivation of signs intrudes. Contrary to expectations, the *CLG* does not maintain that signs are utterly unmotivated. To be sure, it does not go to the other extreme, which would be to defend a Cratylist view of language. But it does introduce the notion of relative motivation (or relative arbitrariness): 'a sign may be relatively motivated' (*CLG*, p. 181). To use Saussure's own example, neither 'twenty' nor 'nine' is in the least motivated, but 'twenty-nine' is motivated relatively to its constituent words. Language is permeated by the tension between arbitrariness (to be found in simple lexical items) and motivation (to be found in complex signs, words, and phrases, but also in rules of grammar). There is a potential contradiction in the following proposition: 'the *system* of language is based on the *irrational* principle of the arbitrariness of signs' (*CLG*, p. 182; my emphasis) – a contradiction between the 'systematic', which is rational, and the 'arbitrary', which is irrational. But this is the predicament of *langue*, a 'naturally chaotic system' (*GLG*, p. 183), in which the human mind manages to introduce a little order – otherwise the complexity of the system would make it unmanageable – by using relative motivation, 'a partial correction' (*CLG*, p. 182).

This is a far cry from the positivist conception of *langue* as a system of rules. Saussure's *langue* is not a stable object, but a locus for the struggle of contradictory forces, a partial cosmos incessantly striving to emerge out of a fundamental chaos, with varying success in various idioms (Saussure suggests that we call 'lexicological' the idioms where arbitrariness dominates, 'grammatical' those where it gives way to motivation). This contradiction Saussure perceives, but at times attempts to deny. His treatment of folk-etymology as pathological is a good instance of this. He hesitates to recognize that the tensions between arbitrariness and motivation, between analogy and agglutination (rational analysis and irrational synthesis), function beyond the limits of the sign, or of grammar, that they also function, for instance at the independent level of the signifier. In other words, he is hesitant about the fact that they mark a *real* contradiction, a contradiction in language, so that what is excluded by *langue* always returns, not only in the proliferation of *parole*, not only in the multiplication of anagrams, but within *langue* itself, in the tensions that shape it. And this is precisely what the remainder is about, why it is constitutive. This is also why its operations deny not only the rules of grammar but also the arbitrariness of the sign, for they seem to motivate arbitrary signs by treating merely phonic similarities as linguistic relationships (this is what happens with puns). As we shall see, the principle of homophony lies at the core of the remainder.

Because the text is essentially apocryphal, because the views he defends are complex and contradictory, it is always easy to enrol Saussure on one's side of the argument. I think that the concept of the remainder, *in statu nascendi*, is not confined to the anagram notebooks, as is fairly clear, but is also implicitly contained in the contradictions that permeate the *CLG*. I also have a feeling that I am referring mainly to the part of Saussure's teaching that was most acceptable to his predecessors and contemporaries, and that the view of language I am defending would not have shocked Victorian linguists, who would have regarded the systematic aspect of *langue*, the focus on synchrony, and the arbitrariness of signs with deep suspicion. I am going back rather than forward. I may not be '*contre Saussure*',[26] but I seem to be '*avant Saussure*', i.e. against the so-called 'Saussurean revolution' in linguistics. That is a price I am willing to pay.

A FIRST APPROACH TO THE REMAINDER:
L'AMOUR DE LA LANGUE

So far, my attitude towards the concept of 'the remainder' has been tentative, indirect, and desultory. The time has come to treat it as a concept. This implies that we answer a preliminary question: within what kind of tradition can such a concept appear? I shall provide two answers to this question. The second will involve a reading of Deleuze and Guattari's *A Thousand Plateaux* and of their metaphor of the rhizome. But the first answer is: in the Lacanian tradition, where what I call the remainder goes, roughly speaking, under the name of *lalangue*.

If I have chosen the works of J. C. Milner as representative of Lacan's views on language, it is because language is his foremost concern. On the port side, he is a Chomskyan linguist of the first order, whose work on exclamative constructions is undoubtedly one of the most important contributions to generative linguistics in France. On the starboard side, he is a disciple of Lacan: *L'Amour de la langue* (*AL*) stems from a seminar given in the department of psychoanalysis at the University of Vincennes.[27]

On the face of it, this Janus-like situation should be as uncomfortable as it was for Saussure, for Chomskyan grammar and psychoanalysis do not go well together, and it would be difficult to describe Chomsky as a warm supporter of the Freudian unconscious. Yet, Lacanian psychoanalysis is notoriously the version of the subject that is most interested in language and closest to linguistics. One does not have to accept Chomsky's philosophy of language wholesale in order to benefit from his grammatical insights. Indeed, Milner is on record as stating that a Chomskyan linguist is not necessarily committed to innatism, for there is at least one Chomskyan linguist, namely himself, who does not believe in innate ideas. The critical nexus is the question of subjectivity. Exclamative sentences, Milner's privileged field of linguistic enquiry, are those sentences that demand a theory of the subject. Psychoanalysis does provide such a theory. We shall see, nevertheless, that this critical tension leaves traces in Milner's work, or rather that it is conceptualized in the opposition between linguistics and poetry (Milner is also known for his work on the theory of versification), between *langue* and *lalangue*. On the one hand, we have a scientific thesis: *langue* is real, and, as is the case with the physical world, this 'real' can be described through a calculus. On the other hand, there is something in language that exceeds scientific enquiry.

The most striking aspect of *AL* is its axiomatic style. The object is to place linguistics firmly within the paradigm of Galilean science, which, according to Milner, has two main characteristics: the propositions of science are formulated by means of symbolic notation, and any technique that produces results is validated. Thus, linguistics is conceived as the logical development of a limited number of axioms, and the attitude of the linguist is that of an epistemologist. Indeed, Milner is not averse to the quasi-prophetic language of foundations: 'Why is there language rather than nothing?' (in which we recognize the initial question in Heidegger's *Introduction to Metaphysics*, as well as a reference to Leibniz).

The first thesis – which justifies the insertion of linguistics within the Galilean paradigm – is that *langue* is real. The object of linguistics, unlike that of other social sciences, is not a fantastical construction of the human mind; it is independent of man, imposed on him, and impervious to manipulation. This is why linguistics, unlike sociology for instance, has always existed (a reference to the quality of Pāṇini's grammar of Sanskrit, which was written centuries before Christ, is to the point here). The concept of 'the real', as opposed to the imaginary and the symbolic, belongs to Lacan. It can be accounted for only through a kind of negative theology: 'the real is the impossible' is one of the best-known, and more obscure, maxims of the master. Its main quality is its independence from man, to whom it is revealed in the epiphany of horror, and who constructs a reality around himself in order to conceal or forget it.[28] Death, as the supreme epiphany, is also the moment when the real becomes inescapable. And what has language to do with the real understood in this sense? Is not the symbolic the natural habitat of language? To be sure it is: Milner's other Vincennes seminar, *Les Noms indistincts*, treats the three notions as a grid, in terms of which any entity can be interpreted.[29] Thus, *langue* is the epitome of what one knows as 'the symbolic'; it can also be viewed in its imaginary aspects; and it is real. And it receives a duly negative definition. To the question 'Why is *langue* as it is and not otherwise?' the only answer is 'parce que c'est comme ca', it is as it is, and that is the end of the matter. The negative aspect in this apparent tautology lies in the arbitrary distinction, which shapes *langue*, between what can be said and what cannot be said, between the linguistically acceptable and the unacceptable – frontiers are not rational entities. The real of *langue* lies in its peculiar form of impossibility, agrammaticality, or unacceptability. As a consequence, the language of mastery, of imaginary mastery, is inadequate for *langue*. The agrammatical cannot be determined by law or prescription, it just is; of language there is no master, not even the linguist, who, contrary to the structuralist vulgate, does not project his constructions onto the flow of language but finds them already in the object. This is why linguistics is closer to natural than to social sciences: it does not imagine its object. Which implies another thesis about 'the real' in *langue*, this time a positive one: it can be represented, that is, presented in symbolic form, translated into formal language.

Langue therefore can be the object of a calculus. Four axioms found it, in which we recognize the basic concepts of Saussurean linguistics, in more ascetic and systematic form: (1) the arbitrariness of signs – *langue* is *causa sui*, it is not determined by anything other than itself; (2) the concept of sign – the real of *langue* can be represented by a calculus, the basic symbols of which are Saussurean signs; (3) the transparent subject of the communication diagram – the speaker is reduced to the position of a mere sender or receiver of signs, in other words, his personal history, his social position, or his instinctual drives are disregarded, and he is placed in the traditional position of an angel; (4) the communication diagram itself – of the variety of actual users of language, *langue* retains only two positions, the addresser and the addressee, necessary for the workings of an abstract situation of communication. From these four axioms, and with the help of the concepts that embody them (arbitrariness, signs, a transparent speaker, communication), the rest of linguistics can be deduced.

The result of the linguist's operations is a scientific object, *langue*, not language. (Here, it must be confessed that the French language allows a systematic ambiguity between '*une langue*' a natural language, and '*la langue*', the object of science.) It has the characteristics of an abstract object. It is distinct from what lies outside it – the construction of *langue* is a process of separation and exclusion; it is also distinct from other *langues*, as a natural language is distinct from other languages, and one cannot combine them unless one takes the extreme precautions of inverted commas and italics; it is always identical with itself, an essentially stable entity, where any diachronic phenomenon can be disregarded as corruption; lastly, it is homogeneous and unequivocal.

Of course, this ideal object falls short of the reality of language, for these characteristics can be shown *not* to apply to the language we all speak, which is corrupt, heterogeneous, not so easily distinguished from its outside or from other languages. This need not trouble us unduly. It merely means that *langue* is an abstraction, an order projected by the linguist onto the chaotic flow of linguistic phenomena. But this nominalist epistemology is precisely what Milner rejects when he insists on the real, not imaginary, character of *langue*. Again, we may consider his position with calm. On the face of it, it amounts to a straightforward claim for the scientificity of linguistics. The science of language is on the same side as the exact sciences, it is a body of knowledge, a set of propositions that picture the reality of language, not a fantastic construction that creates what it claims to describe. The trouble here is that the exact sciences are content to speak in terms of truth. They do not need a contorted concept of 'the real': a straightforward conception of the correspondence between their propositions and states of affairs is usually quite sufficient for them, whereas Milner needs both 'the real' and truth, and his psychoanalytic theory of truth is not based on correspondence. So, beneath the phrase 'the real character of *langue*', he must mean something more. And he does. Or rather his negative concept of the real is supplemented by a positive concept of the symbolic. For *langue*, as we have seen, is the symbolic object *par excellence*. Milner proposes the following strong and contentious thesis: 'the mechanisms of *langue* repeat those of the unconscious, and vice versa' (*AL*, p. 66). He attributes this discovery to Freud, and especially to his thesis of the antithetical meanings of primal words. Three important things must be said here if we are to understand this thesis. First, a repetition is not an image. He does not say: 'the mechanisms of *langue* mirror those of the unconscious'. An image implies two different orders of entities, and a relation of homology between them (as in the early Wittgenstein's picture theory of language, or in Spinoza's 'the order and connection of ideas is the same as the order and connection of things'), whereas repetition implies only one order of entities, and a difference in realization. Far from being a mere representation, *langue* is *articulated* on something else. There is difference, but there is also a point of contact. Second, the 'something else' in question is the unconscious. Milner does not say: 'the mechanisms of *langue* repeat those of language', which would merely be another formulation of the paradox of metalanguage. There is no metalanguage, therefore *langue* cannot be a picture, or even a repetition, of language (of its own object language). It is articulated on the unconscious, something other than it, and yet strangely similar (as

Milner says, the repetition is reciprocal). Perhaps this is merely giving a Freudian twist to Saussure's prediction that linguistics would one day be part of the wider science of semiology. The unconscious is also within the field of that new science, being as it is semiotically articulated. Third, it appears that we are leaving *langue* proper, or at least Saussure's *langue*. The name of Freud is now invoked, at a point where he relies on the pre-scientific linguist Karl Abel, and on one of his erroneous theories. An 'error' in *langue* (for the linguist, there is no such thing as 'the antithetical meanings of primal words') has become a truth about language *qua* symbolic. We are in fact not so much leaving *langue* as thinking its articulation with the unconscious. This is where the remainder appears, for the name of this articulation is *lalangue*.

Strong and contentious as the thesis is, it is susceptible of empirical confirmation (I am aware that I am using 'empirical' in a wider sense than would a logical positivist). We might remember Judith Milner's conception of the link between linguistic frontiers and the frontiers of sex (or sexual roles). We will of course recall the Lacanian thesis that 'the unconscious is structured like a language'. And I have already alluded to Freud's texts on dream-work, joke-work, fantasy, and negation. However, I shall not pursue this line of argument here, but concentrate on a description of *lalangue*.

It must be said that the term, which has all the appearance of *Witz*, is an emblem of its referent – not only because it is an instance of joke-work, but in its very linguistic status. For the word seems to lie outside *langue*, and yet to be part of it (as such, it is a superb example of what I mean by 'the remainder'). It is a word, apparently a noun. In the above phrase 'a description of *lalangue*', it has the syntactic function of a noun, or rather a noun-phrase, for it does not take an article. Indeed, it is produced by the collapsing of an article and a noun, which is no regular way of deriving a new noun. If I force an article on the phrase, and write '*la lalangue*', I have the impression that I am afflicted with a stammer. The article introduces a process of repetition that threatens to become compulsive: what will prevent me from saying '*la lalalangue*' next? An obvious solution to my syntactic quandary is to decide that this is no ordinary noun, but a proper name – *they* do not need articles. But this will not do. If this is a name, it is far too motivated. It not only has reference, it has meaning, and I cannot help dividing it into its constituent words, '*la*' and '*langue*', a thing I should not do with a name. But there is even worse. The word is graphically distinct, and

37

phonetically indistinguishable, from its parent noun phrase, '*la langue*', a deliberate source of endless ambiguities for the speaker (as a coinage, this is almost too Derridean to be true – indeed, it strongly resembles '*différance*' in that respect). So it is both the same as '*la langue*', which it repeats, and different from it – the difference that repetition needs. It is indeed the emblem of the articulation of *langue* on the unconscious. It respects the principle of discreteness on which *langue* is built (at least in its written form) and subverts it; for it is an example of homophonic ambiguity (and homophony is the principal device *lalangue* resorts to in order to subvert *langue*).

The symbolic thesis – *langue* and the unconscious are articulated because of their similar semiotic structures – soon turns out to be a positive thesis on the real of *langue*. *Langue* repeats the mechanisms of the unconscious. 'La Langue supporte le réel de lalangue' (*AL*, p. 29). I suspect that by '*supporte*', we must understand both 'carry' and 'bear as a burden'. *Lalangue* in its relation to *langue* is in a position both of excess ('this function of excess, we name *lalangue*', *AL*, p. 93) and of lack. In the matter of language, science is found lacking; it never has the last word.

There is no point in attempting to construct *lalangue* as the linguist does *langue*. But we can chart a map of the points where it emerges. For the excess makes itself felt. Since *langue* is articulated on the unconscious, *lalangue* returns within it. Whenever desire and language meet, whenever, as the title of Milner's book indicates, a subject falls in love with language, then *lalangue* leaves its trace. So the first map of *lalangue* is a list of its celebrants, language-lovers or logophiliacs. They are the ghosts that haunt the linguist, their dubious practices the shadowy picture of his rational praxis – indeed, they do not analyse language, they make it. And their name is legion. First comes the purist, who defends the purity of language against change and corruption, not with the weapons of science but with those of good taste. His task is to legislate over what escapes legislation, to defend in the name of good taste a status quo for which no conscious choice was ever responsible. Next comes the polyglottal linguist who can never resist the urge to add one more language to his collection – every student of languages suffers from a mild case of this mania. He is followed by the hopeful esperantist, seemingly striving after universal peace and actually realizing his fantasy of power over language. And by the philologist, whose glory lies in writing the grammar of a language, Indo-European, that never existed (he might be called an esperantist of the origins).

After him, the delirious patient rushes on stage. His main symptom – and this includes the Saussure of the anagram notebooks – is an inordinate interest in the workings of language. Last comes the poet, who etymologically makes language, and whose playful but profound activities sometimes border on delirium, as was the case with Artaud and Roussel.

If we cannot describe *lalangue*, perhaps we can find a metaphor for it. The best one is the maternal tongue, the language that for each of us is radically different from all others. It is banal to say that we do not know the grammar of our own language. Yet there is a grain of truth in this, for we apply linguistic rules that we do not remember ever having learnt. Indeed, we have not learnt our mother tongue as we have since learnt other languages. In the case of Latin, or for me in the case of English, memories, often painful, abound; whereas learning our mother tongue appears to us retrospectively as having been a natural and easy process. This is of course due to a rosy vision of our infancy, and the difference between languages is primarily a difference in age. But this is precisely the point: this special tongue is maternal, and the learning of it bound up with our formative Oedipal relationships. This is why we are so attached to it, why it is for us an object of devotion, why the plight of the exile is primarily linguistic (or rather why his linguistic plight remains after he has successfully integrated into another society). The maternal tongue is the language that we inhabit, and that can be said, in Heideggerian parlance, to speak through us.

Langue is unequivocal: it must preserve at all costs the discrete character of signs. *Lalangue*, on the other hand, is equivocal – nor is it, for that matter, homogeneous or distinct from what lies outside it. *Lalangue*, therefore, is not a construct, which can be deduced from the two principles of arbitrariness and discreteness, but a ragbag, rife with the equivocation of homophony. And homophony is not so much another, opposite, principle of construction, as the excess that undermines the two principles. It is obvious that the first rule of a system is that its units must be distinct and unequivocal. Ambiguity and vagueness or uncertainty are the cardinal sins that the creators of artificial languages have always reproached natural languages with. But a natural language *is* equivocal: this, the generalized ambiguity and homophony of *lalangue* capture. *Lalangue* is language at play. 'On joue avec le langage', one plays with language; 'il y a du jeu dans le langage', the parts of the system do not quite fit, there is a certain amount of slippage. But *lalangue* undermines not only discreteness, but also the arbitrary character of signs, for it opens the door to direct motivation. Proper names are ascribed meanings, phonemes are motivated by instinctual drives, relative (and sometimes absolute) motivation rules – arbitrariness becomes so 'limited', to use Saussure's term, as to vanish. There are no simple signs any more. Any item will be analysed, and endlessly re-analysed, for relative motivation. All words will have the same status as the word *'lalangue'* itself. Thus, a male chauvinist view of language, the linguistic counterpart of the myth of Adam's rib, will be supported by (false) etymologies. Women come second because 'female' is derived from 'male'; or because it comes from the Latin *'femina'*, which means *'fe mina'* (lesser in faith) – this etymology comes from the infamous *Malleus Maleficarum*, the medieval treatise on witches; a more modern version would be 'woman' is 'woe to man'. In *lalangue*, language runs wild – but not at random, as we have just seen.

The result is that the excess of *lalangue* 'undoes' *langue* in all the senses of the word (*AL*, p. 118): 'lalangue défait la langue' – it overcomes, it defeats, and it deconstructs *langue*). Which means that *langue* can never be separate and abstract. It is articulated, it is in contact, and therefore there are points in it where *lalangue* is inscribed, and this not only in the accidents of delirious discourse. Milner calls these 'points of subjectivity'. They are the exorbitant points where *lalangue* returns, the interior limits that, within *langue* itself, threaten the system. The best instance of these is the shifters. As we know the sad thing about them is that they shift. They are neither stable nor unequivocal, as appears in the fact that their only definition is circular ('I' means 'the person who says "I"'). What is treated by *langue* as a lack, an exception, and is largely ignored by it as it would like to ignore the points where the system fails, where the structure becomes uncertain and threatens to collapse, is treated by *lalangue* as an excess, a locus for the proliferation of meaning. The map of *lalangue* is the map of the 'points of poetry' where lack is cancelled, where it becomes excess, and where what is impossible to utter is said in a poem.

The dialectic of lack and excess rules the relationship between *langue* and *lalangue*. It also governs the relationship between language and the remainder – it is basically the same relationship. *Lalangue* makes it possible for us to think the remainder in a new, and perhaps in a positive way. Because *langue* is no mere abstraction from *lalangue*, separate and immune from it, the remainder is not merely what is left when the linguist has finished his work, the dross that is discarded when the gold nugget has been extracted. Like *lalangue*, the remainder is not merely to be conceived as what lies outside; it is also within grammar. The process of construction must be understood as an ever-renewed but always failing attempt at disengagement. This is not a case where, if you dig the sand away, Tutankhamun's tomb will be revealed, for the tomb itself is made of sand. We derive from this a rather pessimistic view of the possible achievements of linguistics.

I am going beyond Milner. His positive thesis about the real in *langue* is meant to save science. In his terms, what I have described as a tracing of frontiers, a construction that is either real but arbitrary or rational but imaginary, is not *langue*, the object of science, but grammar, the descriptive result of the purist's explorations. As a scientist, his aim is to defend the formalizations of science against the assault of the irrationalist, that is, to restore and consolidate his authority over language. I am not convinced by the contrast between grammar and *langue*. Nor am I prepared to concede that the linguist's *langue* is 'real' in the technical sense. I think there is something inherently paradoxical in Milner's attempt to combine Galilean science with psychoanalysis, and that the paradox is inscribed in his concept of *langue*. For if it is a characteristic of *langue* that it should be articulated on the unconscious – a thesis with which I have no quarrel – then its autonomy, the axiom that *langue* is *causa sui* (i.e. is not determined by anything other than itself), is at worst untenable and at best paradoxical. *Lalangue*, or in my terms the remainder, is what questions the autonomy of *langue*. If it is articulated on the unconscious, how can we assert that it is in no way *determined* by it? And if by the unconscious why not also by the social-historical conjuncture? At best we shall have to conceive the 'autonomous non-autonomy' of language. How can language be at the same time entirely beyond the mastery of the speaking subject, and the object of innumerable political interventions, mostly, but not entirely, unsuccessful?

In fact, what Milner is doing by articulating the Saussurean axioms of *langue* on the unconscious is imposing on it a full-fledged, debatable theory of language. In other words, having decided that Saussure has achieved an epistemological break (in Milner's preoccupation with epistemology and yearning after scientificity, we find traces of his Althusserian past) and that the

THE VIOLENCE OF LANGUAGE

four axioms state the rational kernel of language, its 'real' character (in the first, negative, sense of 'real'), he projects these axioms onto the unconscious, the workings of which they are supposed to repeat (this is a symbolic thesis, but one that turns out to concern the 'real' character of *langue* in a second, positive, sense of the term: the articulation is real). Thus, he lets the axioms out of the bag of the unconscious, which enables them to pass as the formulation of the real workings of language (the two senses of the word 'real' are now combined into one): Saussurean *langue* is justified by its articulation on the unconscious. This sounds remarkably like circular reasoning. The eager theorist delightedly finds in the object what he has put into it – but by now what he finds is 'real'. It is in fact a symptom of an imaginary construction, of the kind linguists indulge in. We must go beyond Milner. We still need a critique of linguistics, and an analysis of the genuinely subversive nature of the remainder, which will show that language is indeed violent. But in his very paradoxes and aporias, Milner provides us with an invaluable perspective on the remainder. He traces the first map of the remainder, and enables us to think of it in a positive manner.

A SECOND APPROACH TO THE REMAINDER: *A THOUSAND PLATEAUX*

To go from Milner to Deleuze and Guattari's *A Thousand Plateaux* (*ATP*) is to enter an entirely different intellectual universe.[30] Not only do we go from psychoanalysis to an explicitly anti-psychoanalytic tradition (*ATP* is the second volume of *Capitalism and Schizophrenia*, the first volume of which was the celebrated, and eloquently titled, *Anti-Oedipus*), but we also change paradigm. For Deleuze and Guattari, the reference is no longer Galilean science and its linguistic representative, Saussure's *langue*, but a version of pragmatics and the theory of speech acts – a strange and idiosyncratic concept of pragmatics, to be sure,[31] but one that is incompatible with the axioms of Galilean science. The object of '*plateau* no 4' of *ATP* is a critique of these axioms, which is meant to demonstrate that the study of language cannot take the form of positivist scientificity. Thus, Deleuze and Guattari have one thing – but little else – in common with Milner, their starting point: linguistics is based on four postulates. But where he upholds, they tear down. The postulates do not spell out the truth about language, they only build up the illusion of *langue*. The four postulates might, with due precaution, be translated from or into those of Milner. (1) The function of language is to inform and communicate. (2) Language is an abstract machine, which admits no 'extrinsic factor'. (3) Language is a homogeneous system. (4) The object the linguist studies is the standard version of the language, not dialectal variations or individual style. For Deleuze and Guattari, the interest of these axioms is that they provide a good picture of what language is *not*, and therefore *a contrario* suggest what language is. We recognize the type of reasoning of which my choice of the term 'remainder' is typical.

The first postulate, that language informs and communicates, implies an irenic view of linguistic intercourse. A good picture of this would be H. P. Grice's theory of conversation. For him, the basis of all conversation lies in the observance of a 'cooperative principle'. We cooperate in order to communicate; communication is the exchange of informative messages. This view of language is, of course, highly dubious. Grice himself does not ignore this, for the burden of the analysis of actual conversations is placed on the twin concepts of 'implicature' and 'flouting', which analyse the ways in which we do not respect the maxims derived from the cooperative principle. His position is foundational – we may even say transcendental, for it is not through mere oversight that Grice has borrowed the names of his maxims (quantity, quality, relation, and modality) from Kant. So that it is all too easy to invert the position and adopt as a transcendental principle another, agonistic, position, that of verbal struggle, and to deduce new maxims of conversation from it. Thus, an agonistic maxim of quantity would run like this: say as much, or as little, as is necessary to reduce your opponent to speechless rage or to force him to abandon the field. Sometimes a flow of invective, and sometimes a haughty silence, will achieve this end. Or, again, an agonistic maxim of quality would state that you must say not what you believe to be true, but what is most detrimental to your opponent. Sometimes truth, and sometimes falsity, will do the trick. I shall take up the subject again in Chapter 6. It is sufficient to say at this point that the irenic and the agonistic views of language are two sides of the same coin.

Yet Deleuze and Guattari prefer the agonistic tails to the irenic heads. For them, lingistic intercourse is violent, and the agonistic view is closer to the pragmatic basis of language. Logicians and philosophers alike have always attributed a central status to assertions, as bearers of truth and falsity. Linguists like Chomsky have followed suit by deriving imperatives and questions from declaratives. This centrality, as we know, has been questioned by Austin and the tradition of ordinary language analysis. An informative assertion is a special type of speech act, on a par with other speech acts. We might argue from this for an equal status for all speech acts. Questions and imperatives would no longer be marginal, but they would not become dominant. Deleuze and Guattari, however, and this is where they begin to part company with Austin, use tactics of inversion, not assimilation. They ascribe a founding function to one particular speech act: not asserting, but ordering. The basic sentence is in the imperative mode, the basic utterance a slogan. Here, the gap with the analytic tradition widens. Other attempts have been made to ascribe questions, for instance, a central position.[32] But, with the term 'slogan', we are going far beyond this – meaning ceases to be individual, a matter for the speaker's intention. You do not issue a slogan of your own accord, as an expression of what *you* mean to say. A slogan is produced collectively, it is the object of negotiation and collective formulation within a group, generally an institutionalized one (a trade union or a party). In fact, for Deleuze and Guattari, the origin of meaning is no longer in an individual subject, but in a 'collective arrangement of utterance'. Here we find the shadow of another common point with Milner (no doubt a reflection of the French *Zeitgeist*): the subject is no longer master of his language. In Milner, this is due to the intrusion of *lalangue*. In Deleuze and Guattari, the subject is only a mouthpiece for a collective source. The word 'arrangement' stresses that the source is not a collective *subject*, but a non-subjective organization of discourse. The institution speaks, and its speech is not the sum of the discourses of its members. Even if someone invents the words, by the time they become a slogan they have lost their subjective character.

Of course, the production of slogans is a statistically negligible part of our linguistic activity. But since for Deleuze and Guattari slogans have functional value, they argue that they are present in all utterances. In other words, they assert that all speech is indirect speech. What I believe to be my own words is only a reported utterance – another reason why utterances are non-subjective. Most linguists would derive indirect from direct speech, and exercises in school grammars often require such translation. The reason for this is that in direct speech, or in directly reported speech, the author of the reported words is responsible for their meaning, whereas in indirect speech, the primary speaker is responsible for all the words, whether they are his own or those he mentions. This allows him to mingle his own point of view with the words he is allegedly reporting. Thus, the sentence 'President Mitterrand said that that notorious cretin, his Prime Minister, was a very clever man' need not be a contradiction in terms – nor is it necessary that we understand the President to have used such undiplomatic language. The insulting words are not Mitterrand's – he is merely the grammatical subject of the utterance – but those of the primary speaker, myself. Yet they appear to be Mitterrand's: the tricks that indirect quotation allows us to play are well known. What Deleuze and Guattari suggest is that every utterance, even the most innocuous one, contains such semantic tensions and uncertainties. What I believe to be my text is always manipulated by an absent, collective, non-subjective primary speaker; it is originally a slogan. This is not as far-fetched as it seems – it is rather close to what linguists know as the 'performative hypothesis', first proposed by the American linguist, J. R. Ross. Ross draws the linguistic consequences of Austin's evolution from the contrast between performatives and constatives to the recognition that every utterance, and this includes assertions, has illocutionary force. If this is the case, every declarative sentence must contain, in its deep structure, a performative verb indicating its illocutionary force. In common and garden declarative sentences, this performative is erased from the surface sentence. Thus, 'it is raining' has a deep structure of the type: 'I state that it is raining.' I shall not enter here into the arguments pro and contra the hypothesis.[33] Deleuze and Guattari's proposal amounts to something very similar, except that the introductory verb would have imperative, not assertive, force. The addressee of the imperative is the speaker himself, who is both the recipient of and the mouthpiece of the slogan. True it is to say that such a speaker does not speak his own language, but is spoken by a language he can no longer call his own – he only repeats the slogan in which his utterance necessarily originates.

This has drastic consequences for our conception of language. It is no longer possible to think of it as a system of signs – we must view it rather as a locus for contending forces. It is not a structure, but an unstable and potentially violent institution. Transformations are not abstract operations in a computer program but incorporeal events affecting corporeal entities. As is usual with Deleuze, we are going from Saussure back to the Stoics. And it is true that performatives, as incorporeal events (an event occurs whenever words do things), have material effects on the bodies that are subject to their force. The material, even bodily situation of the condemned man is not at all the same as that of the defendant – the noose is now around his neck; he feels it; others around him already imagine it, and behave towards him accordingly; he is placed in a special cell and has special constraints or privileges. Between these two material states, there is only the incorporeal event of the verdict. This is another way of saying that there is not only a politics *of* language, but also politics *in* language.

An example will give us a more concrete experience of what Deleuze and Guattari mean. One of their sources of inspiration is Canetti's *Crowds and Power*. The book contains a chapter entitled 'Question and Answer', which illustrates the type of analysis Deleuze and Guattari are calling for. This is the opening paragraph:

> All questioning is a forcible intrusion. When used as an instrument of power it is like a knife cutting into the flesh of the victim. The questioner knows what there is to find, but he wants to touch it and bring it to light. He sets to work on the internal organs with the sureness of a surgeon. But he is a special kind of surgeon, one who keeps his victim alive in order to find out more about him, and, instead of anaesthetizing, deliberately stimulates pain in certain organs in order to find out what he wants to know about the rest of the body.[34]

The lineaments of *ATP* are already present here. The similes insist on the material, but also on the potentially violent, aspect of language. Since the questioner already knows what there is to find, it appears that the purpose of language is not informative and communicative, i.e. a question's purpose is not, as is commonly thought, to solicit information, but to elicit an answer, to establish a relation of power between questioner and questioned. It is a striking feature of questions that he who asks them establishes, by the very act of asking them, his right to question, his expectation of an answer, and his power to elicit one. Nor is it simply a matter of individual power. Canetti moves from the individual, and apparently innocuous, question 'What is the time?' (uneasiness soon creeps in if the question is too personal, too insistent, too often repeated), to the formal questioning of interrogation (still an interaction between two subjects, even if the dice are loaded in favour of the interrogator, who is invested with the authority of the state), and to the blatantly institutional questioning of state registration. It is often thought, quite rightly, that an important aspect of British democracy lies in the fact that Britons do not have to carry an identity card, that in order to borrow a book from a public library they do not have to produce their paternal grandfather's birth certificate. Canetti, an Eastern European Jew residing in Austria in the troubled times of the rise of national socialism, obviously has another experience of the pervasive nature of bureaucratic questioning:

> A group of questions has taken shape, which is everywhere the same and whose basic purpose is to serve security and order. The state wants to know as much as possible about each person, so as to be able to deal with him if and when he becomes dangerous.[35]

In our days of data banks and connecting computers, this sounds prophetic. The chapter ends with the Welsh legend of a young peasant whom the Noon-woman questioned to death. The moral of this (the first counter-postulate of schizolinguistics) is: language is violent, a locus for power relationships.

This is a long way from the automony of *langue*. Indeed, the second postulate, which describes language as an abstract machine, supports the idea of its non-autonomy. In Saussurean terms, language is a system of arbitrary terms, with no 'extrinsic factor'. Signs – this is what lies at the bottom of their arbitrariness – are separated from the world. Against this, Deleuze and Guattari stress not only the non-autonomy of language, but also its materiality. Language is caught both in the bodies of its utterers and in the society that they form. Artaud's *cri* and Fonagy's conception of the instinctual motivation of phonemes are instances of this materiality. It is no longer a case of a *symbolic* articulation of language and the unconscious which nevertheless turned out to be an essential aspect of the reality of *langue*, as we saw in Milner, but a case of a *real* insertion of words within bodies. Words do not only *do* things; they *are* things. Language cannot be a simple representation of the world; it is also an intervention within it, to be analysed in terms of positions, advance and retreat, territorial markings, and deterritorialization. We are moving here from the body of the individual to the body politic. The non-autonomy of language opens up to the social. Language is an institution with a vengeance. It suffers the fate of all institutions: it is a locus for the exercise of power, and a target for rebellious attacks. As such, it can be revolutionized. Going back to the troubled history of Soviet linguistics, Deleuze and Guattari take Marr's side against Stalin. It will be recalled that Stalin denied that language was a superstructure. For him, it was a neutral instrument of communication, a machine abstracted from the society that used it. On the contrary, Marr maintained, language is part of the society in which the revolution takes place. It not only reflects the revolution, it interacts with it – the Marxist conception of reflection is of an (inter)active reflection, not a passive picture. It is therefore revolutionized when society is. This is another source of the choice of the word 'arrangement' (of utterance). Language is not a rational construct but the product of a historical conjuncture. It is therefore arbitrary, but not random, an arrangement, not a machine that conforms to teleological structure. In language, conjuncture has the upper hand on teleology. Language, therefore, is non-autonomous and material: this is the second counter-postulate of schizolinguistics. If I translate this into my terms, it implies that the remainder, far from being a residue, has now invaded the whole field. There is no longer a frontier, a line of separation.

The third and fourth postulates – language is homogeneous, the object of linguistics is the standard dialect – focus the critique on the existence of universals, both external (universals of language) and internal (universals within one language, i.e. laws or rules of grammar). The critique denies the existence of fixed, stable and general rules. Language is a place for variables rather than constants, for partial and tentative rules. In other words, the critique asserts the primacy of *parole* over *langue* (which is never more than an imaginary construct). It is unfair to say, as a linguist must say, that a speaker of a language speaks only one language. On the contrary, he changes language when he changes addressee. One does not address one's butcher as one does one's beloved or one's banker. A linguist will explain this away as irrelevant. Those are at worst idiolectal or dialectal variations within the same *langue*. But this is precisely the point that Deleuze and Guattari wish to make. For them, *langue* is nothing but a locus for systematic variation, an unstable collection of dialects, a conglomerate of *paroles*. Any attempt at formulating a universal – a rule – will be submerged under an avalanche of dialectal variations. The exception *is* the rule. Deleuze and Guattari make much of one of e. e. cummings's best-known poems, 'anyone lived in a pretty how town'. There is no point in reducing the agrammaticality of this first line by noting that 'anyone' is treated here as a proper name, and that 'how' has been converted into an adjective. This is correct, but it stifles the proliferation that makes itself felt in the line, '"Anyone lived in a pretty town" – "How pretty?" – "Pretty how!"'. Or if this crazy dialogue fails to convince, here is another one, which shows that cummings's line may well be an instance of 'portmanteau dialogue', as Carroll talks of 'portmanteau words': "'Anyone lived *in a big town*' – '*How big?*' – '*Pretty big!*'". In this interpretation, 'pretty how town' is the portmanteau phrase into which the italicized words are collapsed, like a folding chair. What we have here is an instance of dialectal creativity, a type of creativity that is not restrained by grammatical rules and conventions – not even rule-breaking, but rule-dissolving creativity (for the breaking of rules supposes that one recognizes them, whereas they have simply vanished). One of the consequences of this is that the object of the linguist is no longer *langue* but style. Language is not universal, but singular.

There is an obvious danger here. It would appear that I am arguing for that notorious impossibility, a private language; also that the singularity of language contradicts its social character. But singular does not mean individual. A style is a characteristic not of an individual subject, but of a collective arrangement. In any utterance, stylistic analysis maps out the play of variables and the struggles between different dialects and voices. The third counter-postulate is that language is made up of variables. And, as we have just seen, this has repercussions on the type of dialect the linguist studies. Style, not *langue*, becomes the focus of attention: not the standard or major version, but the struggle between major and minor dialects. For, traditionally, one limits the description of a language to its standard version, BBC English or the educated American of the East coast, rather than the dialect of a Durham miner or a farmer from the Middle West. If you happen to be teaching the language to foreign students, this restriction is unavoidable: unity comes before variation. The remainder is abandoned to the marginal studies of dialectology. But, in actual usage, this situation is far from satisfactory, because only a negligible percentage of English speakers like an Oxford don. And it is not enough to claim that they are the sort of speakers that count, and ought to be imitated. The repressed minor dialects – there is such a thing as linguistic colonialism, or glottophagy – return within the major or standard dialect and unsettle it. Do we not, for

instance, detect in the overemphasized schoolmarmish pronunciation of Mrs Thatcher an overcorrected trace of less glorious origins?
The standard version of English is the dialect of cultured, white,
European, heterosexual, urban, adult males. This reads like the
converse of a list of the victims of comedians' jokes: women,
peasants, wogs of all descriptions, trade unionists, lunatics. It is
almost the same list, which means that the major dialect is the
embodiment – and its adoption the practice – of relations of power.
But it is also a symptom of anxiety, the anxiety that the oppressed
may speak in their turn, that questions may be returned rather than
obediently answered, that the possession of linguistic capital may
no longer guarantee academic and social success, that women may
forget that silence is golden, and Harlem blacks claim their own
dialect for a full-fledged version of English. The fourth counter-
postulate is that minor dialects are always threatening to subvert the
standard version of a language.

This is another reason why style is so important. The type of text
where the subversion of the major by the minor dialects is most
apparent is literature. There, texts are open to and aware of the
struggles that make up language. Kafka is for Deleuze and Guatarri
an emblematic figure. A Czech Jew writing in German, his potential
trilingualism makes him a foreigner in his own language. Linguists
have a tendency to find a corpus in the innocuous sentences they
themselves produce – the kind of sentence that is all the more apt to
serve as a grammatical example as it has been formulated for that
express purpose. Literature on the other hand is language at work,
in all its dialectal variety, in all its variables – Bakhtin and his
dialogic analyses of indirect free speech is an obvious source here.[36]
This is why a sentence by Jane Austen is more valuable than a whole
chapter in a textbook of grammar.

The asceticism of the Galilean scientist dominates Milner's conception of language – *lalangue* fails to overturn *langue*. There is no
such constraint in Deleuze and Guattari, because there is no
yearning to save science. The desire for rules has given way to the
rule of desire. In both cases the author's style is an *abyme* of the
view of language he holds. Deleuze and Guattari's is florid and
proliferating: a rhizome rather than an architecture. This is the main
metaphor they use – and it applies to language. The rhizome, a
structureless root, propagating in anarchic fashion, is the second
name of the remainder – except that by now there is no remainder,
because there is no previous abstraction and separation of a

structure from the dross of irrelevant phenomena. The metaphor has turned organic rather than architectural, but it has mainly turned anarchic. The focus is now on the materiality of language, on the literal violence of its interventions and of the struggles and power relationships within it. Acts of language resemble acts of God rather than mere speech acts. And the focus is now also on the social nature of language – Austin rewritten by Marxists. It is easy to understand why Deleuze and Guattari's use of the term 'pragmatics' is based on misprision. They do not so much enable us to think the remainder as force us to go beyond it – to go from the tame description of unruly aspects of language as marginal left-overs from the glories of information and communication, to a conception of violence (literal violence, not the – at best – metaphorical violence of linguistic constraints) as the lord of linguistic misrule.

The dissolution of all structures raises more problems than it solves. The opening up of language to the world, the invasions of the whole field by the remainder, no longer enable us to account for the specificity of language. Perhaps Milner's paradox was not an aporia after all: it indicates the paradoxical locus where we have to dwell. Language is both autonomous and non-autonomous, governed by rules and unruly, arbitrary and motivated, stable and corrupt – the rhizome produces a tree, *lalangue* supports *langue*. I must attempt to have my cake and eat it.

THE COURBET VIEW OF LANGUAGE

This chapter started with a corpus of texts that encroached on linguistic frontiers and questioned the rules of grammar. It developed into a study of the hesitations that can be perceived in the very text that founded linquistics as a science. It found a place for the remainder in an articulation of the mechanisms of language on those of the unconscious: the remainder, or the linguistically repressed, returns. Lastly, with the work of Deleuze and Guattari, it has described the devastating invasion of the whole field by what we now hardly dare to call a remainder, a conception that has at least the advantage of recapturing the unity of the field lost in the process of exclusion and separation out of which the science of linguistics emerged. And we have been able to give the remainder two names: *lalangue* and the rhizome.

Although these two names open the path towards a conception of the remainder, neither entirely fits the object I have in mind. Perhaps *lalangue* is closer to the mark, in so far as it establishes the remainder as exterior, a locus beyond frontiers, in dialectic relationship with an interior. Where there are no frontiers there is no subversion. What I intend to describe is precisely this subversion. I am not, of course, denying the existence of rules of grammar, even if I maintain, contrary to Milner, that linguistics is an imaginary construct, and that the only real in language is that of grammar, i.e. of largely arbitrary and negative frontiers. But the rules are overturned – the smuggler needs the customs officer, and where there is no (linguistic) prohibition, there is no speakeasy. I wish to describe language as a speakeasy, sometimes raided by the grammatical untouchable, where fraudulent imitations of the real stuff are served in the midst of mirth and boisterousness. In other words, I refuse – and here I am closer to Deleuze and Guattari than to Milner – to separate language from the world of which it is a part, to make it autonomous (as *langue* is *causa sui*). Language is both material and social.

I shall express this intuition in a parable. Legend has it that the French painters, Corot and Courbet, used to go on painting expeditions together. Corot, the heir of the Romantic landscape painters, spent hours choosing the place where he would eventually set up his easel: the prospect had to be just right, the landscape must compose itself before he attempted to put it on canvas. When this long and painful process had ended, Courbet, the realist, turned his back on him and started painting whatever was to be seen on the other side. This is my aim: to describe the other side of language. The grammarian and the linguist but also the philosopher of language, choose their objects carefully. The first simplifies in order to formulate clear rules, the second separates the relevant from the irrelevant phenomena, the third is intent on saving rational communication and therefore on ridding natural language of the various impurities that obscure it. These are the frontiers that the remainder subverts and that I wish to cross. I shall dwell in the exceptional and the agrammatical, in the irrelevant and the excluded aspects of language, in the ambiguities and impurities of natural idioms. A countryside less imposing perhaps, and certainly more difficult to paint, but every inch as fascinating as the ordered landscapes of science.

NOTES

1 W. Somerset Maugham, *Cakes and Ale*, London, Pan Books, 1976, p. 109 (first published 1930).
2 R. Quirk, S. Greenbaum, G. Leech, and J. Svartvik, *A Comprehensive Grammar of the English Language*, London, Longman, 1985, p. 140.
3 W. Labov, *Language in the Inner City*, Philadelphia, University of Pennsylvania Press, 1972.
4 L. J. Calvet, *Pour et contre Saussure*, Paris, Payot, 1975.
5 R. Jakobson, 'Linguistics and Poetics', in T. A. Sebeok (ed.), *Style in Language*, Cambridge, Mass. MIT Press, 1960, p. 357.
6 J. Austen, *Pride and Prejudice*, London, 1812, p. 1.
7 L. Carroll, *The Annotated Alice*, Harmondsworth, Penguin, 1965, p. 47.
8 J. Angus, *Hand-Book of the English Tongue*, London, The Religious Tract Society, 1870, p. 313.
9 See N. Chomsky, *Aspects of the Theory of Syntax*, Cambridge, Mass., MIT Press, 1965.
10 H. van Riemsdijk and E. Williams, *Introduction to the Theory of Grammar*, Cambridge, Mass., MIT Press, 1986, p. 175. In modular grammar, this type of structure would not even be treated as a case of extraposition.
11 D. Bolinger, *Meaning and Form*, London, Longman, 1977, pp. 67–8.
12 G. Lakoff and M. Johnson, *Metaphors We Live by*, Chicago, University of Chicago Press, 1980.
13 Riemsdijk and Williams, op. cit., pp. 172–3.
14 J. F. Lyotard, *La Condition postmoderne*, Paris, Minuit, 1979.
15 ibid., pp. 69–78.
16 See L. J. Calvet, *La Guerre des langues*, Paris, Payot, 1987.
17 G. Lakoff, *Irregularity in Syntax*, New York, Holt, Rinehart & Winston, 1970, pp. 70–1.
18 Riemsdijk and Williams op.cit., pp. 286–90.
19 See A. Banfield, *Unspeakable Sentences*, London, Routledge, 1982.
20 S. Freud, *Jokes and their Relation to the Unconscious*, London, Routledge, 1960, pp. 125–6.
21 See J. Milner, 'De quoi rient les locuteurs?', *Change*, 29 & 32–33, Paris, 1977, and J. J. Lecercle, *Philosophy through the Looking-Glass*, London, Hutchinson, 1985, ch. 2.
22 F. de Saussure, *Cours de linguistique générale*, edited by T. de Mauro, Paris, Payot, 1985.
23 R. Harris, *Reading Saussure*, London, Duckworth, 1987, pp. 191–2.
24 For another reading of this chapter, see Harris, op. cit., pp. 79–86.
25 Harris's translation; see Harris, op. cit., p. 96.
26 See Calvet, *Pour et contre Saussure*, op.cit.
27 J. C. Milner, *L'Amour de la langue* Paris, Seuil, 1978.
28 This is the only reason why I have kept the phrase 'the real', which sounds utterly alien to British ears. This tradition distinguishes 'the real' from 'reality', the lived world that the subject constructs around himself, one of the main functions of which is to conceal 'the real'.

THE VIOLENCE OF LANGUAGE

29 J. C. Milner, *Les Noms indistincts*, Paris, Seuil, 1983.
30 G. Deleuze and F. Guattari, *Mille Plateaux*, Paris, Minuit, 1980 (English transl., *A Thousand Plateaux*, London, Athlone, 1987).
31 On this, see J. J. Lecercle, 'The misprision of pragmatics', in A. Phillips-Griffiths (ed.), *Contemporary French Philosophy*, Cambridge, Cambridge University Press, 1988.
32 See, for instance, M. Meyer, *De la Problématologie*, Brussels, Pierre Mardaga, 1987.
33 See J. M. Sadock, 'The evidence for the performative analysis', in his *Towards a Linguistic Theory of Speech Acts*, New York, Academic Press, 1974, pp. 21–50.
34 E. Canetti, *Crowds and Power*, Harmondsworth, Penguin, 1975, p. 311 (first published, 1960).
35 ibid., p. 336.
36 V. Volosinov (M. Bakhtin), *Marxism and the Philosophy of Language*, New York, Seminar Press, 1973.

2

THE RAG-BAG

Some sat her days ago.

(Flann O'Brien)

GATHERING THE RAG-BAG

The time has come to talk of many things. Of shoes, and ships, and sealing-wax, of cabbages, and kings, of why language is fragmented and incoherent, and whether beyond the frontier there is the least vestige of order. Describing the remainder is like gathering a rag-bag. And if, according to Judith Milner, formulating a rule of grammar is a negative process, describing the remainder is the negation of this negation – a matter of reversing the practices of science and dealing, in the manner of Courbet, with the exceptional, the irrelevant, the agrammatical. Yet this reversal is no inversion: the new landscape is not the mirror-image of the old, and it is not enough for us to understand, like Alice in *Through the Looking-Glass*, that in order to stay where we are we only have to run as fast as we can. The world beyond the looking-glass, although distinctly odd, is still fairly regular. Not so the remainder. We are in the realm of chance, of the arbitrariness of the irrational (as opposed to the Saussurean arbitrariness which is the sign of the systematicity of *langue*), and our attitude can only be humble and descriptive. Beyond the frontier, there is no guideline, no structuring metaphor – the tree, for instance – that can be projected on to the chaos of phenomena. We are in the midst not so much of the unknown – for we know where we are, and, since this is our language, the landscape is recognizable – as of the unpredictable. Indeed, we never know in advance what we shall find next. Chance meetings, unnatural *rapprochements*, dubious alliances, awesome and yet

55

pleasurable sights: there is something of Mungo Park in he who ventures into the remainder. He will not be cultivating a linguistic field, tracing the furrows of theory. His progress will involve some ramblings outside the ploughed ground ('*de-lira*', leaving the furrow, is the etymology of 'delirium'), a type of wandering that is compatible not with cultivation but with the primitive custom of picking or gathering. In the big towns of the western world, one sometimes meets old women pushing prams which contain all their possessions. They are known as bag-ladies. I intend to be not a surveyor but a kind of tramp, disrespectful of boundaries and ignorant of by-laws – a rag-bag linguist.

I am not entirely alone in my explorations. I have an illustrious predecessor in the person of Freud, in his book on jokes. The urge to classify and explain cannot entirely conceal the pleasure he takes in telling Jewish jokes, and in adding one more example to an already rich corpus, in giving free rein to the mild anarchism of playing with language. And a new language-game it is, which I shall practise after him: being naughty with language, which means both disruptive and childish. By exploring aspects of language that do not contribute to information, communication, and reference, one lets down the (philosophical) side, one seems to abandon the (de)ontological care for truth. And one appears to go back to the inane babblings of late infancy and early childhood. But of course this is exactly what Freud is saying. Joking implies a return to infantile playing with language and, conversely, this infantile urge, far from being definitively overcome in the adult, constantly returns. The rag-bag linguist listens for signs of protracted or second childhood in ordinary speakers; he is – to revive the most hoary of puns – in his anecdotage. The pun itself, of course, is an excellent instance of the remainder at work.

In this expedition, Freud is not our only predecessor. People have been to Acheron and back. There are plenty of Virgils to our timid Dante. And these explorers have left us their memoirs. We find descriptions of the remainder in accounts of delirium and madness; in collections of jokes and games played with language – there are people like Lewis Carroll, who are compulsive inventors of complex games of this kind; and also in certain types of literature, in poetry or metafiction. In fact, the corpus is so large, and the texts so fascinating, that it is a wonder how linguists have so long managed to ignore them as irrelevant. But this is unfair: it is only the kind of linguistics that is dominant today that has forgotten about the remainder. For there is a now almost forgotten tradition of early linguists in whose works it is, often explicitly, present: nineteenth-century enthusiasts for the life of language, like Darmesteter, practitioners of old-time semantics, like Bréal, or their descendants, like Stephen Ulmann, who, while paying lip-service to the new structuralist orthodoxy, quietly went on with their task of description. In their works, the rag-bag is already gathered, in all its richness and variety: the secret life of words, etymologies true and false, onomatopoeias and tropes of all description. My task will be to reach the second childhood of linguistics by returning to the first – for is not Bréal the founder of semantics, he who left us the name for the subject? Nor is this state of affairs entirely surprising. We have seen with Milner that the remainder does return in grammar, in the form of what he calls points of subjectivity and points of poetry.

Our journey into the heart of the remainder has no guidelines, no certain goal. There is no Livingstone to be rescued. But it is not without a task. My rag-bag will be made up of highly intentional playing with language, attributable to a subject who knows – and enjoys – what he is doing, as in the case of jokes and poetry, and highly unintentional occurrences – cases of possession, etymologies, the workings of language itself, where responsibility cannot be ascribed to an individual, or a determinate, subject. Beneath this, there lurks a thesis about the remainder. If the punster or jokester can be said to be doing violence to language, he does no more that what language itself commonly practises. In other words, using Milner's terms, there lies the real of the remainder. Playing with words is not a perverse and damnable act, as the age-old tradition of hostility to puns would have it; nor is it a marginal and irrelevant practice, as the modern view of linguistics maintains. On the contrary, it is a reflection of the normal workings of language, of the existence of a remainder, of its unavoidable return within grammar itself. If so many jokes on language are made, it is because language allows them, because that is the way it works. 'C'est comme ça': this is always the indication that the real has been reached. As Darmesteter puts it, the daring of the most inventive writer soon becomes linguistic custom, for there is no difference in nature between literary and popular, or grammatical, tropes.[1] Our gathering will follow this intuition.

It appears that mastery over language, possession by language, and the workings of language are not to be as sharply distinguished as we might think. An example will illustrate this. In 1970 Unica

57

Zürn published *Der Mann im Jasmin*, an account of her mental illness. In the same year, she committed suicide. She had been living since 1954 with Hans Bellmer, the Surrealist artist and creator of the celebrated doll, and had produced automatic drawings and a collection of anagrams. The book is a picture of various crises in her life, and a journey into her mental world, into the convictions that possessed her, the signs that were given, the hallucinations that captured her senses. It contains a number of anagrams, for Unica Zürn draws and writes at the same time – and there is an aspect of visual fragmentation and reconstruction in an anagram. Thus, from the phrase *'der eingebildete Wahnsinn'* (imaginary madness), she makes up a thirteen-line anagrammatic text, *'Deine Wege ins Hinterland B'* ('Your paths into the hinterland B').[2]

Here is, at last, what Saussure vainly sought: a text with a pre-text that is entirely intentional. Yet it is also an instance of what Saussure saw but rejected – language at work, by itself, in its own right. For the text is full of contradictions. It is a work of art, a composition – and Unica Zürn did publish some of her anagrams. But it is inserted in the account of fits of delirium (the word is present in the text: *'Weh – Deliria sind Gebete – N-N-N-'*, 'Woe to us! Delirium is prayer. N-N-N-'), a case of both intention and possession. It also gives the reader the impression of a feat of verbal skill. How can juggling with a score of letters produce such a sustained and coherent text? Yet a more careful reading will reveal a certain amount of dissemination of key words, *'Wahnsinn'*, for instance, or *'eingebildet'*, and also the existence of a residue, as in the line quoted above, which ruins the impression of mere skill. Intention gives way to possession, skill to symptom, the master of the subject to the free play of the virtualities of meaning which language contains. There is always something grammatical about delirium, there is always something delirious about language.

The contradiction that appears in Unica Zürn's anagram, between intentional and individual on the one hand, and unintentional and non-subjective on the other, is central to my argument. It makes the existence of the remainder manifest, and gives it its full place within language. A first formulation, to be developed later, will suffice. The speaker is the locus of two contradictory tendencies. He speaks language, i.e. he is the master of an instrument, and he is spoken by language, in other words it is language that speaks. Unica Zürn writes anagrams and demonstrates her mastery of the German language; yet, at the same time, she is not in full control of her words, she follows the path that language opens up for her – paths that lead into the hinterland of the remainder, the hinterland B – and she is spoken by the voices that keep calling to her.

But this, it might be said, is the subjective process of madness. Another example will show that the non-subjective process of language operates along the same lines. Textbooks of rhetoric usually devote a few lines to a trope called catachresis. As often in that field, the term has several meanings. Originally, it meant 'error' or 'abuse'. A mixed metaphor, a malapropism, the illicit adoption of a foreign word that changes its meaning, all these are instances of catachresis – already a mixed bag, where individual error coexists with linguistic usage. Darmesteter explains this development by suggesting that what, in the beginning, was an individual error, was subsequently adopted and became usage. But why should the speaking community adopt an obvious error? Because there is a gap in the dictionary. A word is needed, to denote a new object for instance, and, rather than having recourse to a coinage, we extend the meaning of an existing word. What begins as a crossroads eventually becomes a spaghetti junction. Tables or pianos rest on appendages that are sorely in need of a name. Why not call them 'legs'? And this may have consequences. Legend has it that certain Victorians used to drape cloth round the legs of their pianos, for pianos should be heard, but their legs should not be seen. The French seem to have felt the same need, and made different choices. They talk of *'une bretelle d'autoroute'* (seen from above, what looks like a plate of spaghetti might look, to a different imagination, like a pair of braces) and of *'les pieds d'un piano'*. Catachresis, therefore, is both error and usage, forgetting and invention, a deliberate trope that crosses a frontier, and language at work. Perhaps Darmesteter's definition of catachresis as forgetting is the aptest. Language forgets that someone must have initially forgotten language and made an error. We now talk of *'ferrer un cheval'* or 'shoeing a horse', even if the horseshoe is made of silver and not iron (*'ferrer d'argent son cheval'* ought to be a contradiction in terms, but is not), and even if this shoe is not of the kind we would care to wear. In a catachresis an error has become norm, for such are the ways of language. If I use the device as a trope, I am only following the workings of language. When I speak language, it is always, somehow, language that speaks.

THE REMAINDER AS EXCESS

The example of catachresis shows that the relation of grammar and the remainder is one not of opposition or inversion, but of excess. To describe the workings of the remainder is to describe operations not different from those of grammar, but the same, driven to excess. How do you cross a frontier, if not by taking the main road (the French aptly call them '*voies de communication*') up to the warning sign, and then going across, one step at a time at first, cautiously like Alice on the other side of the looking-glass, but soon giving in to exhilaration and frisking about? In other words, in order to cross from grammar into the remainder – not so much, as we have seen, the discovery of unknown territory as a return to the origins – we take the operations of grammar one step further. And we find their best embodiment in the operations of structural linguistics: the establishment of paradigms, the hierarchization of syntagmata. Analysis and synthesis are the main operations of grammar. One isolates units into paradigmatic classes; one studies their combinations into syntagmatic chains. The genius of Saussure lies in the fact that he made those two operations not only explicit but central to his theory. To cross into the remainder, therefore, is to apply the two operations wrongly and/or excessively. The remainder is the place of excessive (that is, multiple) analysis and false synthesis. The delirious patient and the inspired poet do it; language does it as well.

The principle of linguistic analysis implies that an analysis must be unique. Once a string of words has been analysed, the operation stops, except in the hopefully rare and marginal case of ambiguity. If you re-analyse the same string, you no longer have distinct and stable units, the ultimate requisites for a structure, and the process soon becomes compulsively repetitive. Conversely, the stable – clear and distinct – units obtained by analysis are synthesized into correct phrases or syntagmata, whereas the uncertain and unstable products of multiple analysis produce syntagmatic monsters. The remainder is the realm of linguistic teratology, of false units and illicit constructions. Monsters, however, in addition to their obvious charm, have always been of the utmost interest to science, casting light as they do on the structure of normal phenomena. But we must go further than this. We must let ourselves be captivated by the charm of the monsters, and describe monstrosity for its own sake. Such is the language game that the remainder induces us to play – not only being naughty with language, but doing violence to it, which begins when we become aware of its violence. As an *abyme* of this, I shall coin two names for the monstrous and violent operations of the remainder: Brissetizing language, and Wolfsonizing language.

The phrase 'Brissetizing language' is coined from the name of Jean-Pierre Brisset (1837–1923), the delirious French linguist who believed that man descended from the frog, and who enjoyed ephemeral notoriety in 1912, when, as a result of a hoax engineered by Jules Romains, he was proclaimed 'Thinker Laureate'. The irony of this is that Brisset has fared rather better (he is still in print, and a biography has just been devoted to him) than most of the 'serious' writers and artists who made a fool of him.[3] His method is now well known. It is etymology gone mad. The revelation that God confided to him and that enabled him to make his astounding discoveries is that the history of mankind is contained in language, that etymology does contain the truth, not only about the word, but about the world. In which he was, of course, only following the age-old tradition of speculative etymology – nor was he the last to practise it, as the work of Heidegger demonstrates. There is nothing strange or unusual in the idea that words have a history, and that this in turn reflects the history of the people who speak them. The buns that French people eat for breakfast are called '*croissants*', not only because they are made in the shape of a crescent, but also because they were first baked in celebration of a Viennese victory over the Turks. Why should not our words contain our roots? The core of Brisset's delirium is not in his reliance on etymology, but in his use of *multiple* analysis. The same word or phrase is etymologically analysed not once but many times, each time with equal success. If we take his 'great law, or key to speech' – 'all the ideas expressed with similar sounds have the same origin and all refer, initially, to the same subject' – the example he uses to illustrate it is a good instance of multiple analysis:[4]

Les dents, la bouche	[Teeth, mouth]
Les dents la bouchent	[Teeth block the mouth]
L'aidant la bouche	[The mouth helps this blocking]
L'aide en la bouche	[Teeth are a help in the mouth]
Laides en la bouche	[Teeth are ugly in the mouth]
Laid en la bouche	[There is something ugly in the mouth]
Lait dans la bouche	[There is milk in the mouth]
L'est dam le à bouche	[Damage is done to the mouth]
Les dents-là bouche	[Block, or hide, those teeth!]

My translation closely follows Brisset's explanations. As we can see, analysis becomes interpretation. A narrative, even a dialogue, emerges, for the assertion soon becomes an order, perhaps an insult. The last two items also show that the analysis does violence to language. It is no longer a mere question of homonyms, although their existence is the condition *sine qua non* for the multiplication of analyses; it is a matter of forcing an interpretation out of language.

What is striking is not the proliferation of meanings – Brisset, like all seekers after the origins of language, is able to show that all words come from a few 'primitive' elements, five in his case, as there were four in Marr's 'Japhetic' theory,[5] and his analyses only repeat the original proliferation that must have constituted language. What amazes is rather the multiplicity of analyses. The possibility of this seems to be linked to the fact that a string of words allows itself to be analysed in two ways: as a syntagma, that is, as a hierarchy of syntactic-semantic units (morphemes or words), and as a sequence of syllables, that is, a sequence of 'natural' phonic or prosodic units. In many cases the two divisions coincide, but not always. Everyone knows the misunderstandings to which the wrong segmentation of a sequence of sounds can give rise. According to the social dialect, the sequence '*àvotretour*' in French will be heard as '*à votre tour*' (in your turn: literate) or '*à votre retour*' (on your return: popular).[6] What Brisset does is only to take this situation to its extreme, and therefore excessive, consequences. But the important point here is that there is provocation on the part of language. First, because language offers Brisset too many temptations. A critic once challenged him to account, according to his method, for the French word '*Israelite*' (Jew). 'Nothing is easier', Brisset answered: '*y s'ra élite*', the popular pronunciation for 'he will be the elite'.[7] Who can blame him for not having resisted? Second, because language itself Brissetizes. Brisset's etymology for 'grammar' is '*grand-mère*', an obvious piece of nonsense. But 'grammar' is the real etymology for 'glamour': a metonymy takes us from 'grammar' to 'book of grammar'; a metaphor gives the word the sense of 'book of magic'; a trip to Scotland, and the sounds are duly corrupted; an extension into 'magic' and then 'charm', and the glamour girl is with us. Dare we say that this is less mad, or more rational, than Brisset's version? If another example is needed, here is one in French. A '*chandail*' is a sweater. If I decided to Brissetize, my most obvious choice would be to analyse the word into '*champ d'ail*', a field of garlic. This is demented, in other words popular, etymology. What about 'true'

62

etymology? It will tell you that *'chandail'* is short for *'marchand d'ail'*, a garment typical of garlic sellers.[8] It is clear now that language Brissetizes, or that, beneath Brisset's madness, we find the formulation of a certain amount of truth about the workings of language. One of his early critics said of him: 'starting from a false principle, he developed it to its extreme consequences and crossed the boundaries of ... let us say verisimilitude, to put it politely.'[9] This is doubly unfair. The principle is not so much false as applied to excess, but taking it to its extreme consequences, paradoxically, takes us back to the vicinity of truth. And it becomes clear that the phrase 'Brissetizing language ' has been chosen for its ambiguity: we Brissetize language because it Brissetizes.

The phrase 'Wolfsonizing language' comes from the name of Louis Wolfson (1931–), the Jewish American schizophrenic who could not bear to hear or read his maternal tongue, English, and developed an intricate technique of instant translation according to sound, before writing his memoirs in French.[10] Like Brisset, Wolfson does violence to the sentences he compulsively analyses, and sometimes re-analyses. But there is an important difference. He respects the words of the original text, he does not cut them up into syllables. Rather, he 'translates' them, using homophony between languages and not just within a language, and combines these translations into sentences that, being written in several languages, are linguistic monsters. Thus, when he hears some workmen saying about him 'he's a screwball' – we can understand the urgent necessity of defusing the aggressive potential of the sentence through translation – he produces the following sentence:

$$H(ou)\ i(l) \left\{ \begin{array}{l} est \\ ist \\ yest \end{array} \right\} \left\{ \begin{array}{l} un \\ ein \\ odin \\ achab \end{array} \right\} \left\{ \begin{array}{l} écrou \\ Schraube \end{array} \right\} \left\{ \begin{array}{l} Ball \\ balle \end{array} \right\},$$

where we recognize words in French, German, Hebrew, and Russian, and where I have placed the variants he gives between brackets, because any variation will do, provided it is not an English word.[11] This use of variants reminds us of Brisset, but the most striking aspect of the sentence is the crossing of the most elementary frontier of all, the frontier between languages. There is a cultural – historical element here, for by rejecting and translating his maternal tongue, English, Wolfson unwittingly returns to his mother's mother tongue, Yiddish, the structure of which is based on a mixture of languages. This is how a specialist analyses the Yiddish sentence, '*nokhn bentshn hot der zeyde gekoyft a seyfer*' (following the blessing after the meal, grandfather bought a holy book) : '*seyfer*' is Hebrew, '*bentshn*' Romance, '*nokhn*', '*hot*', '*der*', '*gekoyft*' German, '*zeyde*' Slavic. This is pure Wolfson, down to the choice of languages.[12] But we are of course aware that, although English is obviously absent from Wolfson's sentences, it is still very much present as the absent centre around which the translations are organized. Exactly as the pseudo-Sanskrit or Martian productions of the Swiss medium Helen Smith betrayed their French origin in the arrangement of words, his false syntheses are still, in their very excess, distinctly English. Except that, in the example quoted, it is I who have reconstituted the sentence, for Wolfson dissolves the coherence of the syntax in his lengthy explanations of the phonetic passage from each English word to its foreign equivalents. Wolfsonizing is the mirror-image and consequence of Brissetizing. We must expect our categories to overlap, the frontiers to blur. My two devices are not in fact 'categories' in the Aristotelian sense: there is no imposing taxinomies on an anomic and ataxic remainder. Like the egg in the sheep's shop in *Through the Looking-Glass*, the remainder is always on the periphery of our field of vision, taunting us but always eluding our grasp. The two devices will be used mainly for their heuristic value.

MULTIPLE ANALYSIS, OR BRISSETIZING LANGUAGE

Two characteristics of Brisset's method bear on the reality of the remainder: the multiplication of ambiguities and the exploitation of homophony. As we have seen, the absence of ambiguity explains the superiority of artificial languages, and the reduction of ambiguity is a goal for grammatical analysis. The etymological truth about a word is unique, an immediate constituent analysis univocal. The ambiguity that does subsist in language is an exception to this, but one that only confirms the principle, for there are as many analyses as there are distinct meanings, but only one per meaning. The similitude of homonyms or surface structure is a matter of chance, perhaps of bad luck. It is duly reduced by analysis. There are two entries for 'bank' in the dictionary, so that 'he went to the bank' need not remain problematic too long. And there are two structures for 'the workmen tore up the street', one in which the main syntactic break occurs after 'tore', the other in which it occurs after 'up'.

This is the official line on ambiguity – one can, one must, and one does get rid of it. But does one? For even if it eventually disappears, ambiguity introduces an element of uncertainty into the system. It threatens to increase and multiply, to leave an unanalysed residue, in short to evade the mastery of the speaking subject. This is where the logician can regret 'the deficiency of ordinary language' and celebrate 'the eminent superiority of our technical notation'. Thus, Quine illustrates the defects of natural language with the following phrase:

'pretty little girls' camp'.[13]

A camp for pretty little girls, a pretty camp for little girls, a pretty little camp for girls – will the list ever stop? Of course it does, and technical notation does justice to this incipient proliferation. But we are left with the uneasy feeling that this is merely a fluke. In fact, a fourth interpretation is already looming on the horizon: a camp for girls that is rather small. Or a camp that is a little too much a little girls' camp? Brisset is now with us, his multiple analysis a necessity imposed by language. The phrase is opaque, and language demands, and practises, multiple analysis.

Homophony is as bad as ambiguity. It is present everywhere in our languages – linguists have remarked that French and English, not to mention Chinese, are particularly rich in homonyms. There is something scandalous here. We understand the law of economy that governs the double articulation of language: a limited number of phonemes combines to form an indefinite number of morphemes and words. But with homophony this economy is taken to self-defeating extremes, which sound very much like laziness. There is a traditional explanation for this, which goes back to Aristotle's *De Sophisticis Elenchis*: there are more things than words and therefore we have to use the same words to refer to several things.[14] Darmesteter insists on the scarce resources of language, on the limits of human memory, and concludes that language cannot always express new ideas with new words and has to extend the semantic scope of old ones. Foucault ascribes the same position to Roussel.[15] The dubious character of this position is obvious. We could easily maintain that the opposite is true, that there are many words that do not correspond to a 'thing', or even to a – clear and distinct – idea. As the abundance in our daily life of ontological metaphors – metaphors that call entities like inflation, love, or the mind into being – shows, we rarely resist the Promethean urge to create entities just by naming them. He who would wield Occam's razor always gives in to the inventor of unicorns and concepts. In fact, both positions are equally unhelpful. We must take them as symptoms of the anxiety that the pervasiveness of homophony has always caused. What is at stake in both cases is the autonomous growth of language, unchecked by the constraints of reference or systematic rationality. But this is precisely what the remainder is about.

This is where I begin to sample my rag-bag. Exhibit number one is a case not of multiple, but of excessive, analysis. It consists in motivating the unmotivated, or remotivating the demotivated – in other words, in analysing what cannot, or should not, be analysed. If we start with proper names, we encounter the rhetorical device of *adnominatio*, the remotivating of proper names through etymology, metanalysis, or translation. The best instance I know of *adnominatio* through metanalysis is a piece by the British humorist Paul Jennings, tellingly entitled 'Ware, Wye, Watford'. It has the form of a short lexicon, in which the entries are the names of towns, each followed by a short definition, which functions like an analysis of the name, or a celebration of its 'magical aptness'. Here are a few entries:

> **barnstaple** n. Mainstay, keystone. 'Mrs Thomas is the b. of our committee.'
> **buckfastleigh** adv. (arch. and poet.). Manfully. '*Aye, and right buckfastleigh, lad*' (Hardy).
> **erith** v. (obsol.) Only in third pers., in old proverb 'Man erith, woman morpeth.'
> **kenilworth** n. A trifling or beggarly amount. 'He left her nobbut a kenilworth in his will.'
> **lowestoft** n. A subterranean granary.
> **manningtree** n. A gallows.
> **thirsk** n. A desire for vodka.[16]

Only too rarely dare we indulge in a parody of the NED or in the composition of spurious quotations from Hardy. I confess that, to me, this game is a source of endless jubilation. The irrational aptness of 'man erith, woman morpeth' has indeed something magical about it. And I would like to show that this is no private vice, but public virtue – that the urge to do this pleasurable violence to language is pervasive, an integral part of the way we relate to our words. It is indeed easy enough to find similar playing with names in literature. Any reader of a Dickens novel knows that a man called Uriah Heep is not going to be a pleasant character. There is a rhetoric of fictional names. To quote an obvious example, the names of the characters in Mervyn Peake's 'Gormenghast' trilogy are crying out for remotivation, beginning with the name of the castle itself. 'Gormenghast'? 'Gore', 'aghast', 'ghastly', 'ghost', 'gormless' – all words whose meanings are not entirely indifferent to the narrative and its general atmosphere. 'Sepulchrave'? 'Sepulchre', 'grave' (an obvious portmanteau), but also 'crave', 'rave', 'raven', and countless others, including, why not, the Latin *'pulcher'*. Again, it is not too difficult to establish a link between those words and the atmosphere of the novel or the personality of the characters. We have in fact gone back to the venerable Platonic or Adamic tradition of the veracity of names. The character and fate of Lord Sepulchrave are contained in his name, as are those of Steerpike, the villain, in so far as their names are true. This, of course, is a little facile: the novelist is in full control of his fictional world, and the *deus ex machina* he contrives by his authorial naming does not prove much. He is not even in the position of Adam, who had to guess right – rather in that of the Adam of medieval morality plays who, to the great relief of the audience, named the objects of their familiar world and guessed right every time. Jennings's game is more constrained in so far as he deals with names that he did not invent – and we must note here that he does to those opaque names only what we know can be done to transparent or semi-transparent names like 'Oxford' or 'Chichester'. In other words, he only remotivates what was once motivated but has become opaque. My textbook on toponymy does not account for Thirsk or Morpeth, but it explains Erith, 'a compound of OE *èar* and *hȳ* , "the muddy or gravelly landing place"; "*èar*" ... probably denotes "earth".'[17] It would appear that 'Erith' originally meant 'Mudbath in the Hole'. I prefer Jennings's Brissetized explanation.

Remotivating place names, therefore, is modestly excessive. More contentious is the motivating of common nouns. For they are either complex signs, relatively motivated (this is the case of Saussure's 'twenty-nine'), or purely arbitrary. The French word 'cheval', as a simple sign, is not motivated in any way. Yet this is how Michel Leiris, in his *Glossaire*, accounts for it:

CHEVAL – c'est achevé à ailes: Pégase[18]

'It ends up with wings: Pegasus.' As Alice would say, it fills up my head with ideas, only I don't know which. It is true that Pegasus was a winged horse – but why was he supposed to 'end up' there? The key lies in the spelling of the word. If you read aloud the letters that make up the word, *C–H–E–V–A–L*, you will have uttered something strikingly similar to '*c'est achevé à ailes*', and something which 'ends up on "l".' this, of course, is pure Brisset. People often wondered why he never wrote a dictionary: Leiris has done it for him. Other entries duly play on phonemic dissemination.

vierge fière de son givre [**virgin** proud of her frost][19]

Leiris's autobiography describes the fascination that the form of words always held for him. It begins on the occasion when he discovered that his favourite interjection '... *reusement!*', is short (and incorrect) for '*heureusement!*', and is therefore relatively motivated.[20] This experience became for him the revelation of a truth – not so much the truth that words have correct uses and meanings, but the truth that a word is part of language, a social organism, that it is part of a network of relationships that extend far beyond the grasp of the individual subject. He has, in fact, discovered that words are motivated, that language speaks.

But one might object that this is mere literature, a highly personal and innovative use of language, not one that is central to our everyday use of the system. Not at all – our everyday speech is pervaded with remotivation, and everyone enjoys the game. Daft definitions is one name for it. It is described thus: 'Any number of players, any age, fun rather than competitive.' And it consists in the rawest punning, that is in inventing homonymous definitions for common words. A few examples will do:

DEHYDRATE : proportional excess tax you are charged
with for concealing your true income
EQUIPMENT : he was only joking
GLADIATOR : how the cannibal felt about his mother-in-
law[21]

The last one sounds like a Wellerism. The pleasure we feel in playing that sort of game is due to the fact that we are breaking one of the strictest linguistic taboos: do not tamper with words, for they are not yours. The imposition of a fixed orthography, and the painful need for each of us to learn its senseless rules, is the latest and most extreme form the taboo has taken. It already animated the sixteenth-century purists who insisted on adding a silent 'b' to 'doubt' out of respect for etymology. But in actual usage we do maul our words, we mispronounce, distort, and sometimes eat them ('Could you please articulate!'), and they do not seem to resent it. One is reminded of the famous scene in *Tristram Shandy* where the validity of baptism is discussed. Is the child validly baptized *in nomine patriae et filia et spiritum sanctos*, where only the suffixes are wrong? What if the roots are torn out, and the child baptized *in gomine gatris*? 'My father [says Tristram] delighted in subtleties of this kind, and listened with infinite attention.'[22] So do we, for it is a short step and a pleasant one from mispronunciation to deliberate distortion, or remotivation.

A sure sign of the popularity of the game is its adoption by the authors of slogans, advertisers, protesters, candidates of all description. At one point, one could see on the walls of the London underground the following slogan: 'Foiled again? Try Dillons!' Part of the pleasure we take in this type of slogan lies in its unfair character. Is it not grossly unfair for language to allow one to use the name of a competitor (here, Foyle's), to his detriment? In the 1981 French presidential election, supporters of Giscard d'Estaing produced stickers with this slogan: 'Un mythe errant, ça trompe énormément', where the name of the challenger was analysed and his allegedly Utopian programme dismissed at one fell swoop ('a wandering myth / Mitterand is extremely deceptive'). In this case, we have *adnominatio* combined with pun, for the slogan is based on a popular pun, 'Un éléphant, ça (sa) trompe' (an elephant, it deceives / its trunk).

This injustice is part of the violence exerted by language, the pleasurable violence of arbitrariness, the violence of bad luck. Such improper use of proper names was prominent in the demonstration by French students in December 1986. The name of the minister for universities was made to signify, and I am not certain that such treatment did not contribute to his prompt disappearance from the political scene. This is the best of the slogans I heard: 'Un vaquet ça va, deux vaquets, bonjour les dégâts.' The minister's name was Devaquet. Unfortunately, it can be submitted to an analysis into two morphemes, one well-known ('*deux*'), the other non-existent but not impossible, '*vaquet*'. (Language sometimes does this: in 'cranberry', 'berry' is a morpheme – indeed, it is an independent word – but what about 'cran-'?) The point of the joke is that it was based on a successful slogan for the anti-alcohol campaign on

French television, 'Deux verres, ça va, trois verres, bonjour les dégâts!' (two glasses, everything's all right, three glasses, there's trouble coming). This slogan was itself based on a popular French turn of phrase, '*bonjour*' plus a noun phrase, the ultimate origin of which is, I believe, Françoise Sagan's best-seller of the 1950s, *Bonjour tristesse*. And this title was in turn borrowed from a poem by Paul Eluard. This is a good instance of the way language, as a social organism, works; it has nothing to do with structural linguistics. First, a poet coins a phrase – an intentional act if ever there is one, but a move made against the background of and contrary to the rules of the system. Next, a novelist uses the quotation for a title, a frequent move in the rhetoric of titles. Again, the act is intentional, but the phrase soon grows popular, it becomes common linguistic property. The phrase is then made productive, so that any noun phrase can be substituted for '*tristesse*'. This step cannot be ascribed to an individual speaker – language has taken over. A clever advertising copy-writer uses the phrase for a euphonic slogan, an intentional move again. Last, by pure chance, the slogan fits the name of the minister, and someone successfully parodies it. But who? The Unknown Coiner, the mythical figure who is the necessary and unknowable origin of every linguistic change. It would be more correct to say, 'the student movement', what Deleuze and Guattari call 'a collective arrangement of utterance'.

Adnominatio and punning are, therefore, inseparably intentional and accidental, subjective and collective, a matter of skill and chance. It remains only for me to show that language practises *adnominatio*. And of course it does: chauvinism owes its name to one Chauvin, whose dislike for foreigners became proverbial; '*poubelle*' (dustbin) to a prefect of Paris, who made the object obligatory – a fit punishment for imposing one more regulation; 'pistol' to the Italian town of Pistoia. Examples are legion. Brisset is not the only one to be provoked by language, and we are all in the same *Narrenschiff*.

The next item on our list is a development of the first, motivation not by metanalysis but by translation. The French have a name for it, *traducson*, or translation according to sound. The best-known practitioner is Luis d'Antin Van Rooten.[23] The corpus is now impressive: we have learnt that 'un petit d'un petit' is not the sad story of a dwarf's dwarfish son, and that 'Et qui rit des curés d'Oc?' has nothing to do with laughing at priests from the South of France. An elaborate *mise en scène* surrounds these hermetic pieces. The editor's foreword to *Mots d'Heures, Gousses, Rames* tells us that the poems came to him among the papers of a deceased relative, one Charles Fernand d'Antin, together with a bundle of love letters and a recipe for turbot in saffron. The unintelligible verse is heavily annotated – the notes always stress the difficulty of understanding, for the poems are worthy of Mallarmé and/or the more hermetic French symbolists. Interpretation is needed, and it is impossible. But these notes often begin in a downright cheeky manner – by offering a translation of the line into English. However, for those of us who are more than usually moronic, the editor's foreword has provided a hint. When read aloud, 'these poems assume a strangely familiar, almost nostalgic, homely quality'. As we listen to the sounds, rather than read the printed words, they do become familiar – Humpty Dumpty and Hickory Dickory Dock emerge from their disguise into our linguistic consciousness. (Interpretation is not always that easy – some of the rhymes still baffle the enlightened reader long after he has been given the key.)

In the possibility of a translation according to sound, the remainder is seen at work. Of course, it will be argued that d'Antin's poems can be dismissed as what the French call a *tour de force*, a demonstration of useless verbal skill. The trouble is that it works so well (in a sense, it works too well, for it is *always* possible to translate according to sound), and that language lends itself so readily to such practices. And we have already seen that the structural possibility of the game exists in quotation. With due precaution, I can mix languages. Here is a sentence from Heidegger's *Ueber den Humanismus*: 'Die eigentliche romanitas des homo romanus besteht in solcher humanitas'.[24] In what language is this written? Or is Heidegger the unwitting predecessor of Wolfson? What Luis d'Antin does is to take the possibility of quotation to excess, to the impossible point where the same sentence is both the frame and the foreign quotation, both French and English. This possibility worries even analytic philosophers, at least those who have reflected on the problems of quotation and indirect speech:

> The 'said that' of indirect discourse, like the 'said' of direct, may relate persons and sentences, but be a different relation; the former, unlike the latter, may be true of a person, and a sentence he never spoke in a language he never knew. The trouble lies rather in the chance that the same sentence may

have different meanings in different languages – not too long a chance either if we count ideolects as languages. To give an example, the sounds 'Empedokles liebt' do fairly well as a German or an English sentence, in one case saying that Empedokles loved and in the other telling us what he did from the top of Etna. If we analyse 'Galileo said that the earth moves' as asserting a relation between Galileo and the sentence 'The earth moves', we do not have to assume that Galileo spoke English, but we cannot avoid the assumption that the words of the content-sentence are to be understood in English.[25]

It would be difficult to enrol Davidson as a supporter of the remainder. His concern is clarification, not linguistic excess. But the experience of *traducson* is obviously not confined to a literary hoax like *Mots d'Heures*. It is, for instance, a common one among bilingual speakers. Leonora, a native of the French West Indies, the story of whose life has recently been published,[26] relates her difficulty in adapting to strange foreign languages, while her native creole was forbidden at school. She instinctively retranslated the Latin words of the Bible, which she was made to learn by heart. '*Ave Maria*' became '*lave lari la*' ('*lavez la rue là*': wash the street), '*laudate*', '*dlo glase*' (*de l'eau glacée*: iced water) and '*miséricorde*', '*mizire kord*' ('*mesurez la corde*': measure the rope). There is nothing literary in this. Linguistic contact is a daily experience, sometimes painful, sometimes comic – the mistakes and mispronunciations of foreigners are a source of endless jokes in all cultures. A few years ago, a letter to *The Times* objected to the unfair choice, by the French railway company, of the verb '*composter*' to tell passengers that they were to have their tickets punched before boarding a train. The unwary British traveller could interpret this as a call to make compost out of his ticket. At the time when the communication minister was attempting to purge the French media of English words, a television journalist asked passers-by for the meaning of some of those scandalous words. The answers were edifying. '*Sponsoriser*' (to sponsor) was said to mean 'wash with a sponge'; '*traveling*' (as used in films) as the practice of walking in drag ('*un travelo*' is slang for a transvestite); '*un steeple-chase*' was, of course, a type of '*chaise*', some kind of chair.

Again, language itself practises this, and encourages the practice. Countless words in all languages are corruptions of mispronounced or misunderstood foreign words. The French '*contredanse*', which most French people would gloss as an 'opposite-dance', is a corruption of 'country-dance', as the French '*choucroute*' comes from '*sauerkraut*', where it is '*sauer*', not '*kraut*', that has produced '*chou*'. And everyone knows that coleslaw is so called because it is served cold. A foreign language is a treasury of strange but fascinating sounds, and the speaker is caught between the urge to interpret them, the pervasive need to understand language and the fascinated desire to play with words, to listen to their sounds, regardless of their meanings. Another formulation of the contradiction between 'I speak language' and 'language speaks' might be: 'I need sense' and 'I enjoy nonsense'. The highest summit in Cornwall – its height is modest – is called 'Brown Willie'. It is not brown, and there is no need to be familiar with a hill. The name is a corruption of the Cornish '*bron gwennyly*', the rounded hill of the swallows. *Traducson* is not always poetic, and the need to understand is satisfied with little sense. On the other hand, Edwin Muir, in his autobiography, describes one of his relatives thus:

> Whenever Sutherland got drunk, he began to invent language. I can't remember now many of his feats in this way, but he liked words with a dashing Spanish sound, like 'yickahooka' and 'narrahonta'. He was so pleased with the word 'tramcollicken', which he invented himself, that he gave it a specific meaning which I had better not mention; but the word became so popular that it spread all over Wyre. From somewhere or other he had picked the word 'graminivorous', which struck him by its comic sound, and for a long time his usual greeting was 'Weel, boy, how's thee graminivorous tramcollicken?' Macedonia, Arabia, Valparaiso and Balaclava became part of his ordinary vocabulary, giving him a sense of style and grandeur.[27]

I know who Sutherland is – he is the Unknown Coiner, and he lives on in each of us.

Exhibit number three is re-analysis proper, which I have called, following the practice of etymologists, 'metanalysis'. Not only are words re-analysed, they are also falsely analysed, often on purpose. This is one of the main sources of comedians' jokes. Let us listen to the two Ronnies, in one of the 'But first – the news' sequences of their TV programme:

Foreign news. Uganda. At the state dinner to welcome the German delegation today, General Amin ate a hamburger, two frankfurters and a young man from Heidelberg.[28]

I am not claiming that this is the acme of a centuries-old tradition of British wit – I am offering this as a testimony to the importance of folk-etymology. Far from deserving Saussure's strictures, folk-etymology is the best embodiment of this need for meaning, of this urge to interpret, which governs our relations to our own language. Words must mean, whether they mean to or not; their constituents also must mean, down to the slightest syllable. And since linguistic change conceals their pristine meaning – for words originally did mean – our present knowledge of language will supply the missing link. Folk-etymology is synchronic etymology: 'false' or 'popular' etymologies are based on the community's feeling for language and are therefore etymologically true. They witness to the creative urge that etymologizes words, ascribes symbolic meaning to sounds, and more generally makes us inhabit our language. Judith Milner has studied a popular programme on French radio. Like the television experiment mentioned before, it consisted in asking the man in the street to explain difficult words.[29] No doubt only the best, that is the most eccentric, answers were broadcast. Here are a few. What is an *'analphabète'* (an illiterate person)? 'I know that one – it is a man who has "*des bêtes dans la partie anale de son individu*"(animals in the anal part of his person).' And what is *'la prévention routière'* (prevention of road accidents)? 'Indeed I know, it is the after-sales service for cars, "*l'après-vention routière*".' We note that in the first case the man in the street has a choice between two words within the analysed word, *'anal'* and *'alphabet'*. The choice of the wrong one is probably due to the fact that it precedes the other – indeed, the normal prosodic 'virtual pause' will occur in the middle of the word, *'anal-phabète'*, rather than after the first syllable. Perhaps it is also due to the fact that it refers to a theme that is closer to the speaker, as an object of more direct concern to him than memories of school. In the second instance, the answer involves doing violence to language, for the noun derived from *'vendre'* is not *'vention'*, a coinage, but *'vente'* – the urge to interpret is so strong that it makes the speaker cross the frontiers of grammaticality. And perhaps the most striking aspect of both answers, apart from the fact that they might well have been invented for the two Ronnies, is the way they begin: *'Oui, je sais ...'* – I know that one. When asked about his own language, the subject will not readily confess ignorance. He will behave like what psychoanalysts call *'un sujet supposé savoir'*, the possessor of comprehensive knowledge, which implies that he must and will answer any question.

In the case of metanalysis, it is particularly easy to follow our usual path, from literature to language through popular games or practices. Anthologies of comic verse often contain poems like the following:

A Country Summer Pastoral
(As written by a learned scholar of the city from knowledge derived from etymological deductions rather than from actual experience)

I would flee from the city's rule and law,
From its fashion and form cut loose,
And go where the strawberry grows on its straw,
And the gooseberry on its goose;
Where the catnip tree is climbed by the cat
As she crouches for her prey –
The guileless and unsuspecting rat
On the rattan bush at play ... [30]

The other two stanzas introduce cows nestling in 'cowslip trees', dogs munching dog-wood, and a shepherd turning 'his herd of grasshoppers out to grass.' The interesting point about the poem is that not all the words concerned are cases of metanalysis, but it is difficult to tell which is which without a dictionary. Thus, apart from the obvious 'grasshopper', only 'catnip' (in which the poem betrays its American origin), 'cowslip', and 'dog-wood' are correctly analysed. 'Rattan' is an unanalysable Malay word; 'gooseberry' has nothing to do with geese, and everything with the French word *'groseille'* (red currant); the origin of 'strawberry', although the word does come from 'straw', is modestly stated by my etymological dictionary as 'unexplained'. We realize that folk-etymology is a special case of analogy. A complex situation, the result of historical accident, is made simple through reduction to synchronic analysis. Indeed, in those cases where the analysis is correct, the link between determinant and determined word is also simplified, made 'logical', reduced to spatial relationship – grass-hoppers hop on the grass, hence cats perch on catmint, and cows are found roosting on cowslips. Before I delved into an etymological dictionary, I was convinced, not that strawberries actually grow on straw, but that they were so called because the plant had to be protected against ground frost.

Comic poets play at metanalysis. Comedians use it for their jokes. And language practises in all its forms. Folk-etymology itself, that notorious reaction against the arbitrariness of the sign, is at work everywhere, in every language, in every period. As Ullmann puts it, 'the scope of popular etymology might well be much wider than has been realised so far.'[31] The remainder will insist. But what I would like to stress is the variety of related devices, which are an integral part of the workings of language. I have already mentioned a case of paradoxical analysis in 'cranberry'. What cannot be analysed synchronically can of course be understood in diachrony: a cranberry is a crane-berry, at least in the German original, exactly as 'bilberry', another instance of impossible analysis, has its origin in Old Norse (*bølle* still means 'bilberry' in Danish). Provided the constituent is interpretable, impossible analysis soon becomes re-analysis. Because the old sense of 'mare', an imp or a demon, has disappeared, the modern sense of the word has taken over, giving us the impression that 'nightmare' is the product of a surrealist *cadavre exquis*. We remember the painting by Fuseli, where a young person, reclining on a bed in a state of disarray, is obviously having a nightmare. A horrible imp is squatting on her bosom (this is sufficient to account for her symptoms), while the frightening head of a blind horse appears through the window. Diachronic grammarians use the term 'metanalysis' for cases of resegmentation: an eke-name becomes a nickname; a napron – an apron; a non-peer – an umpire; a *nōēdre* in Old English – an adder, etc. Synchronically speaking, we have, in our life as speakers of a language, witnessed similar phenomena in the shape of back-formation. 'Backseatdriver' is a recent compound. More recent still is the derived verb, 'to backseatdrive'. 'Lecher' has recently produced the verb 'lech', while the classic older example is the singular 'pea' from 'pease', which was falsely understood as a plural. We gladly reminisce, we reluct to contracept. The practice of metanalysis is massive, and there is no end to the violence that the system suffers at our hands – to the point of being forced to accept what is most alien to the structure of English, an infix, as in 'absobloominglutely'.[32]

So far, the phenomena I have described have concerned individual words. This can give the impression that the remainder deals only with words, with languages in contact, and with the consequences of change within the linguistic system, and that the Chomskyan core of language, syntax, is not affected. This is not the case. The remainder is everywhere at work, and this includes syntax. I shall now deal with syntactic ambiguity, either imposed by an author – the rhetorical device called 'double syntax' – or practised by language – ambiguity proper.

There is a famous passage in *The Waste Land*, where Tiresias watches the seduction of the typist by the young man carbuncular:

> At the violet hour, the evening hour that strives
> Homeward, and brings the sailor home from sea,
> The typist home at tea-time, clears her breakfast, lights
> Her stove, and lays out food in tins.[33]

The noun phrase 'the typist' is both the object of the verb 'bring', as the repetition of 'home' shows, and, at the same time, the subject of the verbs 'clear', 'light' and 'lay'. Admittedly, the practice of double syntax demands a playful attitude to syntax, which is more attractive to certain periods and certain authors – we can expect to find more instances of it in Shakespeare than in the Augustans, and there is a history of double syntax as there is a history of the pun, with periods of disfavour and periods of obsessional proliferation. Indeed, Quine's quibble is common fare in Shakespeare. This is Lear offering Cordelia to Burgundy (I,i, 201):

> If ought within that little seeming substance,
> Or all of it with our displeasure piec'd,
> And nothing more may fitly like your Grace,
> She's there, and she is yours.

And this is M. M. Mahood's comment: 'Lear's praise is capable of many interpretations according to whether we read "little seeming substance", "little-seeming substance" or "little, seeming substance", and according to the meaning we put on *seeming*.'[34]

If we analyse the lines in this manner, we are applying the false analysis of folk-etymology to syntax. There is such a thing as folk-syntax. Or again, one can Brissetize syntax, as indeed Brisset himself did not fail to do. We can start with plain ambiguity, which shows us that, here as everywhere else, language encourages and provokes. It is well known that such phrases as 'my aunt's murder' or 'the murder of Gonzago' are ambiguous between the subjective and the objective senses of the genitive, and it is easy to imagine what an author will make of this. In a popular mode, this will give us titles of films, like *Never Say Never Again* – this is an important aspect of the rhetoric of titles – or jokes. Here come the two Ronnies again:

> Following the dispute with the Domestic Servants Union at Buckingham Palace today, the Queen, a radiant figure in white silk gown and crimson robe, swept down the main staircase and through the hall – then she dusted the cloakroom and hoovered the lounge.[35]

In all this, language is used, not forced. It can be argued in fact that double syntax is present in the very structure of language, if we follow the analysis given by certain Chomskyan linguists of sentences like 'John forced Mary to leave', as opposed to 'John wanted Mary to leave'. In the former sentence, 'Mary' is *both* the object of 'forced' and the subject of 'leave', whereas in the latter she is only the subject of 'leave'.[36] In any case, the temptation of violence comes soon enough. M. M. Mahood quotes a line by Thom Gunn, from a poem called *Carnal Knowledge*: 'You know I know you know I know you know.'[37] Apart from being a perfect iambic pentameter, the line, which plays on the existence of recursive rules in English, is syntactically correct. The title of the poem, however, induces the reader to reinterpret this and find other sentences within that sentence: 'I know you' and 'you know I' – we carnally know each other. Punning and double syntax are never very distant. Indeed, it is an irrational and anti-systematic fact of language – an excellent instance of the remainder – that sentences do sometimes contain other parasitic sentences. Yves Lecerf gives the example of the banal sentence 'Le chat de la fermière de mon père croque tous les matins une souris' (the cat of the farmwife employed by my father eats a mouse every morning), which contains, among others, 'mon père croque tous les matins une souris' (my father eats a mouse every morning). He then proceeds to show that this is a frequent, although not always deliberate, occurrence in poems.[38] English instances are not hard to find in comic songs. If we reverse the process, we realize that incremental rhymes like 'This is the house that Jack built' are based on a similar process. It is true that the sentence 'this is the cat that killed the rat that ate the malt that lay in the house that Jack built' strictly speaking contains only one sentence within it, 'Jack built', the clauses that compose it being relative clauses, not independent sentences. But the recursivity that generates the rhyme – apart from the fact that it is a symptom of

78

excess, since it allows the production of sentences of indefinite length – is only the reverse of the remainder's 'sentences within sentences' device. Recursive clauses are added on because the subject decides to do so, even if his sentence may grow to such length that it will threaten to escape his control (linguists usually dismiss this possibility by appealing to the limitations of human memory, i.e. by having recourse to extra-linguistic, ad hoc, explanations). Sentences within sentences are just present in the text, whether the subject has decided it or not. At bottom, both are instances of the same syntactic device. Syntax, it appears, includes the possibility of wild proliferation.

The same applies to words. They may grow by derivation and composition. And they may be pruned, because they contain other, parasitic, words. This is a 'pruning poem' by George Herbert:

> I bless thee, Lord, because I GROW
> Among thy trees, which in a ROW
> To thee both fruit and order OW.
>
> What open force, or hidden CHARM
> Can blast my fruit, or bring me HARM
> While the inclosure is thine ARM.[39]

To go back to double syntax proper, and to the idea that one can conceal a message within another by manipulating syntax: we encounter the linguistic equivalent of visual anamorphosis, which was used for the same purposes as the pictorial version, to celebrate the vanquished in spite of official prohibition. Baltrušaitis mentions anamorphotic portraits of Charles I, and so-called Jesuitical verse is not always an instrument for lewd innuendo.[40] The following poem is known as 'the double-faced creed', and is meant to be read down and across:

I hold for sound faith	What England's church allows
What Rome's faith saith	My conscience disavows,
Where the King's head	The flock can take no shame
The flock's misled	Who hold the Pope supreme.
Where the altar's dressed	The worship's scarce divine
The people's blessed,	Whose table's bread and wine,
He's but an ass	Who their communion flies
Who shuns the mass	Is catholic and wise.[41]

The second characteristic of Brisset's method that is seen at work whenever language Brissetizes is homophony. This it is that radically questions the arbitrary character of signs, and on which the Lacanian concept of *lalangue* is based. The intentional exploitation of homophony is found in puns. I do not feel called upon to prove that puns exist and are widespread. There are whole books on the subject and, for M. M. Mahood, 'Shakespeare's wordplay' can be reduced to his quibbling. Rather, I shall analyse a limited corpus. In Chapter 9 of *Alice's Adventures in Wonderland*, the Mock Turtle recalls the days of its youth ('"Once", said the Mock Turtle at last, with a deep sigh, "I was a real Turtle"') and of its education. The subjects it was taught at school were Reeling and Writhing, Ambition, Distraction, Uglification, and Derision (the four branches of Arithmetic), Mystery and Seaography, Laughing and Grief, and, of course, Drawling, Stretching, and Fainting in Coils.[42] There are two striking aspects to these puns. The first is that they come as a series – puns often do. The other is that they are not particularly clever, which seems to make them even more enjoyable. How can we take Uglification as a successful pun on Multiplication? The obstreperousness of the attempt is three-quarters of the fun. In a way, we can understand why distant paronomasia is preferable to the perfect variety, which rhetoricians call antanaclasis. The wilder the pun the better, because it does violence to language instead of meekly following its call. In antanaclasis, language speaks: the paths are well traced, the diverging meanings clearly in view. In paronomasia, it is I who speak. I make language do my bidding. I take an untrodden path, only faintly indicated by language – I force my way through words.

Indeed, puns do not have to be clever, and their outrageousness seems to be better accepted if they come in a series – the pun is a gregarious species. We remember those old friends of the sea-side picture postcards, Buxom and Lecherous. On one of these postcards, Buxom is lying in bed ill, and the doctor says to her: 'What you need is a little sun and air.' She answers: 'Don't be naughty, not at my age!' The pun on 'sun' is as old as the hills – 'Not so, my Lord, I am too much in the sun' – and by now rather feeble. There is not much wonder in the thought that a monosyllabic word in English should be ambiguous – the Chinese outpun us by far. What is more extraordinary, and more exciting, is that the phrase 'sun and air' should be, as a whole, ambiguous, for the probability of this falls sharply. Extraordinary the situation may be, but it is by no means rare. You can buy in sweetshops a particularly long and revolting looking lollipop called 'So long sucker'. The quality of our pleasure depends not on the wit of the exercise, but on the off-hand manner in which it treats the structure of language – how is it possible to combine a feeble play on 'sucker' with another one on 'so long'? An advertisement for British Gas on television shows an anxious husband walking back and forth in a waiting-room. A man in a white coat comes towards him and gives him the good news: it has been delivered. He rushes into the next room, where his wife looks tired but rather pleased, and, bending towards the camera, which occupies the position of the infant, he asks the expected question, 'Is it a boiler or a grill?'. To which his wife placidly replies: 'both', while the camera pans up to reveal a brand new cooker. The paronomasia on which all this rests is no more 'clever' than Carroll's puns. Yet, supported by the pun on 'delivered' (I cannot remember whether it was explicit or whether my memory has recalled it from its implicit limbo) and the complex setting, it is delightful. And it allows the happy mother to give an answer that, in real life, is hardly possible.

People often wonder why punning ads, which used to be shunned by the profession, are so frequent nowadays. One answer is that advertisers have realized that you do not have to make a clever pun to get a good laugh. The other, of course, is that static advertising can resist the unfair competition of dynamic ads on television only by playing on the other medium, language. Sometimes they go to the extreme of forgetting the most venerable principle of their trade – do nothing that might produce a negative image. This is an advertisement for an Italian make of typewriter: LA STAR LATINE, LA COQUELUCHE DES SECRETAIRES (The Latin star is your secretary's darling). But I have translated the meta-phorical sense of 'coqueluche', which literally means 'whooping cough'. The choice of 'star latine' then becomes clear, for it is a pun on 'scarlatine', scarlet fever. 'The Latin star, the only typewriter which is sure to give you a rash.' One must have a certain confidence in the pleasure we take in playing with language, in exploring the remainder, to risk provoking such unwelcome associations.

I have shown the part motivation played in the slogans used by French students in 1986. Politics in the widest sense is a rich ground for puns. On the one hand, and this is Hamlet's tactics towards Claudius, serious punning is a kind of Aesopian language, which allows one to state the implicit and yet not incur liability for it – it allows one to laugh at the powerful behind their backs, a sort of linguistic Good Soldier Schweik tactics. On the other hand, it also allows one to formulate a demand, to make it memorable, or to understand a new situation by punning on older terms. Jacobean tragedy offers countless examples of the first use, where political innuendo rivals with the sexual kind (for instance in Shakespeare's Sonnet 138, which puns extensively on 'lie'). For the second use, two examples will do. In pre-revolutionary Paris, which was surrounded by walls and to move in and out of which one had to pay a toll at the *barrières d'octroi*, the populace had found a slogan to express the discontent that eventually erupted in 1789: '*Le mur murant Paris rend Paris murmurant*' (the wall around Paris causes the town to murmur). A perfect case of antanaclasis, and a pregnant one, the force of which is increased by the symmetry and repetition in the sentence. In E. P. Thompson's *The Making of the English Working-Class*, we find this Luddite slogan: 'Long live the levelution!'[43] It has two obvious qualities. Alliteration turns it into an easily memorized jingle, of the type one finds in the *Sun* newspaper ('Moors murders monster Myra must rot!'); and the paronomasia, or portmanteau word, clearly enables the militant Luddite to interpret the new political ideas of the French revolution in terms of the older native tradition of the Levellers and to incorporate the two into a new political construct. It is the homophony of a Brissetizing language that allows the incorporation. Indeed, the temptation to pun is as strong as the urge to reinterpret, and the borderline is often difficult to draw, as in this poem by A. N. Neville:

The Masochist's Week

Moanday,
Tearsday,
Woundsday,
Fearsday,
Frightday,
Sufferday,
Stunday.[44]

A fit epigraph for a book called *The Violence of Language*. As in Carroll's school subjects, the puns are valid only within a series. And each of them is the remotivation of an originally motivated but now corrupt and more or less opaque name.

It is, of course, language itself that Brissetizes in this matter. For there are puns in language, which no one ever made, and which make a language less transparent. In the course of linguistic change, sounds converge. One well-known example is 'mail' (of armour), from the French 'maille', '(black)mail', from the Old Norse 'māl', and 'mail' (the post) from the French 'malle'. If a strawberry grows on straw, an attempt at blackmail should be an unsavoury message sent through the post. Language also puns through sheer uncertainty. 'Inflammable' has been borrowed from the French, replacing the older native word 'inflameable'. This is what Fowler has to say about what happened next: 'It must have been a supposed ambiguity in *inflammable* that led to the coining of the word *flammable*. But that could only make things worse, and *flammable* is now rare, usually in the compound *non-flammable*, a more compact version of *non-inflammable*.'[45] How can we blame Buxom and Lecherous for their constant moronic fumbling with words, when language sometimes appears to be half-witted? (And this is not the only case: Ullmann mentions the same hesitation about 'habitable' and 'inhabitable'.[46]) Language also puns because of contagion. The French language allows the speaker to play endless games with the negative and positive meanings of '*personne*': 'cette personne n'est personne.' This is due to the contagion whereby the constant association of negative particle and pronoun '*ne ... personne*' has tainted '*personne*' with negative meaning. Lastly, language just puns, i.e. usage adopts a witticism made by the Unknown Coiner. A French proverb says 'Il raisonne comme un tambour mouillé'. The only reason why anyone should 'reason like a wet drum' is because of the homophony of '*résonner*' (to sound) and '*raisonner*'.

Can we go further still, and state that the very structure of language is based on punning? I came close to this position in Chapter 1 when I mentioned Freud's theory of the antithetical meanings of primal words.[47] The origin of Freud's interest in the work of Karl Abel is well known: having developed a conception of the absence of negation in dreams, and therefore of the antithetical meanings of dream symbols – a white flowering shrub can denote both both sexual purity and impurity – he believed he had found corroboration for it in Abel's linguistic analyses of ancient tongues, particularly ancient Egyptian. Abel's thesis concerned the existence of systematic ambiguity in language: the same Egyptian words were used to mean 'old' and 'young', 'weak' and 'strong'. It is now certain that his interpretations, particularly the Egyptian ones, are erroneous. Philologists have had an easy task in showing that he compares words belonging to different periods of the language, of different origins, where homonymy is the chance result of linguistic change. The foremost critic has been Benveniste, in a famous essay, 'Some remarks on the function of language in Freud's discoveries.'[48] Against Abel, he upholds the Saussurean thesis that it is in principle impossible to distinguish between two notions or referents and yet have only one word for both. If a language uses the same word to mean 'big' and 'small', it only means that it fails to distinguish between the two qualities. *Langue* knows only its own differences, and it is nothing but a network of differences: in this Benveniste is the faithful follower of Saussure. But this critique, in turn, is problematic, as J. C. Milner has shown in his essay on the controversy.[49] First, even if homophony is only a chance result of evolution and corruption, the fact that antonyms are homophonous cannot be totally irrelevant. I know that in 'without', 'with' has the older meaning of 'against', as in 'withstand'. Nevertheless, 'without' does contain 'with' as a word within a word, and for the ordinary speaker, that is, for all of us, this must have its usual meaning in the present state of the language, which makes 'without' a somewhat paradoxical compound. Second, language does ascribe antithetical meanings to the same words: to risk one's life is, paradoxically, the same as to risk death, for risking something is both gambling with what one possesses and would not care to lose – one's life – and being exposed to experiencing what one does not care to experience – death. In this case, it is undoubtedly the same word. Nor is it difficult to produce other examples. To overlook is to look over, but also to fail to do so.[50] If it is easy to look over and dismiss cases like 'cleave' as instances of diachronic ill-luck (the verb comes either from OE *cleōfan*, to cut asunder, or OE *cleofian*, to stick fast), such synchronic cases are harder to overlook. We take medicines '*pour la toux*' and '*contre la toux*' – for and against the cough (the opposition between curative 'for' and preventive 'against', which I believe is felt in English, is not obvious in French). The '*dernière mode*' is also '*la mode nouvelle*'– the French do not distinguish between the last and the latest fashion. Or again, in 'I wonder if Peter did it' and 'I wonder if Peter didn't do it', the negation does not deny anything. This is not properly speaking a case of punning, but it is an indication of a more general, constitutive uncertainty or ambiguity lurking at the heart of the system. *Lalangue*, or the remainder, is not outside but in the middle. Words like '*sacer*', meaning both 'holy' and 'unholy', which Benveniste produces as apparent examples and refutations of Abel's thesis, are words that contain within themselves a frontier (between the two notions, for they *are* distinct in Roman culture) and its dissolution – they are emblems of the remainder.

Brissetizing language means doing intentional violence to it. But it is what the French call *'une douce violence'*. For language provokes, encourages, and practises what the Unknown Coiner and the notorious punster do to it. Multiple analysis, after all, is only analogy taken to excess, one of the organizing principles of *langue* interpreted wrongly. Who are we to say that this excess is wrong? Within a synchronic *état de langue*, an analogy that is perceived by the community of speakers, in the case of folk-etymology for instance, is truly present. Brisset's 'false' starting point appears to state a truth about the workings of language.

FALSE SYNTHESIS, OR WOLFSONIZING LANGUAGE

A striking difference between Brisset and Wolfson is that the former has got rid of most of the constraints that might have limited the proliferation of his interpretations – he has removed the most important constraint on the analysis of linguistic strings by deciding that one may analyse a string more than once. Whereas the latter imposes upon himself one further constraint: the foreign words into which he translates English words must have both the same form and the same meaning; interlingual synonyms must also be homonyms. An easy task if the word has been borrowed from one language into the other, an impossible task otherwise. So that, inevitably, this excess constraint is compensated by an increased freedom elsewhere: in the conjunction of elements that have no right to be combined, in the production of five-legged calves and other verbal satyrs. Of course, the two practices, the imposition of new constraints and the liberation from old ones, are two sides of the same coin. Wolfsonizing is the mirror-image of Brissetizing, and the difference between analysis and synthesis is sometimes hard to tell. Spoonerisms are a good instance of this. One separates, one displaces, one inverts, and one puts together a new, bizarre, string of words. 'May I sew you to your sheet?', as the reverend himself used to say – the innocuous aspect of this Victorian specimen, as opposed to the generally salacious modern versions, is part of its charm. Language too produces monsters of this type. All that is needed is a change of name: spoonerism becomes metathesis, and *'formage'* (a substance placed in a form, Italian *'formaggio'*) becomes *'fromage'*.

The first path we shall take is that of excess constraints. It must be confessed that, in this matter, language is easy. It will accept the most impossible requirements. Suppose I decide that I wish to make up a sentence containing eleven occurrences of the word 'had' in a row – and this without cheating, that is, without turning the word into a proper name. Here is the sentence: 'James where John had had had had had had had had had had had the teacher's preference.' Are the eleven 'had' all there? Perhaps the sentence will become clearer if I punctuate – and it will appear that I have cheated after all, by playing on the word 'sentence'. 'James, where John had had "had had", had had "had"; "had had" had had the teacher's preference.'[51] The cheating I have alluded to is of course the introduction of a semi-colon. But is it not amazing how plastic language can be? By playing on the difference between use and mention, and on the semantic vagueness of the word 'have', a linguistic jack of all trades, it can accommodate the most preposterous demand. (Which, naturally, was made so dramatically only because I knew it could be satisfied; as in all cases of verbal skill, the answer precedes the question.)

This example is isolated and exaggerated. But it sounds surprisingly like one of the games practised by the Oulipo group.[52] On the face of it, the scientific bent of the group (François Le Lionnais, one of its founders, is a mathematician), their taste for 'potential literature' in the sense of the automatic development of rule-governed virtualities, seem to take us a long way from our concern with the free play of language. But the excess of rules and constraints does not conceal, but on the contrary reveals, the remainder. Thus, the Oulipo group practised *traducson* before Luis d'Antin Van Rooten. Only an *esprit chagrin* will refuse to concede that Le Lionnais's 'un singe de beauté est un jouet pout l'hiver' (a monkey of beauty is a toy for winter) is an improvement on the first line of Keats's *Endymion*. However, their typical stance is the imposition of supplementary constraints that automatically produce new texts out of old ones, a sort of intralingual Wolfsonizing. Sometimes the practice is easy enough, as in the 'S+7' method, where each word in a well-known text is replaced by the seventh word following it in a given dictionary – usually, one counts only words belonging to the same part of speech. Thus, using the

Longman Dictionary of Contemporary Engish, S+7 gives 'To beautify or not to beautify, that is the quetzal', while S+9 has a more Shakespearean ring: 'To beckon or not to beckon, that is the quibble.' The infinite potentialities of the method make one shudder: a whole library of Babel is beckoning to us, surrounded by all its quibbles. The remainder shows the tip of its ear in the fact that some of it is bound to make sense. Sometimes, the practice is more difficult, as in the case of anagrams and lipograms. Perec is the author of a long poem, which exploits the 399 possible permutations of letters in the word '*ulcérations*'. This is the first stanza:

> *Coeur à l'instinct saoûl*
> *reclus à trône inutile*
> *Corsaire coulant secourant*
> *l'isolé*
> *tu crains la course intruse?*[53]

> [Heart with drunken instinct
> recluse whose throne is useless
> Corsair sinking, helping
> the lonely
> do you fear the intruding race?]

The translation is fallacious. The only real translation is *COEURALINST* / *INCTSAOULRE*/ *CLUSATRONEI* / *NUTILECORSA* / *IRECOULANTS* / *ECOURANTLIS* / *OLETUCRAINS* / *LACOURSEINT* / *RUSECALOTIN*. We note that the last line of the stanza ends in the middle of an anagram, *RUSE* / *CALOTIN*, that the lines do not correspond to the anagrams, for there is always a residue and that the main difficulty is not to go on but to finish without leaving out anything. Also, we note that the last anagram is independently meaningful: 'wily bigot'.

But Perec is also the author of a history of lipograms, and of *La Disparition*, that famous lipogrammatic novel – he actually managed to write 250 pages of coherent prose without a single 'e', by far the most frequent letter in French.[54] No masculine definite article, most feminine adjectives out, conjugation amputated of the most numerous class of verbs in the present indicative: the obstacles seem insurmountable. But they are not. Most surprising perhaps, which dismisses the facile objection that this is a mere feat of skill, devoid of literary interest, the novel is eminently readable. An obvious pastiche of Roussel, it is an adventure story that progresses at a breathless pace, and the obsessional theme of which is that of disappearance. People and things keep disappearing, while a cryptic sign is encountered everywhere. It has a curious shape: three horizontal lines, joined at one of their extremities by a vertical one.

The inverse constraint consists in imposing the fixed order of language on a narrative. Here, in the most literal sense of the phrase, it is language that speaks, for the tale is in the form of an alphabet. I do not mean by this Edward Lear's nonsense alphabets, where the rhyme illustrating each letter was independent of the others, and the task only became painful when the poet came to the letter X – the existence of Xerxes proved to be a blessing. I mean a very short narrative where the sequence of vowels is combined with a single consonant. This is an instance from Perec: '*dadedidodu*', '*dad est dit dodu*' (my father, an Englishman, is said to be rather podgy). And this is Calvino's Italian version: '*Dà, deh di do! Do!**' The asterisk indicates that the last word is '*in Inglese*'. As to the story, it is as usual very moving: a young American woman, learning the *bel canto*, has the greatest difficulty in producing one of the notes. Her singing master asks her to give him a C, and encourages her in her native language.[55]

This is the stuff that poems are made of. Starobinski has remarked that what Saussure sought to discover in his anagram notebooks may have been fictitious, but it was very close to the practice of poets, who impose upon themselves constaints of sound on top of semantic constraints. This is an extract from Swinburne's *In Sepulcretis*:

> Make bare the poor dead secrets of his heart
> Strip the stark-naked soul, that all may peer,
> Spy, smirk, sniff, snap, snort, snivel, snarl and sneer.[56]

Admittedly, the last line is not the best, and there is a strong element of self-parody in it. But its aspect of excessive, almost perverse, playing is compensated by the intuition it reveals, that there are 'lexical affinities' among English words, that the consonant cluster 'sn-' functions as what Whorf calls a 'phonestheme', possessing expressing meaning. Think of another such series of words: 'nip', 'clip', 'tip', 'sip', 'dip', 'grip', 'pip', 'flip', 'drip', which, Bolinger suggests, all evoke a light blow or its result.[57] This is where the purely intentional monsters of the Oulipo are found to mimic the workings of language.

If language does not practise such games as it practises metanalysis, it allows and encourages them. After all, it has what Jakobson calls a poetic, 'I like Ike', function. Let us remember that mock exam questions from *1066 and All That*: 'Tory acts, factory acts, satisfactory acts,'[58] The reverse of folk-etymology is false synthesis. And perhaps there is one corner of language where it does play the game of one more constraint. Not in tongue-twisters, because someone must have invented 'pick a peck . . .', but in onomatopoeia, a less marginal aspect of language than most linguists would have it. What were the examples above, if not cases of onomatopoeic consonant clusters (according to Bloomfield, 'sn-' has three meanings: a breath noise, as in 'sniff', a quick movement as in 'snap', and creeping, as in 'snail'[59]) and of vowel alternation – from 'snip' to 'snap' the evocative power of the sounds changes? Another example of excess constraint in language itself would be double words with vowel apophony or alternation of initial consonant, like 'pit-a-pat', 'tick-tock', 'namby-pamby' or 'higgledy-piggledy'.

Monsters we see everywhere. By declension (one is reminded of Mr Shandy's declension of modal auxiliaries: 'I wish I were a white bear'), by dislocation, by agglutination. Poets make up portmanteau words or phrases. Carroll's bread-and-butterfly feeds on bread and butter exclusively – a rather sad story, for it dies if it cannot find it, and it can never find it. In Shakespeare's Sonnet 63, 'When his youthful morn / Hath travelled to Age's steepy night', the original text has 'travail'd', which must be understood as a portmanteau.[60] In fact, a pun, if we look at it through the looking-glass, is nothing but the perfect form of a portmanteau. But this is still literary and intentional, even if, in the case of 'travail'd', language helps. There are portmanteaux among our words. A dictionary will tell you that when a mouse scurries, he scatters in a hurry. Under the name of 'blends', linguists describe the device as productive: the Chunnel, it is hoped, will be completed at last in 1993; a dawk is an American politician who is not very firm about foreign policy, until he becomes a hawk and gives in to wargasm.[61] Blends may not be numerous, but they are very much alive. And the seductiveness of 'wargasm', the sense that the word is deeply right, like a good metaphor, shows that the remainder is at work. It is at work in all coinages. Not all of them are irregular, and not all the irregular ones are interesting. Acronyms, for instance, can be innocuous (BP, NATO), but they can also be inventive. The former French prime minister, Raymond Barre, has a name short enough to be turned into an acronym. He duly headed a group of B-A-R-R-E candidates in a local election. I have forgotten what the letters were supposed to be the initials of – it never mattered in the least.

In the matter of dubious synthesis, language shows the same forgetfulness as in folk-etymology (which is another means of coining new words: 'burger', 'copter'). This plainly appears in what is known as exocentric compounds. A ladybird is no lady. Nor is it a bird. At least birds fly: my etymological dictionary informs me that the beast used to be called a lady-cow. Of course, I am playing dumb. The *Marienkäfer* is the beetle of Our Lady, although the reason for this distinction is unknown to me, and the word is no more strange than innumerable plant names. But, precisely, the lexical field of the names of plants and insects is one in which the English language is most imaginative and poetic, where the remainder runs wild, and we can understand Carroll's temptation when he invented the snapdragonfly. Here is a French example. French people, when dressed in their Sunday best, are said to be '*sur leur trente et un*'. Nobody knows why the phrase was adopted, or what it originally meant. The sanest explanation is the only one that is very likely false: '*trentain*' was a rare name for a rich kind of cloth, the woof of which was made up of thirty times a hundred threads. Other, more fanciful, accounts are less improbable: thirty-one is a lucky number in certain card games; an old military proverb says '*trente et un, jour sans pain*', a pretext for extended leave of absence or a cause for (ironic?) festivities. Worse still, the phrase seems to have been preceded by another, still extant in Quebec, where thirty-one is replaced by thirty-six. The least wild explanation of this is that 'thirty-six', like 'a thousand and one', is a magical number, and denotes an exceptional occasion.[62] Nevertheless, the result is a linguistic monster. I understand every single word and yet I do not understand the phrase as a whole (or rather, which is in a way even more disquieting, I understand the phrase as a whole, but I fail to understand the relationship between its global meaning and the meaning of its constituent parts). A false synthesis is like a riddle, the meaning of which has been lost. There is a picture in the Uffizi gallery in Florence, long attributed to Giorgione and now to Bellini. It is entitled *Allegory*. The problem is that no one can tell what it is an allegory of. On the bank of a river, with a rocky landscape in the background, a few figures stand on a marble platform. One of them appears to be St Sebastian, but the others have not been convincingly identified, and no one can tell why they have been placed together. This strange syntax gives us the clue to the allegory: it is a premonitory representation of the remainder at work, of false composition and undue analysis.[63]

Composition is the right word. If the coinage of portmanteau words produces *monstres de langue*, to use Judith Milner's phrase, it is because it uses the monstrous composition of traditional chimeras. A little lion here, a little eagle there, and you have a gryphon. A dash of breakfast here, a modicum of lunch there, and you can eat your brunch. The subverted element is Saussure's *langue*, in so far as portmanteau words deny the arbitrary character of signs by introducing motivation everywhere, and the linearity of the signifier by compelling the interpreter to find 'words beneath words'. Thus, a mental patient addresses her doctor in the following words: 'Cher merdessein, est-ce que j'ai une tu meurs?'[64] Beneath the coinages (this sounds very much like a case of folk-etymology), a multitude of words appear: *'médecin'*, *'merde'*, *'sain'* *'sein'*, *'tumeur'*. And they form, as A. Grésillon shows, a narrative: Dear doctor, from the depth of my misery, or 'shit', can you tell me whether I am healthy or suffer from a breast tumour, in which case the verdict will be 'you die'? We also sense a certain glee in the possibility, which the remainder gives, of calling the dear doctor a piece of shit without incurring responsibility for the insult. This example shows that coinages are the mirror-image of folk-etymology, and that the remainder talks about the subject's body, and carries the violence of its affects. It also shows that forgetting frontiers is not always temporary, that whereas Carroll's portmanteaux respect the structure of *langue*, belonging as they do to determinate parts of speech and following the rules of syntax, these 'insane' coinages are no respecters of rules of any kind, especially those of syntax. If false analysis is often lexical, false synthesis is primarily syntactic.

The word 'syntax' must be understood etymologically, as the combination of dubious strings of words. Sometimes this involves merging, as in those two provocative 'words' from the first page of *Finnegans Wake*: 'twone nathandjoe', where 'two in one' and 'Nathan and Joe' are graphically represented by the fusion of the words. This sounds like a parlour game again: *'aiferferferferr'* means *'les quatre fers en l'air'* (being flat on one's back) because four occurrences of *'fer'* have been inserted within *'air'*. In 'upturn-pikepointandplace', each morpheme becomes the beginning of a new compound, and the difficulty is, as usual, to end the sequence rather than to continue it – it would not be too difficult to add another word after 'place'. Sometimes, such false syntax involves mere semantic incongruity, which is a definition of zeugma. This is the leitmotiv in Carroll's *The Hunting of the Snark*:

> They sought it with thimbles, they sought it with care;
> They pursued it with forks and hope;
> They threatened its life with a railway-share;
> They charmed it with smiles and soap.[65]

An implicit zeugma is the cause of a well-known misunderstanding between uncle Toby and the widow Wadman. If she indulges in the art of declension, 'L-d! I cannot look at it / What would the world say if I looked at it? / I should drop down, if I looked at it / ... / I will look at it', it is because she has got hold of the wrong end of the trope, for Toby was wounded in the leg and in Namur, and what the widow eventually sees is a map.[66]

Zeugma is blatant and playful. Oxymoron is more insidious, but it plays the same game. Burning ice and icy ardour, darkness visible and true falsehood are our daily linguistic fare. It has been noted [67] that the trope is particularly important in fantasy, a game where contradictory extremes are held together and sustained in impossible unity, without solution or resolution – witness Bram Stoker's name for his vampires, 'the undead'. It also plays a noticeable part in the rhetoric of titles. A subgenre of American bestselling romances is known under the name of 'sweet savage love romances', after the title of the novel that set the trend.[68] The memorable aspect of a title – no doubt a prime concern for the commercial side of publishing houses – is often partly due to overt or covert oxymoron. This is the title of a romantic novel: *Forbidden Rapture*.[69] It is phonically striking, an iambic dimeter (fŏrbǐddĕn rāptŭre) showing a nice sense of symmetry. And it is also semantically evocative, in its quasi-oxymoronic opposition of pleasant and unpleasant – a rapture, yes, but one that is forbidden: this is the topos of sinful pleasure, a notorious oxymoron. Or take another bestseller, Victorian this time, Miss Braddon's *Lady Audley's Secret*.[70] She may have been a lady, but she had a (presumably guilty) secret. Oxymoron consists in combining into a single phrase what lies on either side of this 'but', thus evincing a taste for linguistic antithesis that reminds us of those mythical primal words.

At first sight, it would seem that we cannot offer examples of language producing and preserving such 'syntactic' monsters on its own accord, except in the shape of clichés or proverbial phrases.

The violence done to the structure of *langue* is perhaps too great to be absorbed – it must be acted anew each time by an individual speaker. But language certainly offers the subject the requisite weapons to exert it. Monstrousness is a consequence of the formal character of *langue*. A syntactic system will reject coinages like those of the mental patient or of *Finnegans Wake*, but it will accept zeugma and oxymoron – all that syntax requires of 'with' is that it should be followed by a noun phrase, and all it requires of an adjectival phrase like 'forbidden rapture' is that the adjective should precede the noun. The way the speaker fills the slots is indifferent to the system – at least *qua* syntactic system. One of the results of such indifference is Chomsky's sentence, 'Colourless green ideas sleep furiously.' but it must be added that if Chomsky accepted this sentence as 'grammatical but meaningless' in the *Syntactic Structures* model, one of the aims of his subsequent models was to filter out such sentences – a sure sign that the remainder is at work in them.

If I cannot produce syntactic monsters of this kind in ordinary language, if the destruction of syntax is left to the responsibility of the individual, I can produce their diachronic equivalent, known as conversion. He upped his score, downed a pint, and garaged his car. Will the haves and have-nots out-Herod Herod? 'But me no but', as I am told Walter Scott said.[71] Nouns, adverbs, proper names even, become verbs. Verbs, even in the negative, become nouns. Confusion now hath made his masterpiece! Most sacrilegious Mixture hath broke ope. Witness this poem:

> Across the moorlands of the Not
> We chase the gruesome When;
> And hunt the Itness of the What
> Through forests of the Then.
> Into the Inner Consciousness
> We track the crafty Where;
> We spear the Ego tough, and beard
> The Selfhood in his lair.[72]

This is not a piece of nonsense, although found in an anthology of the genre: it is a denunciation of the most frequent types of offenders, for whom conversion is no longer a diachronic collective process, but synchronic and individual – philosophers and psychologists who, contemning Occam's razor, write about ifs and cans, and invent the Ego and the Id. But I am unfair to the profession, and indeed I am wrong to present the process as mainly diachronic. Any respectable grammar will tell you that conversion is a synchronic possibility, and a most productive one at that – at least in English, which in this matter is more plastic than French. Noun to verb, verb to noun, and noun to adjective conversions are normal in the system. Only think of the expressive potential of the last type mentioned: you can turn any noun into an adjective by anteposing it to another noun – a London taxi driver, a Cambridge undergraduage, a brick house. Whereas the French have only limited access to the device: 'il est très cinéma' (he is a movie addict) still have the flavour of syntactic daring. It is only the minor categories of conversion that are judged 'anomalous', 'less productive', and 'informal', like the conversion of grammatical words to nouns ('this is a must') or of phrases to nouns and adjectives ('he was one of the also-rans'; 'he had that under-the-water feeling'). Tame monsters, but syntactic monsters all the same: exactly as it Brissetizes, and for the same reasons, language Wolfsonizes.

The core of Wolfsonizing language remains the portmanteau word, as metanalysis is the core of Brissetizing language. In Saussurean terms, if folk-etymology or false analysis are natural perversions of the general principle of analogy, coinage and false synthesis are variants of the opposite principle of agglutination. In Chapter 7 of Part Three of *Cours de linguistique générale*, Saussure draws an explicit contrast between the two notions: agglutination is synthetic, analogy analytic; the former is syntagmatic, the latter paradigmatic; one is a process, *un procès*, which does not involve intention – only the natural course of usage has turned '*au jour d'hui*' into '*aujourd'hui*' – the other is a device, *un procédé*, which implies intelligence and intention.[73] The last point is dubious, the Unknown Coiner, that master of analogy, being nothing but a convenient fiction. The first two show that agglutination is the monster-creating faculty in language. This takes us beyond teratology. Not so much because the production of monsters, in its chaotic proliferation, casts light on the normal productions of the system as because the operations of the system and of the remainder are *the same*: there is no fixed frontier between the allowed and the disallowed. The same language follows Saussure and is seduced by Brisset and Wolfson. Speakers give the same welcome to the children of the legitimate and of the illegitimate union.

OVERVIEW

What happens when the remainder is encouraged to break loose?
When it pervades the text, when it prevails? Not all instances of this
are to be found in the *textes bruts* of lunatics. For it takes the highest
form of literary talent and control over words to let language speak
for itself. As an illustration, I have chosen to examine the opening
paragraphs of Christine Brooke-Rose's *Amalgamemnon*:

> I shall soon be quite redundant at last despite of all, as
> redundant as you after queue and as totally predictable,
> information-content zero.
>
> The programme-cuts will one by one proceed apace, which
> will entail laying off paying off with luck all the teachers of
> dead languages like literature philosophy history, for who will
> want to know about ancient passions divine royal middle class
> or working in words and phrases and structures that will
> continue to spark out inside the techne that will soon be
> silenced by the high technology? Who will want to read at
> night some utterly other discourse that will shimmer out a
> minicircus of light upon a page of say Agamemnon returning
> to his murderous wife the glory-gobbler with his new slave
> Cassandra princess of fallen Troy who will exclaim alas, o
> earth, Apollo apocalyptic and so forth, or else Herodotus, the
> Phoenicians kidnapping Io and the Greeks plagiarizing the
> king of Tyre's daughter Europe, but then, shall we ever make
> Europe? Sport. Rugger. The Cardiff team will leave this
> afternoon for Montpellier where they will play Béziers in the
> first round of the European championship, listen to their
> captain, Joe Tenterten: we're gonna win.[74]

The novel appears to begin straightforwardly enough. A voice of
authority, an authorial 'I' takes command, in the customary fashion.
'Longtemps, je me suis couché de bonne heure' is the untypically
short opening sentence of *Du Côté de chez Swann*.[75] But the reader
soon realizes that something is wrong. For the author, in true
remainder-like fashion, has imposed one more constraint upon her
text, turning the novel into a syntactic lipogram. She will use only
what she calls 'non-realized tenses', to the exclusion of the narrative
past or present. If the text is to be a lipogram, the element that
disappears must be by far the most frequently used. However, the
disappearance of the two natural tenses of narration does not just

make the novel an obstacle course. (Will she, like Wolfson, manage this up to the end? Of course she will – logophiliacs always do.) It introduces deep changes into the narrative mode, for it precludes the two 'effects' on which a mimetic text is based: the *'effet de réel'* and the *'effet de reconnaissance'*. A mimetic novel, in order to establish a correct relationship between narrator and reader, must somehow convince the latter that 'it is all real, or very much like reality'. We follow the travels of a Hardy character on an ordnance survey map; we treat *Mary Barton* as a representation of the situation of the English working class in 1848. Besides, we easily find our bearings in such a novel. We recognize this world, and above all we recognize our place as readers, a well-disposed, obedient audience ready to grant the narrator due mastership and authority. Choosing only non-realized tenses deeply alters this situation. For a narrator usually knows how to keep at a distance from the story he or she is narrating – if necessary, as in *Jane Eyre*, we shall distinguish between the narrating adult and the narrated child. This involves a global point of view, a sense of narration always being after the event – hence the normal use of 'narrative' past. Not so in *Amalgamemnon*. There is a narrator, Cassandra, or Mira Enketei, a history teacher recently made redundant, but she never knows how the story will develop – she makes hypotheses, feigns to decide, and the reader has the impression that *it*, the story, really decides for itself. There is no distance between the narrator and her characters: they invade her home and her life, protest against their narrative fate, force her hand.

Which means that they are not characters in the usual sense, as Cassandra is not so much a round character as a shifter, a redundant 'I', as redundant as 'u' after 'q', and the reader a 'you', a network of shifting addressees, with none of whom we can identify. True, the characters increase and multiply in the approved fictional manner, along genealogical trees, which are duly provided – there is a certain excess there, for the novel gives us too many of them, and they are somewhat fanciful, beginning as they do with Charlemagne. But we soon realize that their origin is linguistic. Language is the master, it speaks in its own right, producing subjects on the rebound of its sentences, out of an intertext. Thus, the narrator is called Enketei after the Greek phrase *'en ketei'*, inside the sea-monster. A Jonah-like persona, she is not merely a consciousness, imagining people and events, but a part of the constellation Cetus, language become the cosmic creator of the world. Her lover, he who plays

Agamemnon to her Cassandra, is duly called Willy, the embodiment of the modal that replaces realized tenses, but also he who
hath his will of her and hath her will (there is a long tradition for
this pun, the climax of which is in Shakespeare's Sonnets).

At first sight, this is only mild Dickensian excess: we have seen
that *adnominatio* was rife in Victorian novels. But it goes much
further than this – a question no longer of names, but of voices. The
text intertwines them, so that it is sometimes difficult to decide who
speaks, or when a new voice replaces the old one. This babble is a
sign that the remainder is speaking, that language is not meant for
the exchange of messages between already constituted subjects, but
what constructs them, letter after letter. Such intertextual characters
are often nothing but embodied metaphors. In the course of the
novel, a group of extremists kidnap an important statesperson. We
soon understand that the victim is an allegory, Poundian *Usura*
herself. This causes problems for the kidnappers, as ontological
metaphors feed not on cornflakes but on abstractions; in this case,
naturally enough, on capital. The solution, however, is not so
difficult to find: it only requires a metonymy. The prisoner is fed on
Das Kapital, a fate that she richly deserves.

Pierre Clastres tells us that among the Guayaki Indians, when
night falls, the men start singing, not in a chorus, but individually,
each singer lost in his solitude. They live in a tribe where the meat
the hunter brings home is taboo for him – thus forcing him to
depend on the community for his food – and where a dearth of
women has imposed the adoption of polyandry – thus forcing a man
to share his wife with others, a situation to which Guayaki men
have resigned themselves, but which they resent. Guayaki men,
therefore, are caught in a compulsory system of social exchange.
This is why, when they sing at night, they transform the third type
of exchangeable commodity, words, into the expression of individuality and solitude, why they attempt to forget its use as a social
bond. Language allows them a space for personal freedom because
of the duality of its functions. During the day it is a means of social
integration and communication; at night, it allows men *not* to
communicate, it lets them be alone in the midst of the tribe. The
burden of their litany is the endless repetition of a single word:
'I!I!I!'[76]

This anecdote must not be taken as an illustration of the
opposition of expression and communication within language. It
seems to me that it illustrates the constitutive power of language, its

role in the construction of the speaking subject. The singer can intone 'I' because language has created him a subject. The situation in *Amalgamemnon* is similar. The real narrator is not Cassandra, but language itself, or rather that part of language that speaks the speaker, the remainder. The first page is indeed a festival of Brissetizing or Wolfsonizing tropes. Each word becomes a character who calls and answers other words, establishing a network of relationships that sustains the text, evokes voices, and creates a world. Thus, a pun on Europe – hardly a pun at all, merely an incipient piece of anachronism – marks the appearance of the voice of a newscaster in the middle of an evocation of Ancient Greece. The name of the captain of the rugby team is naturally meaningful, an emblem of this time-shift: Joe Ten-to-Ten.

Words speak. They alliterate ('who will still want ...'), they proliferate in the inventories of subjects and passions, they Miltonize ('ancient passions divine', 'middle class or working': an unusual repartition of adjectives reminiscent of the master's style), they quibble ('middle class or working in words' is an excellent instance of double syntax; 'paying off with luck all the teachers of dead languages', an implicit zeugma), and of course they endlessly pun. Homophony is the law of the remainder, as in 'Apollo apocalyptic and so forth' (this is adapted from a famous pun in Sophocles), and words constantly plagiarize each other (an etymological pun on 'plagiary', the original meaning of which is 'kidnapper'). Who will deny that such use of paronomasia or of etymological tropes is pregnant with meaning, at the Heideggerian play on 'techne' and 'technology' shows? The result is complex, but eminently pleasurable. The remainder is full of verve and joy, and *Amalgamemnon* is, among other things, an extremely funny novel.

CONCLUSION

What I have tried to show is the sheer size of the rag-bag. The remainder is everywhere in the system, in our everyday use of words as in our playing with them or in our attempts at *écriture*. It is present at the two extremities of the spectrum: the authorial voice of the writer, rich in *procédé*, and the autonomous development of language, a mere process. Brissetizing or Wolfsonizing is a matter not of being demented, or gifted with words – there are people who are geniuses at crossword puzzles or suchlike games – but of giving in to the provocation of language, of letting oneself go.

The main consequence of this is that we can no longer treat the remainder as negative, as excluded, as the shady side of the frontier. It is the other side of language, but not a shady verso to a rightful recto. It is rather like one's shadow: a constant companion, which one tends to forget, but whose absence – conceivable only in tales of the uncanny – would be sorely missed. There is something *unheimlich* in the remainder. It shares the antithetical meanings of this primal word: it is homely yet disturbing.

Since the uncanny has been mentioned, one last distinction. Brisset and Wolfson are often celebrated – or dismissed – as practitioners of '*la linguistique fantastique*'. I have treated them here not as linguistic eccentrics, but as the discoverers of a certain type of truth about language. We must go beyond the quirks and oddities that account for their exclusion from the field of serious research. '*Linguistique fantastique*' is best defined as the form of linguistics that is no longer admitted in recognized research programmes: speculations about the origin of language, the search for a universal tongue, etc. But the remainder, which is so much present in Brisset and Wolfson, cannot be excluded as mere speculation or irresponsibility. A physicist who supports the second principle of thermodynamics will not encounter instances of perpetual motion; but a linguist who believes in the syntagmatic and paradigmatic axes of language will come across cases of glossolalia – he will meet the remainder in all its various and enticing shapes.[77]

NOTES

1 A. Darmesteter, *La Vie des mots*, Paris, Champ Libre, 1979, p. 46 (first published, 1887).
2 U. Zürn, *Der Mann im Jasmin*; French transl., *L'Homme-jasmin*, Paris, Gallimard, 1971, pp. 111–12.
3 J. P. Brisset, *La Grammaire logique*, Paris, Tchou, 1970; M. Décimo, *Jean-Pierre Brisset, prince des penseurs*, Paris, Ramsay, 1986.
4 Brisset, op. cit., p. 146.
5 On Marr, see F. Gadet *et al.*, *Les Maîtres de la langue*, Paris, Maspéro, 1979.
6 R. Jakobson and L. Waugh, *The Sound Shape of Language*, Bloomington, Indiana University Press, 1979, ch. 1.
7 Décimo, op. cit., p. 143
8 S. Ullmann, *Semantics*, Oxford, Blackwell, 1962, p. 41.
9 Décimo, op.cit., p. 146.
10 L. Wolfson, *Le Schizo et les langues*, Paris, Gallimard, 1970.
11 Ibid., pp. 184–9.
12 Quoted in R. Robin, 'Le Yiddish, langue fantasmatique?', in S. Auroux

et al., *La Linguistique fantastique*, Paris, Clims/Denoël, 1985, pp. 225–35.

13 W. V. O. Quine, *Elementary Logic*, New York, Harper & Row, 1965.

14 Aristotle, *De Sophisticis Elenchis*, 1, 615a, 11; see W. Redfern, *Puns*, Oxford, Blackwell, 1984, p. 7.

15 Darmesteter, op. cit., p. 40; M. Foucault, *Roussel*, Paris, Gallimard, 1963, p. 22.

16 P. Jennings, *The Jenguin Pennings*, Harmondsworth, Penguin, 1963, pp. 15–17.

17 P. H. Reaney, *English Place Names*, London, Routledge, 1960, p. 141.

18 M. Leiris, 'Glossaire', in *Mots sans mémoire*, Paris, Gallimard, 1969, p. 78.

19 M. Leiris, *Langage, tangage*, Paris, Gallimard, 1985, p. 63.

20 M. Leiris, *Biffures*, Paris, Gallimard, pp. 9–12.

21 D. Partlett, *The Penguin Book of Word Games*, Harmondsworth, Penguin, 1982, p. 21.

22 L. Sterne, *Tristram Shandy*, Oxford, Oxford University Press, 1951, p. 297 (IV, 29).

23 L. d'Antin Van Rooten, *Mots d'Heures, Gousses, Rames*, London, Angus & Robertson, 1968, p, 13.

24 M. Heidegger, *Ueber den Humanismus*, bilingual edition, Paris, Aubier, 1964, p. 46.

25 D. Davidson, *Inquiries into Truth and Interpretation*, Oxford, Oxford University Press, 1984, p. 99.

26 D. Bébel-Gisler (ed.), *Leonora*, Paris, Seghers, 1986.

27 E. Muir, *An Autobiography*, London, Hogarth, 1959, p. 19.

28 The Two Ronnies, *But First – The News*, London, W. H. Allen, 1977, p. 25.

29 J. Milner, 'La Voix publique', in *DRLAV*, 21, Paris, 1979, pp. 101–7.

30 C. Wells, *A Whimsey Anthology*, New York, Scribner, 1903 (Dover, 1963, p. 164).

31 Ullmann, op. cit., p. 103.

32 L. Bauer, *English Word-formation*, Cambridge, Cambridge University Press, 1983, pp. 231, 18.

33 T. S. Eliot, *Collected Poems*, London, Faber, 1963, p. 71.

34 M. M. Mahood, *Shakespeare's Wordplay*, London, Methuen, 1957, p. 43.

35 The Two Ronnies, op. cit., p. 28.

36 For various analyses of this type of sentence, see R. A. Jacobs and P. Rosenbaum, *English Transformational Grammar*, London, Ginn, 1968, and P. M. Postal, *On Raising*, Cambridge, Mass., MIT Press, 1974.

37 Quoted in Mahood, op. cit., p. 108.

38 Y. Lecerf, 'Des Poèmes cachés dans les poèmes', *Poétique*, 18, Paris, 1974, pp. 137–59.

39 Quoted in J. A. Cuddon, *A Dictionary of Literary Terms*, Harmondsworth, Penguin, 1982, p. 539.

40 J. Baltrušaitis, *Anamorphoses*, Paris, Olivier Perrin, 1969, p. 107.

41 Wells, op.cit., p. 142.

42 L. Carroll, *The Annotated Alice*, Harmondsworth, Penguin, 1965, p. 129.

43 E. P. Thompson, *The Making of the English Working Class*, Harmondsworth, Penguin, 1968, p. 733.

44 A. N. Neville, 'The Masochist's Week', *Times Literary Supplement*, 4 September 1987, p. 951.

45 H. W. Fowler, *Modern English Usage*, 2nd edn, Oxford, Oxford University Press, 1965, p. 283.

46 Ullmann, op. cit., p. 157.

47 S. Freud, 'The antithetical sense of primal words', in S. Freud, *On Creativity and the Unconscious*, New York, Harper & Row, 1958, pp. 55–62.

48 E. Benveniste, 'Remarques sur la fonction du langage dans la découverte freudienne', in *Problèmes de linguistique générale*, Paris, Gallimard, 1966, pp. 75–87.

49 J. C. Milner, 'Sens opposés et noms indiscernables: K. Abel comme refoulé d'E. Benveniste', in Auroux, op. cit., pp. 311–23.

50 Redfern, op. cit., p. 45.

51 I owe this sentence to a lecture by Peter Hacker. He is not, of course, responsible for the use I make of it.

52 Oulipo, *La Littérature potentielle*, Paris, Gallimard, 1973.

53 Oulipo, *La Bibliothèque Oulipienne*, Paris, Ramsay, 1987, vol. 1, p. 3.

54 G. Perec, *La Disparition*, Paris, Denoël, 1969. On translating Perec, see John Lee's comments in *Times Literary Supplement*, 2 September 1988, p. 958.

55 G. Perec, 'Petit Abécédaire illustré', in Oulipo, *La Littérature potentielle*, op. cit., p. 240; I. Calvino, 'Piccolo sillabario illustrato', in Oulipo, *La Bibliothèque oulipienne*, op. cit., vol. 1, p. 106.

56 A. G. Swinburne, *Selected Poems*, Manchester, Carcanet, 1982, p. 230.

57 D. Bolinger, *Forms of English*, Cambridge, Mass., MIT Press, 1965, pp. 245–7.

58 W. C. Sellar and R. J. Yeatman, *1066 And All That*, Harmondsworth, Penguin, 1960, p. 101.

59 Quoted in Ullmann, op. cit., p. 89.

60 See Mahood, op. cit., p. 104.

61 Bauer, op. cit., pp. 237, 96.

62 I owe my knowledge to C. Duneton, *La Puce à l'oreille*, Paris, Stock, 1978.

63 For a more serious account of this extraordinary painting, see R. Caillois, *Cohérences aventureuses*, Paris, Gallimard, 1976, pp. 150–5.

64 A. Grésillon, 'Le Mot-valise, un "monstre de langue"?', in Auroux, op.cit., p. 257. The case history originally comes from A. Fernandez Zoïla, 'Mots en jeu/enjeu de mots', *L'evolution psychiatrique*, 44 (1), Paris, 1979, pp. 29–42.

65 L. Carroll, *The Annotated Snark*, Harmondsworth, Penguin, 1967, p. 73.

66 Sterne, op. cit., p. 569 (IX, 20).

67 R. Jackson, *Fantasy*, London, Methuen, 1981, p. 21.

68 See J. A. Radway, *Reading the Romance*, London, Verso, 1987.

69 V. Winspear, *Forbidden Rapture*, London, Mills & Boon, 1973.

70 M. E. Braddon, *Lady Audley's Secret*, London, Tinsley, 1862.

71 Ullmann, op. cit., p. 52.
72 C. Wells, *A Nonsense Anthology*, New York, Scribner, 1902 (Dover, 1958, p. 36).
73 F. de Saussure, *Cours de linguistique générale*, edited by T. de Mauro, Paris, Payot, 1985, pp. 242–4.
74 C. Brooke-Rose, *Amalgamemnon*, Manchester, Carcanet, 1984, p. 5.
75 In *Amalgamemnon*, the voice reminds us of Beckett, for the first sentence is a false quotation of the opening sentence of *Malone Dies*.
76 P. Clastres, *La Société contre l'Etat*, Paris, Minuit, 1974, pp. 104–8.
77 This argument is borrowed from Auroux, op.cit., p. 26.

3

A THEORY OF THE REMAINDER

But this is neither here nor there—why do I mention it?——
Ask my pen,—it governs me,—I govern it not.
(*Tristram Shandy*, VI, 6)

LANGUAGE SPEAKS, I SPEAK LANGUAGE

The land of fairy tales is peopled with characters who hide a heart of gold under a gruff appearance. In our wanderings through the remainder we have met one such figure, the Unknown Coiner. The origin of all arbitrary and irrational changes in a language, a major source of its corruption, he is also the only selfless poet, he who imagines and creates, and whom language forgets while it preserves his creations and benefits from them. Thus, we saw that the '*bonjour* NP' phrase, which was used to make fun of the name of the French minister for universities in December 1986, went from poet to novelist, from novelist to common parlance, and from there to an advertising copy-writer and to the student movement. In this long chain, the poet, Paul Eluard, is in the position of the (un) known coiner – someone (in this case we can give him a name, and a famous one at that) and yet no one, for the speakers who now use the phrase are not interested in its origin. The progress of the phrase along the chain, going as it does from literature to language and to politics, and from individual speaker to collective speaker or no speaker at all, is an excellent embodiment of the contradiction that is at the heart of language, because it is the core of every speaker's experience of his language: when the subject speaks, it is always also, or always-already, language that speaks. Language speaks only if someone speaks it, if *langue* is actualized in *parole*; it speaks only if someone has already spoken it. Each generation appropriates the

THE VIOLENCE OF LANGUAGE

system anew, and we are all the heirs of the Unknown Coiner. Yet, nobody speaks: the speaker is cast in the mould of a system exterior and anterior to him, he negotiates his meaning with the expressive potentialities that language allows him. Sometimes he is even convinced, in exhilaration or sorrow, that the words he utters are not his, but someone else's, usually God's. For God, or Nobody, is the source of speech. As the Red King might have said in *Through the Looking-Glass*: 'To be able to hear Nobody speak! And at that distance too! I wish I had such imagination.'

I have described this contradiction elsewhere,[1] in the context of nonsense texts. I tried to show that in those texts it takes the form of a (logical) progression from 'language speaks' to 'I speak language', which goes through several stages. Stage one – the starting point – is one pole of the contradiction, 'language speaks': meaning is an effect of the free play of language, not the product of the speaker's control over an instrument. In stage two, 'language speaks through me', I am possessed by words: the sounds are mine, since they come out of my mouth, but somebody else, God or Nobody or language, is speaking. The third stage, 'language speaks to me', gives me the status of an addressee. The progression describes the constitution of a speaking *subject*, his or her liberation from the tyranny of language. Although at this stage I still speak from a place that is imposed upon me by language (certain utterances, and not others, are expected of me, as *this* speaker, speaking from *this* place), it is I who speak. The fourth stage is 'mine is an empty speech'. In the joy of individual utterance, the speaker – like someone who has just acquired their first television set and watches episodes of *Dallas* twice – falls into *bavardage*, into endless garrulousness. The exhilaration, however, does not last, and the speaker goes on to stage five: 'I speak about language.' When I seek to give a content to my logorrhea, the first object of my speech is naturally language itself: I become a linguist or at least a language-lover, a Wolfsonizing or Brissetizing logophili. *:. One last step will take me to the sixth stage, the other pole of the contradiction, 'I speak language', where at last I have become the masterful subject the dreams of linguists are made of, and where I use language as an instrument.

This raises two questions. Is this relationship between the speaker and his language restricted to nonsensical or delirious texts? What role does the remainder play in this contradiction? In other words, is it merely the embodiment of that aspect of our experience of language that tells us that it is language, not us, that speaks?

What I have said so far clearly indicates that the answer to the first question is no. The contradiction 'inhabits', to use a Heideggerian phrase, every speaker. Our experience of language, unless we give in to the devastation of delirium or to the asceticism of grammar, is one of compromise between the two poles of the contradiction. On the one hand I am fully aware that I speak language – a fortunate state of affairs, since it has allowed me, among other things, to write this book – and this conviction is dominant in me. On the other hand, at the very moment when I become reflexively aware of my mastery over language, the slightest uneasiness creeps in, and a slip of the tongue, a lurking solecism, an unwelcome anacoluthon reminds me that, even within my most rational or reflective statements, language speaks in its own right.

The answer to the second question is that the contradiction – and the compromise it entails – are more complex than appears at first sight. In order to speak, I must worm my way out of two apparent paradoxes. On the one hand, language is material and even corporeal, while on the other hand it is abstract and immaterial; on the one hand, language allows individual expression, while on the other hand it is a collective institution, which allows only collective meanings. The term 'paradox' must be taken calmly. Since we do speak, we know that there is a solution, other than speechless rage or resigned muteness. But the type of solution that we choose is not innocent. Two paradoxes – this means four propositions:

(1) Language is material. My body, a concrete object, utters sounds and absorbs sounds produced by other bodies. I whistle, I scream, and I also produce articulated sounds, words, and sentences. I cannot bear the shrieks of my neighbours' children or of their favourite pop musicians. It will of course be argued that language resides not in the capacity of my body to produce sounds – any parrot can do that – but in the intellectual faculty to articulate them according to an abstract system; in other words that there is no paradox. But there is. There is an inescapable materiality to language. My words emerge out of this body; other people's words penetrate it, an effraction that in the case of Wolfson has the direst consequences. Language is material not because there is a physics of speech, but because words are always threatening to revert to screams, because they carry the violent affects of the speaker's body, can be inscribed on it, and generally mingle with it, in one of those mixtures of bodies the Stoics were so fond of.

(2) The English language, *qua* system, is an abstraction. It is

105

independent of this body, in so far as it is the common property of a whole speech community, past, present, and future. In so far as it is a system of rules, it is immaterial. Its only materiality is contingent – it takes the dusty form of textbooks of grammar. In this sense, language, far from coming out of or entering my body, is what I must enter in order to become a member of the community. Karl Kraus talked about language as a universal prostitute. Language talks about itself in the metaphor of the mother, of the maternal tongue. In this opposition between *la maman* and *la putain* we have an illustration of our first paradox – language is both material and abstract.

(3) The subject *qua* individual says what he or she means. Chomskyan creativeness, which states that I utter sentences that have never been uttered before, because I use the rules of syntax in my own original way, gives a weak version of this. The creativeness of discourse goes far beyond the individual application of universal rules, the realization of *langue* through *parole*. This is my own meaning, these are my words: a relationship of inalienable property – there is a law against plagiarism – is established between the subject and his utterance. Karl Kraus also said that the writer is he who restores her virginity to the universal prostitute, language. Every speaker is a writer in that he is not the mere user of a common set of rules, but an individual voice, who appropriates language in his own way. In English, this verb has a euphemistic meaning that is absent in French: it means 'to steal'. This is a good image of the speaker's individuality: I waylay and transform for my own ends what is supposed to be common property. Some people call it style.

(4) What I appropriate *is* common property. For language is undoubtedly social and collective. Meaning belongs to the community before I make it mine, and in spite of the individuality of my style I can only state what is made available to me by the system. This is not yet another version of the conduit metaphor, whereby I cast my thoughts in the constraining mould of a collective language. It is rather the linguistic version of Kant's forms of intuition. What I want to utter is always-already language, framed by the structure of the tongue I speak only in so far as it speaks me. Straying off the linguistic path presupposes the existence of paths – we recognise a version of Judith Milner's concept of frontier. In more historical terms, the subject can say only what is made available to him by the historical conjuncture – he speaks within a collective arrangement of utterance.

Propositions 1 and 2, and 3 and 4, are contradictory and form two paradoxes. The solution consists in displacing the paradox by holding one proposition in each couple and discarding the other. This gives us two possibilities: 2 and 3 – language is both abstract and individual – or 1 and 4 – language is both material and collective. These new oppositions are no longer strictly paradoxical: I can conceive of an individual relationship to an abstract system, perhaps also of a collective materiality.

A commonsensical view of language will adopt the first solution, and hold both 2 and 3. Language is an instrument for communication: the individual subject freely uses his abstract tool for his communicative and expressive purposes. But choosing one solution leaves out a residue, or a remainder – the opposite solution. If I hold both 1 and 4, a position that smacks of sulphur and the bottomless pit, I shall maintain – not an easy thing to do, for this time the weight of tradition is against me – that language is both material and collective. And I find it much more difficult to give a content to this opposition than I did for the previous one. Arguing for the existence of an entity that possesses those two apparently incompatible qualities smacks of extravagance. I can do so only via a detour through the Marxist conception of ideology. This type of materiality, at first only conceivable in metaphors like 'the body politic' – but there is wisdom in such metaphors – is to be found in institutions, in what Althusser calls state apparatuses, and in the rituals and practices of an ideology. I shall argue that language, far from being a neutral instrument placed at the disposal of each individual speaker, is an institution in that sense; that it is pervaded not only by the violence of affects but by the symbolic violence of institutional struggle.

It would be too simple to say that the remainder is the part of language that is excluded by the commonsensical view, and focused upon by the opposite view. The two conceptions, the commonsensical and the nonsensical, the dominant and the dominated, are in a state of mutual implication; they are two sides of the same coin. As in the venerable story of master and slave, commonsense needs to reassure itself in the contemplation of excess. Because the first, commonsensical, solution is dominant, the second can only appear as derivative and dominated. But this is what enables it to return within commonsense, as the remainder returns within *langue*. In the excess of the second solution commonsense finds its models, both positive and negative. I shall try to capture this complicity.

The commonsensical solution (which holds propositions 2 and 3) enables us to conceive the relationship between an individual speaker and an abstract system: this is what Saussure captures in his *langue/parole* dichotomy. It will contain the two poles of my first contradiction, 'language speaks' (LS) and 'I speak language' (ISL). I follow usage, and faithfully reproduce the language invented by the Unknown Coiner, but in my Chomskyan creativeness I explore avenues of meaning, even if those are commonplace and it ends up in my producing only clichés. A Bouvard and Pécuchet figure, I labour under the illusion that in uttering clichés I express my own meanings.

But the commonsensical view of *langue* and *parole* will project, by exclusion, two other figures – the central figures of the second solution, which holds propositions 1 and 4: the delirious madman, who lets language speak him, and whose productions have the false originality of an individual expression that expresses no individual subject; and the poet, who truly speaks language and uses it for the highest form of expression. Both do violence to the system – one by treating it as mother, the other by giving it back its lost virginity. The first talks irresponsibly – he cannot be made liable for his utterances; the second exerts linguistic responsibility in the highest sense. Whereas the speaker of *langue* is both responsible, when he follows usage (it is an attitude of moral responsibility to accept the necessity of being spoken by the system), and irresponsible, when he hides himself behind the well-established convictions carried by clichés, when he takes refuge in the fact that language is a common prostitute and that it allows him to forget his individual responsibility in linguistic consensus.

This rather complicated map will, I hope, be made clearer by Figure 3.1. By crossing the two aspects of my original contradiction (LS and ISL) with the notion of textual responsibility and irresponsibility (What does it mean for a speaker to be held responsible for his text? Is this the same notion as criminal liability?), my diagram focuses on four types of text, i.e. four types of relationships between the subject and his words: delirium, usage, cliché, and poetry. The central pair corresponds to the commonsensical view of language, and shows that it is only an unstable compromise between the individual and the collective, where usage always threatens to freeze into cliché. The outside pair corresponds to the excess of the other view of language: two poles of attraction and repulsion, both similar, in that they are closer to individual expression than to collective meaning, in that they are both outside the system, and strongly dissimilar, for the expression of poetry cannot be assimilated, not even in the wildest dreams of the Romantics or of the disciples of Lombroso, to the irresponsibility of delirium.[2]

Figure 3.1

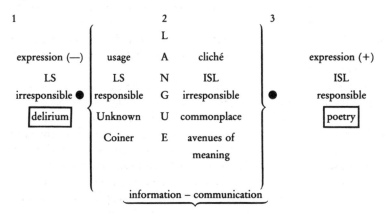

I have not yet answered my second question, about the exact locus of the remainder. In fact, what I have tried to show is that the remainder is everywhere and nowhere. It is the instability that affects every region of the diagram. It lurks within *langue*, as the return within usage of the corrupting work of the Unknown Coiner, as the irresponsibility that condemns cliché to follow the paths fixed by language. And it emerges in the two projections from *langue*, as that against which, but also with which, the poet constructs his style, and as the subversive medium for the speech of the delirious madman. But perhaps it is mostly to be found in the two dots that in my diagram mark the frontier between *langue* on the one hand and delirium and poetry on the other. The remainder, as we have had occasion to understand, deals with frontiers; its favourite location is always a wasteland, for the only territory that truly escapes all rules is no man's land.

DIE SPRACHE SPRICHT AND CODICE DI AVVIAMENTO FANTASTICO

By placing the remainder on the frontier between positions 1 and 2, and 2 and 3 on my diagram, I mean to draw attention to two

aspects. My conception of the remainder owes its origin to the idea
that it is language that speaks. And it owes a great deal to the
concept of linguistic imagination or fantasy: there is fantasy in
words, and not just in thoughts and mental pictures. The first point
comes from Heidegger's famous dictum, *'die Sprache spricht'*; the
second will be illustrated with a short story by the Italian writer
Gianni Rodari, entitled *Codice di avviamento fantastico* (Fantasy
expedition code).

It is a well-known fact that from the mid-1930s onwards, when
Heidegger focused his interest on poetry, above all on the poetry of
Hölderlin, and made it a major theme in his writing – some would
say: when he became dissatisfied with the politics of national
socialism – he began to defend a conception of language that gives
pre-eminence not to the speaker but to his *Sprache*. A quotation
from his collection *Vorträge und Aufsätze* (Essays and conferences),
first published in 1954, provides a clear formulation of this: 'Man
acts as though *he* were the shaper and master of language. While in
fact *language* remains the master of man.'[3] It would not be difficult
to find similar statements in the pieces on Hölderlin, in the
Holzwege collection, or in *Unterwegs zur Sprache*. Here is a similar
quotation, from the last of these texts: 'Only language is that which,
to speak properly, speaks; and it speaks *on its own*.'[4]

It would appear that, once I have tipped my cap to the intertextual source of 'language speaks', I must stop and express serious
doubt about the similarity of my conception of language to what
Heidegger means by *Sprache*. For it will soon be clear that
Heidegger's view goes far beyond my rather modest remainder, or
even language conceived as a coin whose two sides are *langue* and
the remainder. Language in my sense is a historical object, the
accidental result of blind chance – my position in this matter is still
Saussurean; whereas for Heidegger language acquires the utmost
ontological value – it discloses Being. The essence of language is the
language of essence, of Being. Ontology is only the explicit
formulation of the *Sage* of Being, the 'dictum' of Being that is also
its legend.[5] Hence the 'poetic' maxims that abound in his work after
1935: 'Die Sprache is das Haus des Seins. In ihrer Behausung wohnt
der Mensch' ('Language is the house of Being. In its home man
dwells'[6]); or again, 'Das Sein kommt, sich lichtend, zur Sprache'
('Being comes, lighting itself, to language'[7]). I make no such claims
for the remainder. Language has no message for me beyond the
proliferation of its paths, or beyond its easy victory over my feeble

attempts at mastering it. Yet, in my plodding, centipede-like progression, as my little paws are industriously striving to overcome the obstacles in my path, I have an intuition that, high above, the eagle is flying in the same direction.

Indeed, the trajectory followed by Heidegger from the early dissertation on the pseudo Duns Scot to the period of the Hölderlin texts opens up vistas on the remainder. He went, roughly speaking, from a classic position where, like Bergson in the *Essai sur les données immédiates de la conscience*, he regretted the fetters language places on the fascinating nuances of our emotions and sensations (that is, from a critique of the limitations that language imposes on thought), to a celebration of the powers and centrality of language. We cannot remain indifferent to this evolution. In his essay 'Bauen, Wohnen, Denken',[8] which contains the celebrated description of the bridge as a 'place' or 'site' (*Ort*) gathering the four elements ('*das Geviert*' – the earth and the sky, the Gods and the mortals), he develops an argumentative strategy that starts from the idea that man, before he begins to think, must acknowledge the fact that he is steeped in language, that he must listen to what words have to say. This enquiry into the practice of building and inhabiting, which will end in mundane and conjunctural considerations on the shortage of dwellings in post-war Germany, starts with an analysis of what the verbs '*bauen*' and '*wohnen*' tell us. The etymology, which purports to show that *bauen* was originally the same word as '*ich bin*' or the verb 'be' in English, may be dubious. Yet, it points to the fact that we inhabit our language, that we are what it says through us, or, to use Hölderlin's phrase (which provides the title for another essay in the same collection), that 'man inhabits this earth poetically'.

To inhabit this earth poetically, i.e. in language – there is food for thought in this. All the more so as Heidegger's description of this practice often sounds like a journey through the remainder. The essential equivalence that is established between language and poetry ('language itself is poetry in the essential sense. ... Poesy takes place in language because language preserves the original nature of poetry'[9]) implies consequences that will remind us of familiar landscapes.

The first is that language takes on an Adamic quality. By naming beings, it allows them to come into Being. Which means that language, far from being merely an instrument for communication, a tool for exploration and comprehension, the function of which is to circulate meanings that are already manifest, always – already formulated in thoughts or ideas, has the much higher task of disclosing Being, for 'naming nominates beings to their being from out of their being'.[10] This is why language is in essence poetic.

The second consequence is that language cannot be entirely dealt with through formalization. There is truth in the metaphor of a 'natural' language. The technical view of language understands the 'natural' aspect of language only as that which has not yet been formalized (we have already encountered the Chomskyan myth of module $n + 1$). This is a mistake, for *natural* language is not susceptible of formalization. In his essay 'The path towards language',[11] Heidegger proceeds in three stages, which will be familiar to us. In the first stage, natural language is an embarrassing remainder for the theory of information. In the second stage, one realizes that the definition of natural language, even if the remainder is conceived as constitutive and permanent, and not merely temporary, is still negative, and therefore dependent on the theory of information it seeks to deny. The third stage, therefore, consists in stating that the naturalness of natural language – a move that preempts all formalization – comes from its origin in *Sage*, in the legend that is the self-disclosure of Being in language. Even if the centipede cannot follow the eagle when it soars to these mythological and dizzying heights, where language is the saga of the four elements of Being, we understand that, for the first time, we have a conception that hails the remainder as the positive essence of language, as the bearer of an intuition (*Einblick*) into the essence of Being.

The third consequence is that natural language, which cannot be formalized, is also the maternal tongue. In *Holzwege*, Heidegger comments on a maxim attributed to Anaximander of Miletus. How, he asks, can we capture the essential meaning of the maxim, how can we listen to a speech that comes to us from such a remote past in a language not our own? In other words, how can we guard ourselves against the arbitrariness of translation? 'We are bound [says Heidegger] to the language of the saying. We are bound to our mother tongue. In both cases we are essentially bound to language, and to the experience of its essence.'[12] The answer is that we must go beyond psychological or philological calculus, and apprehend the originally poetic quality of thought, the dialogue between thought and its 'legend'. Translation is the importation of this legend from the Greek language to the German. It is by going deeper into the original being of one's maternal tongue that one can 'translate' from the Greek, a practice that owes more to etymology than to what is usually known as translation. Both languages, in so far as they are maternal, have this original relation of disclosure and concealment to Being. They communicate at this deeper, original level, where Being opens up in language, rather than at the superficial level of linguistic organization. Again, the remainder, the part of language that is maternal and cannot be formalized, acquires the highest positive value.

The fourth consequence is that the relationship between word and mouth, between language and human body, will be conceived in a new light. Heidegger, naturally, does not wish to reduce language to the physics of speech, to a series of sounds or vibrations produced by a human body. His conception of language as the legend of Being implies that there is more at stake than this. But it is also incompatible with language as pure abstraction, as ideality. These sounds are more than sounds not because they carry ideal significations, but because they have rhythm, because they make up a melody. Here again, language itself helps, for, in *Unterwegs zur Sprache*,[13] Heidegger notes that in German dialects are called '*Mundarten*', 'mouth-types'. In these dialects, the earth itself speaks: the mouth is not a mere bodily organ, it belongs, with the human body, to the *Geviert*. Language, to use Hölderlin's phrase, is 'the flower of the mouth'.

Being a centipede, I am not sure I can follow the eagle to the ultimate consequences of these consequences. My business is to describe aspects of language that are left out by linguistics. I can only note that Heidegger, when he talks about language, seeks to occupy precisely this ground. I therefore share with him, if only that, at least his critique of linguistics as a technical approach to language, reducing language to a mere instrument (not even a tool in the sense of *Sein und Zeit*). There are some prophetic-sounding pages in *Ueber den Humanismus* on the objectification of language, which tends to become a mere means of exchange, on its submission to the tyranny of 'publicity' (*Oeffentlichkeit*), and on the necessity, in order to counter this devastation, to take care of language. I am not convinced by the theme of the dereliction of language, for each generation sees in the language of the next a devastation of its dearest values, and falsely prophetic pronouncements are not missing in our tradition. There is a history, from Swift to Orwell, of 'the decay of the English language', where the repetition, generation after generation, of the same intimations of apocalypse encourages disbelief. I wish, therefore, to take Heidegger's prophecies in another sense: he insists on the independence of language from its functions of communication and information, on the necessity of paying attention to language as it is, not according to an ideal structure, but according to its 'naturalness', its arbitrary rhizomatic proliferation. The only devastation of language is its technical reduction to a means of communication. Of course, since the remainder is constitutive, there is no chance of this happening completely or definitively. We must remember, however, not to forget the remainder, for it is shy and does not thrive in the glare of 'publicity'. In other words, there is a basic aspect of Heidegger's conception of language for which I am deeply grateful: the founding tautology, *'die Sprache spricht'*. As we know, it is not the only one he ever committed (see *'Welt weltet'*, *'das Ding dingt'*, or *'das Nichts selbst nichtet'*). But this one has the very valuable quality of reversing an age-old philosophical tradition of pride in man's control over his language. There is a lesson in humility to be learnt from this apparently extravagant statement.

One last point about Heidegger's method. His views about language are not held at a safe distance from the object. They determine his practice, for everyone knows that he relies heavily on etymology, thus following the ancient but not venerable tradition of speculative etymology. And everyone knows that his etymologies, being speculative, are dubious – perhaps the best example is the very etymology of 'being', which he borrows from the somewhat fantastic Grimm. I take this reliance as a sign that the remainder is at work in his style, that he lets language speak through him. Heidegger is in no way the victim of an etymological conviction, as Brisset is. The important matter, he states in his essay 'The Thing', is not that there is truth in etymology, but that etymological analysis considers the essential relations that words, as part of language, disclose and conceal at the same time. In other words, etymology is all-powerful in so far as it is true. It must be relevant, not random, and Heidegger's relation to truth is different from Brisset's – it is based on the deconstruction of a whole metaphysical tradition that begins in the Greek language, and, in so far as it deconstructs it, it relies on it. This use of etymology focuses our attention on the contradiction that I attempted to describe in the first paragraph of this chapter. Heidegger phrases it in the following manner: 'Sprache ist lichtend-verbergende Ankunft des Seins selbst' (language is the coming, both in lighting and concealment, of Being itself).[14] In the terms of Figure

3.1, Heidegger is trying to map the frontier between positions 2 and 3 – one of the places where I have located the remainder. He is trying to account for the emergence of poetic truth – i.e. position 3 – out of the garrulousness of usage and cliché, that is, out of the form of language that betrays Being for the preoccupations of the commonplace, for which Heidegger finds a name in the indefinite pronoun *man* in German (the usual English translation is 'the They'). One of the best-known aspects of his theory of language is the celebration of silence as one of the highest forms of speech. When the babble of glib interlocution has at last come to an end, then, in the silence that is the essence of speech, we can at last listen to the monologue of language, in which the remainder makes itself heard.

A map of the same frontier between positions 2 and 3 in my diagram can be found in an essay by Sartre, 'Qu'est-ce qu'écrire?',[15] where he seeks to give philosophical grounding to the opposition between poetry and prose. The main difference with Heidegger, however, is that the positive pole of the opposition is prose – the right side of language (*l'endroit du langage*') – whereas poetry is 'the other side of language', *l'envers du langage*'. Poetry, or, as we shall see, the remainder, is again given a negative definition.

The opposition is based on a different attitude to language in the speaker of prose (*le parleur*) and the poet. For the speaker dwells within language, he is '*en situation*' in it, and words are to him like spectacles or antennae, like instruments or artificial limbs, which provide greater scope for his senses. He goes in fact beyond words, which he uses, towards other ends and other things. To him, language is transparent, a useful convention providing disposable tokens for getting closer to things. In short, the speaker does not bother with words, for with them and through them he acts. Not so the poet, who refuses to be content with words and withdraws from language *qua* instrument for the communication of truth. Far from striving to get closer to things by forgetting about his words, the poet treats words as things, not signs. As a result, the poetic word takes on a life of its own, it becomes a microcosm. Words become natural objects that grow on the earth like grass or trees. But this reverses the relationship between man and his language. In the case of poetry, it is rather a matter of language and its man, for his words capture the poet. They do not express his passions but carry them – and carry him away.

The main characteristic of the poet, as opposed to the more down to earth but rational and active *parleur*, is his faculty of linguistic imagination. Except that faculty is an ill-chosen name, for it suggests a certain control in the speaker – whereas what is meant here is rather an effect of language on the subject, the work of the remainder in and on him. This is how Sartre describes the situation; 'Florence est ville et fleur et femme, elle est ville-fleur et ville-femme et fille-fleur tout à la fois. Et l'étrange objet qui paraît ainsi possède la liquidité du *fleuve*, la douce ardeur fauve de l'or et, pour finir, s'abandonne avec *décence*'[16] ('Florence is a town and a flower and a woman, a flower-town and a woman-town and a girl-flower at the same time. The strange object that thus emerges has the liquid quality of a *flow*, the soft russet ardour of *gold* and eventually abandons itself in all *decency*'). The remainder is indeed at work here, for Sartre is practising *adnominatio* and phonetic dissemination (why, for instance, is this gold russet-coloured, if not because of the 'f' in *'fauve'*?). He is abandoning himself, in all decency, to his linguistic imagination, i.e. he lets his language speak for him, which produces the beginning of a fiction: a strange object emerges, and with it the embryo of a tale.

The preference for prose that is discreetly expressed in the essay – one can sense a certain irritation at this interfering language that hinders the involvement of prose in a world of significations and actions – is bound to be paradoxical. At the very moment when the author celebrates the asceticism of prose, he gives in to the seductions of a feminine, and therefore wily, language. The *'douce ardeur fauve'* turns out to be a *douce violence* done to the prose writer, who finds himself in the situation of Jonathan Harker when he is on the point of being raped, or vampirized, by Dracula's sisters: he is a little apprehensive but, on the whole, he likes it.

We must go further into this poetic gift of linguistic imagination, even if it is conceived by Sartre as a loss of transparency rather than as the opening up to or unveiling of Being. After the fable of the Eagle and the Centipede, we deserve a parable – the parable of the Fantasy Code.

Codice di avviamento fantastico is a short story by Gianni Rodari, a writer of children's books.[17] It takes the form of a letter, in which an insomniac narrator thanks the Postmaster General for sending him the post-code book, in which the names of Italian towns are listed, together with their post codes. (The nearest British equivalent would be the list of telephone dialling codes: Grays Thurrock 0375, Great Alne 078 981, Great Ayton 0642, etc.) The perusal of these lists has temporarily put an end to the narrator's insomnia: there is something hypnotic in this combination of alphabetical order and complete meaninglessness. 'Things (the poet said) fall apart, the centre will not hold.' For this narrator at least, owing to the cosmic force of the post-code book, things no longer fall apart.

But the effect is only temporary. The code may have the structural advantages of all codes (it is perfectly regular), it also has their defects. It is too static; it lacks action. The narrator tries to animate it by forming subsets, for instance the subset of seaside resorts the names of which begin with 'Marina': 'Marina d'Ardore, Marina d'Andore, Marina di Asceo, Marino di Belvedere Marittimo.' But this only gives the impression of a football team that would not go beyond the official photograph before the match, and never actually plays a game. The centre holds so well that it all becomes a little boring. In desperation, the narrator decides to turn the post code into a *madeleine* and load the name with personal memories. 'Bude, Cornwall, 0288': I remember paddling up the canal, watching the spring tides roar against the breakwater, buying my Cornish pasty in old Mrs Rattenbury's shop on the corner of the Strand. But reading only the names of the towns he has visited does not help the narrator's insomnia, it makes it worse. Mere subjectivity tears the cosmos apart; it disturbs its regularity and causes unwelcome excitement, not the sought-after *ataraxia*. Suddenly, like Brisset, like Wolfson, the narrator has an illumination: the key lies not in subjective control, but in letting language, or the remainder, speak. As he reads the words 'Sambruson, Venezia, CAP 30030', the word '*trombon*' comes into his mind, together with a jingle, in which a shepherd from Sambruson teaches his goats to play the trombone. A solution has been found, insomnia is vanquished. A grateful narrator suggests to the minister that he should publish a revised post-code book, a fantasy code, in which the name of each town would be followed by a short poem. He offers to write the jingles himself, and, being as modest as he is grateful, does not even ask for his name to appear on the title page. It would be enough it it were included in the alphabetical index, followed by a postal number. As we see, the code, or language, has finally captured the subject, who is now only, to parody Lacan's phrase, a signifier among and for other signifiers.

What has happened? The remainder has taken over. An English version of the tale might go like this. After reading 'Bude, Cornwall,

0288' in my telephone book, I am seized with inspiration and I find myself uttering the following wild unmeaning rhyme:

> There was an old person of Bude
> Whose deportment was vicious and crude;
> He wore a large ruff, of pale straw-coloured stuff
> Which perplexed all the people of Bude.[18]

This, of course, is by the father of all limericks, Edward Lear. What the narrator has discovered, after Lear (who was always a source of inspiration to Rodari), is that every place-name is the virtual source of a limerick, which will develop out of it according to the rules of rhyme and linguistic fantasy.

For 'linguistic imagination' I shall substitute 'linguistic fantasy', a characteristic of the work of the remainder to be raised to the same level as homophony. The reason why we must abandon 'imagination' is that it is the name of a faculty, which, as we saw, presupposes a (controlling) subject – in this sense, I do not even believe in a Chomskyan 'faculty of language'; whereas fantasy can be ascribed to language itself: a Lacanian theory of fantasies, for instance, will insist on their dependence on and origin in sentences. But in order to see linguistic fantasy at work, I must forget my transposition of Rodari's ditty into an English limerick, and read it in the author's maternal language. For here the Italian language is speaking. The remainder is not merely an aspect of language in general, it is always linked to a particular language, the speaker's maternal tongue:

> Un pastore di Sambruson
> Insegnava alle capre
> A suonare il trombon.

This is short, and particularly pointless, therefore nonsensical. But it is so only if we decide that the origin of a text must be found in an intention of meaning. Clearly, the author does not mean to mean, or rather he means not to mean. Yet the text is not meaningless, for in it language speaks. Why for instance does this shepherd teach goats rather than sheep, cows, or crocodiles? Not for 'meaningful' reasons of verisimilitude – the answer lies in the post code for Sambruson, 'CAP 30030', in which the initial syllable of 'capre' is present. And why does he teach them to play the trombone? For obvious reasons of rhyme, but also because the number following CAP, 'trenta mille trenta', contains the initial consonants of '*trombon*'. Far from being the product of arbitrary pointlessness, the ditty appears to be an intricate network of phonic relationships, the result of the linguistic fantasy of the remainder. It is easy, for instance, to show the massive presence of phonetic dissemination in the text, in the form of the consonant cluster 'br'/ 'pr', with its dental variant 'tr', which also appears in diluted form in '*pastore*'; or of the nasal syllable 'on' (which provides the rhyme and appears in '*suonare*') with its variants 'un', 'am' ('*Sambruson*'), 'in' ('*insegnava*'), 'om' ('*trombon*'). Rhyme, prosody (four accents per line), phonetic dissemination, alliteration, and assonance: the whole text functions exactly like one of Saussure's anagrams, complete with *mannequin* (since the name '*Sambruson*' is explicitly present in the first line). The ways of the remainder are the ways of poetic imagination – if the word 'imagination' creeps back here, it is because I am trying to show that linguistic fantasy is the source of what is interpreted, in psychological terms, as 'poetic imagination'. And it has become clear that the remainder is not averse to rules and constraints, but often proceeds by adding new ones. An analysis of Lear's limerick about Bude would come to the same conclusions. There appear to be constants in the work of the remainder: we must attempt to define them.

RULES FOR THE REMAINDER?

I shall not enter the vexed question of rules more than is absolutely necessary. The ground is slippery, a Chomskyan beast is growling threateningly on my left, and in the distance I can hear Wittgensteinian dragons tuning up their flame-throwers. If I must be devoured, I shall plump for the Wittgensteinian dragons, for I prefer the colour of their scales.

Yet I must justify my use of the term. The easiest way out would be to say that I have kept it for sheer lack of another. I could even support this inglorious move by the latest post-modern devices. I could write the word in inverted commas, or cross it out (write it '*sous rature*') in the approved Heideggerian manner. Nor would such tactics be entirely inappropriate. In being compelled to treat *langue* and the remainder as separate entities, I am separating the inseparable. The remainder-work must and yet cannot be described in terms of rules.

But the argument goes further, and becomes more interesting. For the phrases 'linguistic rules' or 'rules of grammar' have a paradoxical flavour. If we divide the set of what we normally call 'rules' into two mutually exclusive subsets, descriptive and normative, i.e. rules that necessarily follow or necessarily precede their application (the rules of conversation v. the rules of chess), we shall, to our dismay, find that rules of grammar paradoxically belong to both subsets.

Linguists usually conceive their task as the observation of regularities and the formulation of rules that account for these. In this, rules of grammar seem to be rather similar to the laws of the natural sciences. One observes, one formulates hypotheses. When these are sufficiently verified, they acquire the status of rules. Indeed, in certain limited cases, one does talk about laws of language (in the diachronic cases of Grimm's law or Verner's law). And such rules *are* posterior to their application – they are the object of what Chomsky calls 'tacit' knowledge. I do not need to be read the Gravity Act in order to comply with the law of gravity when I trip on the family cat and fall downstairs. Nor do I need to learn the rather complex rules of English phonotactics before I produce acceptable logatoms (i.e. senseless coinages).

Differences, however, soon appear. There is wisdom in the phrase 'rule of grammar' (in the fact that we do not normally talk of 'laws of grammar'). For rules of grammar are, as we have seen, defeasible. Laws are not. If, having tripped over that blasted cat, I fail to break my neck, because I have operated an ingenious device of my own invention called an interior parachute, I have not broken the law of gravity, but merely adapted my behaviour to it. Whereas, in spite of the impressive and often hardly intelligible diagrams produced by linguists to spell out the canonic form of the legal syllable in English, I can produce the illegal syllable 'Hjckrrh!! (this is what the Gryphon says to Alice in *Alice's Adventures in Wonderland*), and I shall still be within language. Laws (like rules) can be exploited; only rules can be defeated.

Yet I am still within my first, descriptive subset. Even if they are defeasible, my rules of grammar are still posterior to their application. But are they? For they are, after all, learned. The child, the foreigner, and Eliza Doolittle (in other words, everybody) are taught rules of grammar in the best normative manner: Say this! Don't say that! The model for language-learning proposed by generative grammar, Chomsky's LAD, even if it captures certain aspects of actual language learning, is too abstract to account for the process satisfactorily. It is true that the child learns his language by formulating relatively constrained hypotheses and testing them. But that is not the whole of the picture. The tiny tot may collate his notes and exclaim: 'By gosh! Aunty Meg, like mum and dad, does say "went" instead of "goed", so I must be wrong. Memo: try "went" on Uncle Jack.' But it is highly likely that, before he reaches that experimental stage, aunty Meg will have told him, in no uncertain terms, that one says 'went' and not 'goed'. We are not in the situation of the prehistoric tribe that becomes civilized as false scientific hypotheses are slowly replaced by sounder ones – a century-long process. The child's ontogenetic development does not recapitulate this slow phylogenetic improvement, for his social environment plays the part of a *deus ex machina* by telling him where he goes wrong. Rules are normative – not only because one is always, to a large extent, *taught* them (again, this is an idealization: not all rules, not all of these rules), but because normative intervention can change them. This is an obvious source of linguistic change. New conventions replace older ones, ditto new fashions. And it is not only a question of a group of teenagers inventing a new in-word for a cigarette: phonology and syntax are affected by this type of change.

Rules of grammar, therefore, are both descriptive and normative. Learning a foreign language, for instance, involves taking a plunge into it, exploring it like Aladdin's cave, and coming to feel at home in it (a phrase popular wisdom uses about language). Making one's home in a foreign language does not mean that one will acquire a reflexive knowledge of it and formulate rules – this can come only after the event. Rather the process involves what Paul Veyne calls 'pre-conceptual' rules. Such rules are neither in our consciousness nor in our unconscious – they are nowhere, not even in the margins of consciousness, in implicit limbo. It takes grammatical reflexion to invent them, but in the archaeological sense, for they are not created at random: 'they are logically implied by our sentences, that is all.'[19] Rules they are, for they have normative force, but we do not need to be aware of them in order to play the game. The best way to phrase this paradox is to talk of *retroactive normativity*, or normativity after the event ('I order you to have conformed to my instructions'). This expresses the normativeness of rules, but in the mode of the always-already.

If rules of *langue* are paradoxical in this way, I no longer have to apologize for keeping the term. The paradox is only another aspect of the uneasy peaceless coexistence between *langue* and the remainder.

The mastery that is implied in 'I speak language' always comes after the event. *Langue* is an order imposed through exclusion on a chaotic language where tendencies towards regularity coexist with tendencies towards disorder. Language is an unholy brew, a mixture of the stuff that *langue* will be made of and of the stuff that will be left over in the remainder. Since my object is not *langue*, but the other side of language, I must try to describe these tendencies towards disorder, for which I have already suggested the general characteristic of 'defeasibility'.

The first rule of the remainder is the rule of *exploitation*, or flouting. The main lesson that can be drawn from my initial corpus, and from my sampling of the rag-bag, is that in language all rules, not merely pragmatic rules, can be defeated and give rise to exploitation. This is where the remainder is negative and subversive, locked in endless combat with tendencies towards order. The concept has its origin in the work of H. P. Grice. For the only reason he can maintain an irenic view of conversation that is so alien to our experience of real conversations or to the collective wisdom of dead metaphors ('argument is war') is that the irenic maxims are meant to be exploited in order to produce implicatures. Exploitation, therefore, is the central concept of the Grician system, and conversation conforms to rules that are not meant to be followed, or rather an important function of which is to be deliberately flouted.

I think this structure can be extended. Conversation in this matter only reflects the workings of language. The following is a sentence from Christine Brooke-Rose's *Amalgamemnon*: 'I must get himself out.'[20] This is strange English, or a gross exploitation of the syntactic rule of reflexivization. But in the context of the novel it is entirely rational. The narrator, Cassandra, is in the process of creating one of her fantasy characters, Orion, a prisoner in a Soviet camp. The new-born character has just reached the stage when he is independent enough of her who dreams him to say 'I', and think of escaping. But he is not totally independent yet, the male Athena is not entirely out of the head of the female Jupiter, and this dependence is marked by the third-person pronoun, where Orion still has the status of an object of discourse. Syntactically, the sentence is a portmanteau, combining two voices or two points of view. A brilliant case of syntactic exploitation.

The exploitation of the remainder works through either excess or lack – by imposing yet another rule or constraint (the $n + 1$ constraint) or by discarding one (this is the operation of an $n-1$

constraint: deleting a rule may come to the same thing as imposing another constraint). I have described the complicity between operations $n + 1$ and $n–1$ in Brisset and Wolfson. In order to show that the remainder is no mere weakening of order, delirium through dissolution, I shall insist on the typical $n + 1$ operations of palindrome and lipogram. Despising the meagre result of the most famous palindrome of all, 'Roma-amor', Perec prides himself in having written a palindrome of more than 5,000 letters. Here are the beginning and the end: 'Trace l'inégal palindrome. Neige. Bagatelle, dira Hercule. ... lucre: Haridelle, ta gabegie ne mord ni la plage ni l'écart.'[21] Perec was also a compulsive writer of lipograms. Here are the first lines of *La Disparition*: '*Trois cardinaux, un rabbin, un amiral franc-maçon, un trio d'insignifiants politicards soumis au bon plaisir d'un trust anglo-saxon, ont fait savoir à la population par radio, puis par placards, qu'on risquait la mort par inanition.*'[22] Any attempt at translating this is bound to founder upon the Charybdis of literalness (if I say 'three cardinals', I have translated the first words, and broken the lipogram) or the Scylla of transposition (these cardinals can be two or four, but not three; the admiral will not be a free mason – will a *carbonaro* admiral do?). The interest of the text, however, is not merely the total absence of the letter 'e', but the readability of the lipogram, whose tale of sound and fury is found to be significant on every page.

Let us take an extreme example of the opposite operation of deletion, and admire the resilience of language. Here, it is not so much a question of discarding one constraint, as of discarding part of a text and making do with what remains. In *Langrishe, Go Down*, a novel by Aidan Higgins, the heroine, while emptying the drawers of an old desk, comes across a letter, which has been torn into two equal pieces. The left part is missing. This is the result:

> She thrust in her hand again; and this time brought out to her surprise something she had not seen before. A single carbon copy of a sheet of typescript, torn down the centre in an irregular line, the left half of which was missing. She put on her spectacles to read.

> non
> moment ago was; if you were aware
> present or other examinations
> or made you waver in your opinion,
> e? No, you wouldn't.

ay, you can exaggerate sweating
s a far more important factor
sweating at one examination
erent things, – what the frame of th
t, whether she was nervous at that
mean the woman was full up after

e state of her nerves? It might.
ve a neurotic case without any of
s? Yes, it could.
it may be held to you, when these
you know the woman's full history
before? I don't know what you
tory because she gave me details
d past history since childhood.
patient for numerous years would it
be a help?
Delaney who knew her for close

ient. His evidence was that he met
accident but never beforehand
ing her as a patient, I suggest to you
her as a woman for twenty years and
ion to judge her genuineness than you
e.
examination of her? I had two
to to my satisfaction,
think I could decide in that time.

> Imogen read this through twice; but it yielded up nothing. She
> could make nothing of it. She replaced it in the drawer which
> she then closed.[23]

Although the heroine cannot make head or tail of it, the more astute
reader thinks he can. Is this not an extract from some doctor's notes,
or from a case history? We feel we know both who wrote the letter
(a doctor) and what the text is about (a female patient), so that we
must interpret the heroine's refusal to understand as a symptom.
The author is using this text to tell us something about her. He is
also having his little joke at our expense, in the tradition of Lewis
Carroll's 'They told me you had been to her', a poem that on the
whole fails to make sense because the referents of the shifters are

never made clear. In our text, the violence done to language is exaggerated because arbitrary. A (presumably) perfectly innocuous piece of informative prose, a letter or a report, has been turned into the wildest nonsense by being physically torn in two. The result is the same as if the rules of syntax had been made looser in delirium: the remainder takes over (the plasticity of language is due to the fact that where *langue* fails us, the remainder remains), and the reader's irrepressible need for meaning is satisfied, by filling the blanks (a kind of syntactic or narrative implicature), and also by letting language have its say and establish its own 'meaningless' regularities. If we forget about the gaps and treat this as a text, not as half a text – and nothing will convince us that this half-text has not been deliberately and carefully written *as such* – a whole network of intratextual references will soon appear. 'Non' (l.1) and 'No' (l.5) versus 'ay' (l.6) and 'Yes, it could' (l.14); 'it might' (l.12), 'it could' (l.14), 'it may' (l.15); 'history' (l.16), 'tory' (l.18), 'history' (l.19); 'examination' (lines 3 and 29, i.e., symmetrically, three lines after the beginning and before the end of the text). Let us not forget the author's obvious glee at our bafflement in the last two lines: 'to my satisfaction' (his, but not ours) and 'think I could decide in that time' (he may, but we cannot). But in a way we have decided, we are satisfied. The text shows that even in the most adverse circumstances language survives: the rule of exploitation celebrates this capacity for survival.

The second rule of the remainder is the rule of *paradox*. This is perhaps the longest recognized of all. Natural languages have always been accused of allowing paradoxes, for instance by confusing logical types. We do not need to share the general belief in the superiority of artificial languages in order to recognize that this uncertainity is a fundamental characteristic of language as a whole, because it is an important aspect of the workings of the remainder. Let us remember the sentence, mentioned in Chapter 2, that contained eleven occurrences of 'had' in a row. The astonishing fact here is not that we can produce such a sentence, but the facility with which we can 'cheat', i.e. accommodate the constraint. I could have cheated by turning the eleven 'had' into a name (the longer the hyphenated name, the grander the family; and Haddad is a common family name in the Lebanon). The proposed solution, which is considerably more subtle than this, does cheat by introducing a syntactic break in the guise of a semi-colon, and by crossing the frontier between use and mention. But this uncertainty over use and mention *is* an important aspect of language and a cause for paradoxes. The best formulation of this comes from an unlikely source, Noam Chomsky in *Aspects*.[24] In the course of a discussion of the location of selectional restrictions within his 1965 model, which is not relevant here, he notes the following paradox: an agrammatical string of words can always be turned into a sentence by being embedded as the subject of certain predicates, or by undergoing certain types of negation. Thus, in 'John frightened sincerity', selectional rules are violated, and the sentence is, to say the least, odd. But it becomes perfectly natural when embedded in or transformed into the following sentences:

(i) it is nonsense to speak of frightening sincerity
(ii) sincerity is not the sort of thing that can be frightened
(iii) one cannot frighten sincerity.

This even applies to what he calls 'strict subcategorization', the violation of which produces even odder sentences, like 'John elapsed a book' (intuitively, the difference is that I can easily construct a metaphorical reading for the first sentence, but not so easily for the second). By simply going from use to mention, one can always have: '"John elapsed a book" is nonsense'. Note, however, that Chomsky does not offer this simple solution and that his sentences, which are all somehow metalinguistic, are syntactically more complex than this. The ways of paradox in language are as numerous as they are devious. Chomsky's solution states that the lexical entry for 'nonsense' and such words will allow them to be predicated of any sentence, grammatical or ungrammatical: one may plausibly maintain, he says, 'that base strings that deviate significantly from grammaticalness are nevertheless constituents of sentences that receive nondeviant interpretations, by virtue of the semantic properties of certain lexical items and certain constructions. In further support of the argument that grammaticalness cannot, in any event, coincide with the intuitive notion of "deviance", one can cite cases of perfectly grammatical strings that are incongruous on nonsyntactic grounds.'[25] In this opposition between grammaticality and deviance I think I can read the paradoxical workings of the remainder. It is not a question of a nonsensical sentence, like 'colourless green ideas ...', being grammatical – it is a matter of grammar accommodating agrammaticality within itself. The predicate 'nonsense' launders a solecism as one launders ill-gotten money. Rules are made to work paradoxically against themselves.

The superordinate sentence, 'S is nonsense', conforms to rules that the subordinate sentence S flouts. The result is a paradox: there are rules of syntax, and yet anything goes.

This is, I think, the rationale for the production of such a syntactic oddity as I evoked in Chapter 1: 'A poem is a poem is a poem.' For if the sentence does flout a major rule of English syntax, it is also superficially similar to – and deeply deviant from – a pattern of recursive embedding, where a quoted sentence becomes the subject of a certain type of predicate:

'A poem is a poem' is a problem.

I can, with the help of recursivity, produce endless 'acceptable' sentences of this type, which, however, need bracketing if they are to be disentangled:

((((A poem is a poem) is a problem) is true) is utter nonsense).

Not a very prepossessing sentence perhaps, but definitely a recursive pattern – we shall have to appeal to the limitations of human memory again (an easy way out as we have seen) if we want to be rid of it. We can even give this recursive embedding the characteristic hesitation of paradox:

(((S is true) is nonsense) is true).

(An extraposed version of this would be more palatable: 'It is true that it is nonsense that it is true that S' I am not claiming, of course, that this sentence is a *logical* paradox – it is the linguistic image of a paradox.)

All this tends to suggest that the remainder disrupts the orderliness of syntax by introducing two rogue 'rules', the result of which is paradox. (1) Sentences can have ANY LENGTH. In other words recursivity threatens the communicative and informative function of language. (2) ANYTHING GOES as a subject of certain predicates, for even '"setmul gsap" is utter nonsense' is a correct sentence. In other words, reflexivity also threatens communication.

Having said this, and at the risk of waking the Wittgensteinian dragons from their beauty sleep, we must admit that it is no chance if the rule of paradox – which is the rule of exploitation taken to its limit – finds its formulation in Chomsky. The subversiveness of the remainder is exerted against a core of rules of syntax. If there is to be general defeasibility, there has to be, at the centre of language, a body of syntactic rules. Chomskyan grammar is not abstracted from a void; it is not just an illusion in the fertile mind of an American linguist. Language *is* the unholy mixture of potential *langue*, a certain tendency to order, to be embodied in rules, primarily in rules of syntax (I am still a Chomskyan in this, for I believe in the centrality of syntax), and of the remainder, a subversive tendency to exploitation and paradox.

This, however, is not the end of the matter. The third rule of the remainder is the rule of *rhizome-work*. The remainder 'works', but not like syntax – its work is much more reminiscent of Freudian dream-work or joke-work. Conversely, the different types of 'work' described by psychoanalysts always have something to do with the workings of language. I have tried to show elsewhere, following Lacanian psychoanalysts, that the work of fantasy is linguistic in essence.[26] Since I have already alluded to joke-work in Chapter 1, I shall concentrate on the third type, the Freudian 'dream-work', with reference to M. Safouan's account in his *L'Inconscient et son scribe*. In a way, the case of dreams is more interesting, for, unlike jokes, they are emphatically not language. They deal with scenes and images, not words, and as such have no syntax, except the elementary one of succession and inversion – the succession of scenes in a dream, with or without inversion of the (chrono)logical order, is relevant to its meaning. This state of affairs is to be related to Freud's statement that the unconscious ignores negation: rules of syntax as such have no business down there. Yet Freud himself compares dreams to pictographic writing, to a succession of hieroglyphs, a conception of which Safouan reminds us by introducing the fictional character of the scribe, he who writes down our dreams. His point is that since the unconscious is structured like a language, dreams must have some sort of syntax. In fact, the case of fantasy already shows that an activity, day-dreaming, that is visual in the main ('I see the following scene: ...') is deeply related to an unconscious process (fantasy proper) that depends on the formulation of a sentence and the grammatical transformations it undergoes. ' I see this scene: a child is being beaten.' What Safouan demonstrates in Chapter 5 of his book, 'Decyphering dreams: syntax and abstract meaning', is that dreams have their own syntax, which may not be strictly equivalent to the syntax of *langue* (as the syntax of fantasy appears to be) but is nevertheless linguistic in essence – in other words, dreams conform to the syntax of the remainder.

The first example of this is negation. It is simply not true to say that the unconscious knows only declarative sentences, or rather that the latent thoughts of a dream are limited to assertions. Nor is it merely, as in the case of *Verneinung*, a matter of adding a negation, in correct syntactic fashion. Having no direct access to words, dreams cannot do this. But they have access to words, if indirectly. And they *will* express negation, only indirectly. Thus, because in French the phrase '*je n'y vois goutte*' expresses nothing but a strong negation of the verb ('I am practically blind'), dreaming of a drop of blood is a way of expressing the latent thought, '*de sang, il n'y a goutte*' – there is absolutely no blood, not even a drop.[27] The dream image is related to the latent thought through a pun on *goutte* and through the practice of rebus – dreams are indeed like hieroglyphs.

The second example plays on the blurring of the distinction between use and mention – a game at which we have noted the remainder is singularly proficient. How can a dream, which cannot use quotation marks or indications of point of view, express a metanarrative comment like 'this is absurd!'? It can do it in two ways – either by introducing absurd sequences, which will eventually suggest the same judgement, or by taking metaphorical phrases literally, thus making them absurd. The French usually say of someone who is absent-minded that he has '*la tête en l'air*', that he has his head in the clouds. The dreamer will dream just that – a head without a body, as in the well-known case of the Cheshire Cat.

We are so close to the remainder that we are actually in the centre of it. For this device, Safouan claims, is the universal device used by dreams to transpose 'abstract meanings'. They draw on the 'treasury of language' – not only idiomatic phrases, but proverbs, nursery rhymes, slang, and the poems that everyone has learnt at school. 'Certain dreams [he adds] are from beginning to end based on this device, to the point that their decipherment need not draw on the dreamer's associations.'[28] Indeed, one of the major operations of Freudian dream-work, displacement, is particularly sensitive to the workings of the remainder. It has recourse to homophony ('*un décor minable*', a shabby environment, for '*des corps minables*', ugly bodies), punning (a fire represents '*feu Monsieur Untel*', the late Mr So-and-so), paronomasia ('*une partie de tennis*', a tennis game, for '*une partie de pénis*'), portmanteau words ('*il calait son bateau*', he was propping up his boat, for '*il calait à ses examens*', he was failing his exams), and lastly Brissetic metanalysis ('*un cadavre macéré*', a macerated corpse, for '*un cadavre m'a serré*', a corpse took me in his arms), not to mention numerous cases of *adnominatio*.[29] To be sure, not all 'verbal associations' are cases of displacement, nor does displacement always consist in verbal associations, but the extensive use of Brissetizing and Wolfsonizing in dream-work shows that the origin of the censored latent thoughts is to be found in 'another place', where no controlling 'I' dwells – *'le lieu de l'Autre'*, the place where language comes to the subject. There is a deep-seated link between the semiotic activity of dreaming and language. Naturally enough, the syntax of dreams is close not to the censored syntax of *langue*, but to the 'other side' of language, to the side of the Other. In this case, there is philosophical benefit to be derived from an apparently negative or secondary determination of the remainder – except that the position of the remainder is not so much negative as foundational.

Langue and the remainder are intertwined. An apparently different approach will lead us to the same conclusion. Psychoanalysts of the Lacan school, like Safouan, often refer to Jakobson's seminal essay on two types of aphasia, where he systematically develops a correlation that takes him from linguistic units to dream-work (see Figure 3.2).[30] We can safely dismiss columns 5 and 6 as conceptual jumps beyond the limits of the credible – although I must confess to being convinced by the metonymic aspects of Tolstoy's description of Anna Karenina when she is on the point of committing suicide. We shall note that the correlation starts with the two organizing principles of *langue* – analysis and synthesis. The interest of the correlation, therefore, lies in the two series, paradigm – metaphor – condensation and syntagma – metonymy – displacement. This seems to state that displacement is based on one of the operations of *langue*, not of the remainder. But, stated like this, it is too simple. What we have is a correlation, that is, not only a statement of equivalence, but a passage from column to column – a not so gradual passage from *langue* to the remainder, demonstrating their inextricable reciprocal penetration. From this point of view, the position of the rhetorical column, which provides a kind of fulcrum for the whole correlation, acquires strategic importance. Metaphors are paradigms gone wild, metonymies syntagmata gone illicit: if columns 1 and 2 are solidly in *langue*, after column 3 the frontier of the remainder has been crossed. And we have seen in my description of the rag-bag that a frontier interrupts a road that is the same on both sides. Metaphor or condensation are only paradigm taken to excess, that is Brissetized.

But perhaps I am reading more than the text can bear into

Figure 3.2

1	2	3	4	5	6	7
Linguistic units	Linguistic operations	Aphasia	Rhetoric	Literature	Painting	Dream-work
Paradigm	Selection (analysis)	Combination aphasia (selection is preserved)	Metaphor	Romantics	Surrealists	Condensation
Syntagma	Combination (synthesis)	Selection aphasia (combination is preserved)	Metonymy	Realists	Cubists	Displacement

131

Jakobson's essay. Even if the correlation implies moving from one end of it to the other – and there is no doubt that, in order to follow Jakobson, one must be prepared to drift – it does imply some sort of equivalence. Against this, I would like to argue that there is something specific in the work of the remainder, which I have called rhizome-work, with reference to the works of Deleuze and Guattari.[31]

One cannot be too careful about one's metaphors. The results of the operations of structural linguistics – analysis and synthesis – are traditionally represented as a tree. An apt metaphor, because you can actually write down an immediate constituent analysis in a form that is reminiscent of a tree (see Figure 3.3). If I turn this tree, the fruits of which are words, upside down, and give a name to the nodes, I shall have a Chomskyan 'tree', or phrase-marker. The main characteristic of such trees is that they offer a limited number of paths along which words can enter into relationships. Thus, in my sentence, 'simile' and 'smiling' will be related only through their belonging to the predicate phrase, or the highest VP in the sentence – not a particularly close relationship. But if we go into the remainder, of course, they are related through proximity (only two words separate them) and paronomasia ('a smile like a secret simile', C. Brooke-Rose, *Amalgamemnon*). I must invent different paths for the remainder, a world in which sister nodes and Chomsky-adjuncts are unknown. Relationships in the remainder conform to rhizome-work.

Figure 3.3

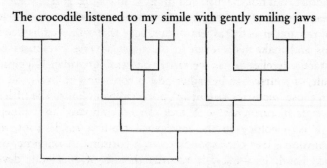

The crocodile listened to my simile with gently smiling jaws

Like the tree, the rhizome is more than an image – it is a concept. It has, therefore, distinct characteristics. Deleuze and Guattari call them 'principles'. The first is the *principle of connection*: a point in the rhizome can be connected with any other point. There are no fixed paths, as in a tree. The remainder is unstructured: in the matter of relationships, anything goes, be it proximity, phonic similarity, or obsessional recurrence. The remainder has no master root, no centre: its relationships are eccentric, as we have just seen. The second is the *principle of heterogeneity*: the tree imposes the coherence of order, and all segments are treated in the same manner. Phrase-markers deal with equal morphemes. The rhizome-like remainder does not accept this constraint. It Wolfsonizes from one language to another and knows only a medley of contending dialects, heterogeneous styles, and idiosyncratic punning. It Brissetizes by jumping from one level to another, by blurring the distinction between discrete units. The result is that there is no homogeneous speech community or ideal speaker-hearer. The third is the *principle of multiplicity*: the remainder, having no coherence and no structure, has no unity. There is no One there (*'il n'y a pas d'Un'*), by which we must understand that there is no unified controlling subject to grasp a proliferating linguistic production (the unified subject has given way to collective arrangements of utterance), and the proliferating production does not let itself be grasped as a single object. There are no fixed points or positions in a rhizome (as there are in a tree) that a subject might occupy in order to structure an object, to make sense of it. The fourth is the *principle of non-signifying breaks*. A tree, being a coherent structure, cannot be transformed in any odd way, or have its branches lopped off at any point. Thus, in the sentence quoted above, I can erase the 'with gently smiling jaws' prepositional phrase without damaging the structure, but not the 'listened to my simile' verb phrase. Not so the remainder, for if you break a rhizome, it just starts growing again. The remainder is the aspect of language that will establish connections and make sense even in the most adverse circumstances of syntactic dereliction, as we saw in the case of Aidan Higgins. The result, of course, can be rather odd, a confusion of levels and units, as in those *'monstres de langue'*, portmanteau words. The fifth is the *principle of cartography*. A tree can be compared to a blueprint: there is teleology in its emergence from a single root, and a Chomskyan tree corresponds to an algorithm. A rhizome, on the other hand, is a map: it records the lie of the land, develops according to its own lines of flight; it has arbitrary branchings off and temporary frontiers. That the remainder is concerned with the question of frontiers, I have amply demonstrated: it takes a cartographer to delineate it.

Five unmistakable marks – as many as in the Bellman's description of the Snark. And they fulfil the same function: they produce a paradoxical object. They enable us to follow an anarchic growth, not to survey the smooth unfolding of an orderly structure. There is order in language – it is abstracted into *langue*; there is also deep-seated chaos, as the remainder sprouts into a rhizome.

The fourth and last rule of the remainder is the rule of *corruption*. If *langue* is constructed on the exclusion of diachrony, or rather if the construction of the concepts of synchrony and diachrony is meant to exclude linguistic corruption from the field of science, the remainder is the part of language that is sensitive to the historical conjuncture. For in the remainder corruption rules, and also conservation. The paradoxical fact is that language is always changing and threatening to destroy the dearest values of the individual speaker, but that it is also the main instrument for the conservation of his past.

An '*état de langue*' is an untenable abstraction. The noble symmetry and stability of *langue* is always unsettled by the multiplicity of creative idiolects or social dialects; it must always come to terms with the consequences that its own past projects onto its present. There is no Hegelian 'instantaneous present' for *langue*, allowing the '*coupe d'essence*' of synchrony, but different regions with different times.[32] From the historical point of view also language is an unholy mixture.

The postulate of synchrony must be criticized, like the others. Language is both inclined to change and impervious to it – in those two tendencies, the relevance of synchrony is seriously questioned. On the one hand, we have ever-renewed disquisitions on the dereliction of modern speech and the need to return to origins that always turn out to be mythical. As we have seen, Heidegger offers one of the modern versions of this. But, on the other hand, his constant recourse to etymology, justified by the fact that language is subject to corruption, is also a recognition of the fact that language conserves – the meaning may have changed, but the word is the same (Saussure was already keenly aware of this). Let us remember the history of the word 'glamour', or let us consider what are known as 'ontological' metaphors, in which ancient theories often survive long after science has abandoned them. Thus, 'temperature' has meant 'our state with regard to heat and cold' only since the seventeenth century, i.e. since the work of Boyle, who acclimatized the word in English. Before this, it referred to a mixture of humours (a meaning that is the source of the modern word 'temperament', for the due mixture of the four cardinal humours constitutes our natural disposition). In other words, the metaphor carries the trace of ancient scientific theories, for instance the conceptions of Aristotle, (in *De generatione et corruptione*) who believed that 'cold', 'hot', 'dry', and 'wet' were discrete, not relative, qualities, the combination of which distinguished the four elements, as shown in the matrix in Figure 3.4.

Figure 3.4

	dry	wet
hot	fire	air
cold	earth	water

Medieval doctors prescribed medicines to temper the hotness of the human body, i.e. to restore the natural balance between heat and cold. This tempering became objectified in temperature when it was decided that heat and cold formed a continuum, that they could be treated as two opposite poles on the same scale, that there were, in other words, degrees of temperature. No doubt the invention of the thermometer was both a consequence of this evolution and a help towards its general adoption. The word 'temperature' reflects this complex history: like all words, but perhaps more explicitly than most, it bears witness to the past of a language – a past of which the remainder must take charge, since it is excluded from *langue*.

I shall come back to this later, since it is the theme of my fifth chapter. But the fourth rule raises a problem as to the nature of the remainder. If, in my account, I reject the term 'structure' and the corresponding metaphor of the tree, and if, on the other hand, I adopt the image of the rhizome and insist on the historical nature of the remainder, it might seem that I am implicitly treating language as a kind of organism – an entity endowed with a life (it proliferates anarchically) and a history of its own. There is a certain amount of temptation in this. Adopting the term 'organism', however, involves unwelcome consequences. Since I would not be the first to talk about language in those terms, it would imply importing into my account the linguistic Darwinism of linguists like Schleicher and Humboldt.

Perhaps this need not frighten us. By going back to Humboldt, I find myself in impressive company, as it is notorious that both Chomsky and Heidegger have acknowledged their debt to him. But the presence of these two names in the same sentence hints at the existence of a problem. For what Chomsky has found in Humboldt is a form of linguistic teleology. If language is an organism, it develops according to a plan – it is the actualization of a pre-existing faculty. What to Humboldt was the expression of the spirit of a nation – the complexity of a language reflects the state of development that a nation has reached – has become in Chomsky a language faculty inscribed somewhere in the mind-brain. This may be seen as a logical consequence, but it is one that is unwelcome to me. Similar ideas would be found in the word of Schleicher (who introduced the word 'morphology' into linguistics as a borrowing from biology). The main problem is that the teleological development of an organism is not the same as its history, and that language conceived in this way is ahistorical.

This logical consequence itself has a consequence, which is the idea of linguistic progress. Humboldt considers not the development of a single language so much as that of language in general. As a result, he produces a classification of languages – this is anathema to the modern linguist, quite rightly so – in terms of superiority and inferiority. His preference for flexional languages is well known: there lies the source of the superiority of Greek over Chinese, as he argues in his *Lettre à M Abel de Rémusat*.[33] For these reasons, it is difficult to suggest that language is an organism.

Heidegger's admiration for Humboldt has an entirely different source. He believed that Humboldt had achieved a Copernican revolution in the field of language, for he had tried to conceive the essence of language from the point of view of language itself, as if 'under the dictation of language'.[34] In other words, Humboldt may have been the first linguist to let language speak, to treat it as the real human *Umwelt*. This, of course, cannot leave us indifferent. And it is fair to say that a perusal of the works of Humboldt and Schleicher offers many glimpses of the remainder. For Schleicher, language is an organism, but it is a *material* organism: 'Languages are real natural beings, having material existence.'[35] The opposite view would be that language is merely a function – against this, Schleicher stresses the maternal aspect of language, an important part of its materiality. But it is in Humboldt's *Einleitung in das Kawi-Werk*, an essay on language in the form of an introduction to the description of a Malay dialect, that we find intuitions about the 'other side' of language. He introduces the concept of '*Beredsamkeit*', the 'volubility' of language, the capacity of a language to become discourse (*Rede*), that is, to actualize its potentialities and create a world. This fictional capacity of language is the result of the creativeness that resides in language, not merely in the speaker. In his *Lettre*, Humboldt refers to a specifically linguistic form of imagination, whereby ideas are clothed with sounds, acquire an existence separate from their speakers, and come back to them as words that in turn suggest 'ideas fixed by language'.[36] In this detour, language becomes independent, a source of ideas for man rather than a means of expressing them. The parable drawn from Rodari's story states just this.

In spite of these temptations, however, we must conclude that even if language is a separate entity rather than a mere function, even if it has material existence, even if it is not a mere instrument for the exchange of ideas, it cannot be considered as an organism. We must – this is the essence of the fourth rule of the remainder – maintain its historical character. By which I mean that its development reflects not some teleological pre-formation, but the arbitrary changes in the historical conjuncture. There is no progress in language, and the historical survival of languages is not due to linguistic factors that would make some fitter than others. A language does not even 'develop'; it corrupts and conserves.

The ultimate failure of the four 'rules' of the remainder is programmed. Being neither laws nor rules in the usual sense, they are rather unstable. At best they are only variants of one meta-rule, which is the true characteristic of the remainder: ignore all rules, whenever you feel like it. Defeasibility, thy name is remainder. If the remainder has one rule to impose on the speaker, it can be only a form of double bind: I order you to disobey. Which just goes back to the mutual implication of *langue* and the remainder, that is, to our main contradiction.

THE REMAINDER, THE DICTIONARY, AND THE ENCYCLOPAEDIA

Among the rare references to Deleuze's concept of the rhizome, one of the most interesting is to be found in Umberto Eco's *Semiotics and the Philosophy of Language*:[37] 'the model for a semiotic encyclopaedia is not the tree but the rhizome.' Eco is trying to find a solution to the frustration felt by linguists who are interested in discourse analysis about the semantic component of linguistic theories. For this component, which has the form of a dictionary (a list of lexical entries), simply will not do. It aptly captures the semantic meaning of words, with more difficulty that of phrases and sentences, but it is incapable of dealing with their contextual meaning. Or, in the words of another type of theory, it is good at denotation and hopeless at connotation. Take, for instance, the word 'cat'. A dictionary entry, in the shape of a tree, will account for the relationship of the word with its hyponyms (Birman and Burmese are two varieties of cats) and its hyperonyms (a cat is a feline is a mammal). Or again, it will provide an ordered semantic marker, indicating semantic features, such as [+ animal], [+ mammal], etc. – a semantic dictionary of this type is a pretty gloomy sight. There lies the rub. What the speaker needs to know when a cat is mentioned is not only this, which distinguishes a cat from a hair-dryer. He needs to know that the cat was worshipped by the Egyptians, that a member of the tribe greatly helped the Marquis of Carabas in *Puss-in-Boots*, that witches were rather fond of the animal, and T. S. Eliot even more so. In other words, says Eco, he needs to possess a vast number of *interpretations* of the term. He needs to have recourse to an encyclopaedia, which cannot be reduced to tree-like structures but looks more like a rhizome, composed as it must be of potentially unlimited and only partially structured pieces of knowledge. You cannot represent your culture in a systematic manner, as a series of trees.

The question that naturally arises here is: do we need a separate concept of the remainder, and will a rhizomatic encyclopaedia not do? My answer is that it will not.

To show the difference between the semiotician's encyclopaedia and the remainder, I will use three examples. The first is the title of an article in the *New Statesman*, published in March 1987:

THE STRAIN IN SPAIN

We may wonder what it is that the reader must know in order to understand the title, even before he has read the article, which deals with social unrest in Spain. A dictionary will provide the conventional meanings of the words. It will be a great help to a reader who has not yet gone beyond lesson 5 in *Teach Yourself English*. The encyclopaedia is much more helpful, for it provides the reader with a real understanding of the title: it points out the source of the allusion, a sentence (mis)pronounced by Eliza Doolittle in *Pygmalion*,

'The rain in Spain falls mainly in the plain.' It will even, perhaps, remind him of Audrey Hepburn's cockney accent as she painfully works her way through the tongue-twister. The reader has now understood the origin of the title. But has he understood the title completely? Not yet. For now comes the work of the remainder, which is contained not in any body of knowledge, but in the reader's close relationship to his own language. For the title is successful in so far as it plays on assonance (as in the original phrase), contains a word within a word ('strain'/'rain') and has added on an alliteration, 'the strain in Spain', that was not present in the original sentence. At the beginning, we have a jingle (used by Professor Higgins as he plies his sinister trade), which is produced not with a view to making sense but according to homophony. The title re-semanticizes this jingle, makes it relevant to the current political situation in Spain by following the paths of the remainder. All this is covered not by an encyclopaedia, because it all remains within language; not in the dictionary, which is the semantic component of *langue*; but in the remainder.

The second example is a collection of essays on William Tell by Swiss historians. It is entitled *Quel Tell?*.[38] The dictionary will not be much help. Indeed, the whole of *langue* will not be very informative. It will presumably tell us that the title is in French, that it is an elliptic interrogative sentence, formed with an interrogative pronoun and a proper noun. And that is all. As usual, the encyclopaedia fares better. According to the age and culture of the reader, it will refer him not only, of course, to the historical character, but also to the journal *Tel Quel*, an ephemeral minor star in the intellectual world of post-1968 Paris, to the origin of its title in a collection of essays by Paul Valéry, perhaps even to the Latin grammar of his childhood (*talis, qualis*). But whatever the point of entry we choose, the work of interpretation will have to proceed beyond the encyclopaedia into the remainder. For here the remainder uses the encyclopaedia as its raw material: it plays on it, produces not only a pun (*Tell/tel*) but an inversion. The path of interpretation goes from language (the dictionary) to extralinguistic knowledge (the encyclopaedia) and back into language again (the remainder).

Of course, I must not make too much of those two examples. Indeed, in both of them, access to an encyclopaedia is essential if the title is to produce its full effect. Yet, is there not a sense in which a reader who had no access to the encyclopaedia would still be able to understand the point of each title – i.e. would understand that 'The

Strain in Spain' involves more than the syntactic and semantic rules of *langue*?

The global work of interpretation involves the cooperation of three levels:

- *Langue*, which contains a syntactic component as well as a dictionary, interprets the utterance in terms of syntactic structures and semantic trees, which spell out the utterance meaning, i.e. the meaning of the utterance within the language, without a context.

- The encyclopaedia provides contextual meaning. It deals with pragmatic interpretation, with cultural references, some of which are collective, but some are not. Thus, 'cat' suggests to me not only the connotations evoked above, but also the cat Charlemagne in Vikram Seth's *Golden Gate* (dubbed, in true remainder fashion, a 'magnificat') and an old tom called *Mine Mine* whom I happened to love as a child. We have no tree here, but a rhizome, and the motto of the encyclopaedia is: unto each according to his rhizome.

- Not so the remainder, which is the same for the whole linguistic community. The paths towards meaning it offers are open to one and all, and exploration here is always rediscovery. In front of our language, we are all '*des sujets supposés savoir*' – we all practise the same legal (paradigmatic) and illegal (homophonic) associations. With the remainder we are back in language, but not in *langue*. And it is not a question of marginality (the remainder is language gone wrong) or subtraction (the remainder is language minus *langue*). We must think both the negative aspect of the remainder (it reaches parts of language that *langue* cannot reach) and its positive aspect (there is a specific remainder-work,

Figure 3.5

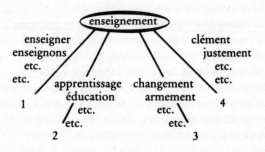

140

independent of the structure of *langue*). Perhaps Saussure had more than an inkling of this when he produced his notorious association diagram (Figure 3.5):[39]

As we can see, legal paradigms (syntactic, semantic, and morphological: 1, 2, and 3) coexist with an entirely illegal one, 4, which works according to homophony.

In Saussure, the remainder is coming through the back door, but it is coming. My contention is somewhat bolder. The remainder can never be dismissed, at least in an utterance couched in the subject's maternal language, even if its presence is vestigial (this is the source of notorious difficulties in translation). For it will be present in the apparently most innocuous and least poetic utterances. Here is my third example:

THE CAT IS ON THE MAT

Langue will provide a straightforward phrase-marker for this, together with a semantic marker, in the shape of what semioticians call a 'Porphyrian tree'.[40] The encyclopaedia may not be of great help in this case: a spelling bee;[41] and a sentence favoured by analytic philosophers: 'the cat is on the mat, but I don't believe it is.' It is the remainder that will explain why analytic philosophers, in order to formulate Moore's paradox, choose precisely this sentence. Although the utterance is deliberately flat and literal, it contains a paronomasia, which is the real reason for the presence of the cat on a mat, rather than a rug or a radiator. The sentence projects a paradigm – a minimal pair – onto the syntagmatic axis. But it is through this type of projection that Jakobson defines the poetic function of language. Thus, the sentence may be literal, but the work of the remainder makes it poetic.

This is what a theory of the remainder involves – an account of the complex relationships between the two sides of language, the remainder being the 'other' of *langue*. This implies a constant hesitation between on the one hand a negative definition of the remainder – as that which de-structures *langue* – and on the other hand a positive definition, where the remainder is equivalent to Heidegger's *Unumgängliche*, that which cannot be bypassed (or the remainder as constant reminder), where it is the core of naturalness in natural languages against which *langue* is constructed, but which no structure can overcome.

NOTES

1 See J. J. Lecercle, *Philosophy through the Looking-Glass*, London, Hutchinson, 1985, ch. 2.

2 See J. J. Lecercle, 'Textual responsibility', in A. Montefiore, I. MacLean (eds), *The Political Responsibility of Intellectuals*, Cambridge, Cambridge University Press, forthcoming.

3 'Building dwelling thinking', in M. Heidegger, *Poetry, Language, Thought*, translated by A. Hofstadter, New York, Harper & Row, 1971, p. 146.

4 My translation; see 'The way to language', in M. Heidegger, *On the Way to Language*, translated by P. D. Herz, New York, Harper & Row, 1971.

5 '*Sage*', Heidegger reminds us, has the same origin as 'saga'.

6 'Letter on humanism', in M. Heidegger, *Basic Writings*, edited by D. F. Krell, London, Routledge, 1978, p. 193.

7 ibid., p. 239.

8 'Building dwelling thinking', op. cit.

9 'The origin of the work of art', in *Poetry, Language, Thought*, op. cit., p. 74.

10 ibid., p. 73.

11 In *On the Way to Language*, op. cit.

12 See 'The Anaximander fragment', in M. Heidegger, *Early Greek Thinking*, translated by D. Krell and F. Capuzzi, New York, Harper & Row, 1975, p. 19.

13 'The essence of language', in *On the Way to Language*, op. cit.

14 'Letter on humanism', op. cit.; my translation.

15 In J. P. Sartre, *Situations, II*, Paris, Gallimard, 1948.

16 ibid., p. 66.

17 G. Rodari, *Il gioco dei quattro cantoni*, Turin, Einaudi, 1980.

18 E. Lear, *The Complete Nonsense of Edward Lear*, edited by H. Jackson, London, Faber, 1947, p. 193.

19 P. Veyne, *Le Pain et le cirque*, Paris, Seuil, 1976, p. 39.

20 C. Brooke-Rose, *Amalgamemnon*, Manchester, Carcanet, 1984, p. 21.

21 Oulipo, *La Littérature potentielle*, Paris, Gallimard, 1973, pp. 10, 106.

22 G. Perec, *La Disparition*, Paris, Denoël, 1969, p. 11.

23 A. Higgins, *Langrishe, Go Down*, London, Calder & Boyars, 1966 (Paladin, 1987, p. 64).

24 N. Chomsky, *Aspects of the Theory of Syntax*, Cambridge, Mass., MIT Press, 1965, pp. 157–8.

25 ibid., p. 158.

26 See *Philosophy through the Looking-Glass*, op. cit., ch. 4; also, J. J. Lecercle, *Frankenstein, mythe et philosophie*, Paris, PUF, 1988, ch. 4.

27 M. Safouan, *L'Inconscient et son scribe*, Paris, Seuil, 1982, p. 113.

28 ibid., p. 129.

29 ibid., p. 140.

30 R. Jakobson, 'Two aspects of language and two types of aphasic disturbance', in *Selected Writings, II*, The Hague, Mouton, 1971.

31 See G. Deleuze and F. Guattari, *Rhizome*, Paris, Minuit, 1976, and *Mille Plateaux*, Paris, Minuit, 1980.
32 See L. Althusser, 'L'Objet du capital', in *Lire le capital*, Paris, Maspero, 1965.
33 G. de Humboldt, 'Lettre à M. Abel Rémusat', in *De l'Origine des formes grammaticales*, Bordeaux, Ducros, 1969.
34 See A. L. Kelkel, *La Légende de l'être, langage et poésie chez Heidegger*, Paris, Vrin, 1980, pp. 351–2.
35 Quoted in P. Tort, *Evolutionisme et linguistique*, Paris, Vrin, 1980, p. 79.
36 G. de Humboldt, 'Lettre à M. Abel Rémusat', op. cit., p. 119.
37 U. Eco, *Semiotics and the Philosophy of Language*, Bloomington, Indiana University Press, 1984, p. 81.
38 A. Berchtold *et al.*, *Quel Tell?*, Lausanne, 1973.
39 F. de Saussure, *Cours de linguistique générale*, edited by T. de Mauro, Paris, Payot, 1985; see also F. Gadet, *Saussure, une science du langage*, Paris, PUF, 1987, p. 94 (English translation published by Radius).
40 U. Eco, op. cit., ch. 2.
41 It can be traced back to a Victorian primer, Mrs Mortimer's *Reading Without Tears*.

4

METAPHOR

The sheep were a miserable-looking lot, dingy, close-cropped,
undersize and misshapen. ... They made the exposition of
Wordsworth's lovely 'fields of sleep' as a compositor's error
for 'fields of sheep' seem no longer a jibe at that most excellent
man.

(Samuel Beckett)

HINTS ABOUT METAPHOR

It is not my intention to offer yet another theory of metaphor. At
that hubristic thought, the mind, as Bertie Wooster might say,
boggles. I feel no compulsion to out-Aristotle Aristotle, and I know
how brief is the life expectancy of new-fangled conceptions in the
field. But I intend to persist in my line of thought and follow up the
consequences of my exploration of the remainder. My question,
therefore, is not, What is metaphor? but, What can a theory of the
remainder say about metaphor? And it must be confessed that such
a theory has a fair amount to say on the subject. In the preceding
chapters, we have already, on several occasions, come close to the
question of metaphor – when I evoked the Lacanian concept of
lalangue in Chapter 1, when I sampled a number of tropes from my
rag-bag, or when I mentioned Jakobson's all-encompassing theory
of metaphor and metonymy as the two poles of language. From this
series of partial insights, we may derive a few hints.

The first hint is that the relationship between the literal and the
metaphoric might well be reversed, or at least envisaged in a new
light. If the remainder is constitutive, if it is always threatening to
return even in the most orderly, informative, and literal discourse, it
is not easy to relegate metaphor to the position of a mere trope, a sin

144

against the order of *langue* or a fortunate accident. On the line that goes from univocal to plurivocal meaning, there is no privileged starting point or goal. Here is the scale on which A. Grésillon plots ambiguity and metaphor:[1]

	Absolutely univocal utterances
LANGUE	1. Literal (univocal) utterances 2. Ambiguous utterances
LALANGUE	1. Jokes about *langue* 2. Portmanteau words 3. Metaphors
	Absolutely plurivocal utterances

On such a scale, metaphors appear to be the extreme point – and also the core – of the remainder (of *lalangue*). But the distance that separates them from literal utterances is no exile. The scale can be climbed up or down indifferently. One could indeed decide that if there is to be a dominant side, the plurivocal pole ought to be chosen. This idea – of the all-pervasiveness of metaphor in language – is very old, and from Vico to Max Müller a long chain of philosophers and linguists have entertained it, sometimes in exhilaration, sometimes with resignation. Eco remarks that theories of metaphor centre around two conceptions.[2] The first is that language is a rule-governed, conventional machine and metaphor a breakdown in the machine, which allows in a certain amount of creativity. The second is that language, by nature and from its origins, is metaphorical, and rules and conventions are only *a posteriori* attempts at reducing this profuse inventiveness. As Eco notes, this opposition is similar to the age-old oppositions between *nomos* and *phusis*, analogy and anomaly, motivation and arbitrariness. Since my account of the remainder has drawn on the second member of each of these oppositions, it seems that my task will be simple. It will be sufficient to state that metaphor is the same thing as the remainder (or the remainder as metaphor). This has the obvious inconvenience of drowning the specific operations of metaphor in what I have called 'remainder-work', and my modest disclaimer at the beginning of this paragraph would seem to have been well founded. There appears to be no theory of metaphor proper because there is a theory of the remainder. This, of course, will not do. The specificity of metaphor must be accounted for in non-trivial terms. Any treatment of it as the centre of our linguistic activity will either dissolve metaphor in the undefined creativity of language or reduce it to a trivial trope, where the metaphorical meaning replaces the literal, which it nevertheless maintains and presupposes. Such is, for instance, the unsatisfactory definition that Grésillon uses.

Yet, there is something to be learnt from her diagram, and from our first hint. Being an integral part of the remainder, metaphor is concerned by our description of the remainder-work. As a result, its analysis must be firmly grounded in language, in the uneasy combination of *langue* and the remainder, not in truth-functional semantics, pragmatics, or cognitive science. In other words, metaphor is a matter for sentences, not propositions or concepts. And the points of comparison, from which metaphor must be distinguished, are other tropes or linguistic games, like puns and portmanteau words, rather than literal sentences used for purposes of information and reference.

The second hint follows from the first. Most theories of metaphor, especially of Anglo-Saxon and analytic origin, treat it as a purely synchronic phenomenon. Thus, in his well-known essay, Davidson suggests that the sentence 'He was burned up' is no longer metaphoric, the only meaning evoked being, literally and straightforwardly, 'he was very angry'.[3] The argument fails to convince me, perhaps because I am not a native speaker and therefore have a more distanced or less blasé relationship to the language. I cannot help associating the sentence with the idea of fire, thus reviving that most dead of dead metaphors. In any case, even if we accept Davidson's native linguistic judgement, and agree with him that the former metaphoric meaning is now the literal meaning of the sentence, there must have been a time – the time of the shift from one to the other, the time of meta-phor – when the two meanings coexisted. From which it may well follow that the old literal meaning is still, somehow, even if vestigially, present. Metaphor is one of the points where synchronic *langue* is riddled with diachrony. Every metaphor contains, and will reveal on the slightest provocation, a history of its own. All we have to do, in order to retrieve the diachrony implicit in a dead metaphor or simile, is to translate it into another language. There is no duller statement of comparison than 'they are as like as two peas'. Yet, *'ils se ressemblent comme deux petits pois'* sounds delightfully metaphoric. The French *'se gargarisent de mots'*, they use words without paying much attention to their meanings. Try and state this in English by saying that they 'gargle with words'.

Going from synchrony to diachrony does provide an insight into metaphor. It will make us wonder about the life expectancy of a metaphor (how long does it remain 'fresh' or 'live' ?); reviving dead metaphors will appear as a possible, even a fruitful strategy; and the freezing of a live metaphor into a dead one will remind us of the similar case of cliché. After years of assessing metaphors against the yardstick of true propositions or literal sentences, perhaps the time has come to compare them not only to puns, but also to clichés. A metaphor has a history in so far as its status changes, as it goes from live to dead, becomes a cliché, and goes back again to revived metaphor. Thus the daily newspaper *Libération*, well known for its punning headlines, once referred to *LA MAJORITÉ LICENCIEUSE*. Once upon a time there was a live metaphor, which claimed that the majority of the electorate did not care to make their views explicit. When dead, the metaphor became the kind of cliché that adorns the daily speech of our politicians ('at the end of the day ...'). The headline in *Libération* revives the cliché by punning on it, thus creating a new metaphor. On the whole it appears that, even when it is at its quietest, because at its deadest, a metaphor is a source of instability in language. Which is another way of saying that it belongs to the remainder. There is a famous instance of this in Milton's sonnet, *On His Blindness*:

> When I consider how my light is spent
> Ere half my days, in this dark world and wide,
> And that one Talent which is death to hide,
> Lodg'd with me useless, ...

The word 'talent' must, of course, be understood in its modern meaning: as the title of the piece indicates, it refers to the sense of sight. Yet, Milton uses the word as an etymological pun, for the immediate context ('which is death to hide') refers to the parable of the talents, in which the word had its original, and by now archaic, meaning of a coin. The passage from the coin to the faculty was a straightforward instance of metaphor – a metaphor long dead by the time Milton revived it as a pun. Which goes to show that the injection of diachrony into metaphor reveals the fact that it belongs to the remainder, here to category 1 in Grésillon's *lalangue*.

The third hint derives from my account of the 'rules' of remainder-work. One of them was the rule of paradox. There is indeed something paradoxical about metaphors, of which the analytic tradition, notably Davidson, is fully aware. On the one hand a metaphor is blatantly false: to use Davidson's example, 'Tolstoy was a great moralising infant' is said of the adult, not the infant Tolstoy. But, on the other hand, it has a certain relationship to truth. Many students of metaphor are committed to the idea that there is such a thing as metaphorical truth. Of course, the solution to this dilemma is, on the face of it, simple. A strict definition of truth, within a Tarskian theory of truth for instance, will show that the first proposition – that metaphor is false – is literally true, whereas the second – that metaphor is true – is at best metaphorical. This does not even entail a condemnation of metaphor, merely a separation between a semantic (truth-conditional) and a pragmatic level (where metaphor is not so much true as successful). I do not intend to follow up the idea of metaphorical 'truth' and I will refrain from mystic pronouncements about the deeper truth of blatantly false metaphors. Yet I am not prepared to dismiss the paradox entirely. The opposition between the two propositions does not, strictly speaking, constitute a paradox, but it has the flavour of one. A metaphor is truly false and falsely, or apparently, true. This, I believe, is due to the fact that metaphor is a matter for language, not thought. What gives metaphor this appearance of truth is that it conforms to the rules of language. We are dealing not with truth proper but with truth-in-language, the representation of truth in language, the effect of truth produced by language, notably by syntax. In other words, we are dealing not with 'appearances' but with the reality of a linguistic *effect*. This is the origin of Barthes' (in)famous maxim, 'language is Fascist'. There is an inevitability in syntactic regularity that gives the proposition that a sentence conveys the force of truth, irrespective of its semantic coherence or referring capabilities.

At first sight, it is easy to dismiss such claims. 'Snow is white' is true iff snow is white, not iff the sentence is well formed, for 'snow is red' is equally well formed and untrue. But this is precisely the point. Because 'snow is red' is well formed, i.e. has the aspect of a true statement, I will try and construct a metaphorical meaning that will save the sentence. To be sure, this is a classic move in a pragmatic calculus, for language itself practises this game, so that the frontier between true and metaphoric utterances soon becomes blurred. Let us go back to that silent majority. If I wish to use the adjective 'silent' in a sentence conveying a 'true' proposition, I will

148

choose, to be on the safe side, a sentence like 'this man is silent'. The truth conditions in this case are easy to define. Simple verification, here and now, will do, as a result of which the proposition is straightforwardly true or false. But what if I say 'he is a silent man'? I am now extending the meaning of 'silent' into a perennial, not a deciduous, quality, and I can without contradiction state that 'the man who is at present talking is a silent man.' True, I can still deal with the matter in terms of truth-conditions (the set of truth-conditions for 'silent' being in effect a dictionary definition of the term). However, this extension of meaning is close to metaphor. A wide enough concept of metaphor might even cover it – for even the most silent of men sometimes chatters, thus belying his reputation and the immediate truth of my proposition. And the extension is not so different from straightforward metaphors like 'Gorbachev is red', by which I do not always mean that he is red in the face after an interview with Walesa. I can even go one step further, and talk about 'a silent majority', where a collection of individuals, a set with extremely fuzzy boundaries, has been personified into what Lakoff and Johnson call 'an ontological metaphor'. It is clear now that the people that form this majority are not always silent; nor are they all silent people.

It is time to note that the passage from the literal to the metaphoric does not involve a shift from truth to falsity, for the truth or falsity of all but the very first proposition is at best contingent and at worst undefinable. What it involves is a decisive change in syntax, which occurs in the position of the adjective when we go from 'the man is silent' to 'he is a silent man'. In the first sentence, the fact that the adjective is used predicatively suggests a determinate, 'he is being silent' interpretation, whereas in the second the attributive use of the adjective entails a generic, 'he is usually silent', meaning. Syntax has turned the account of a perception (I perceive that I do not perceive any sound coming from his mouth) into the expression of a quality. This quality will normally be ascribed to the referent of any other noun inserted into the correct syntactic slot, thus giving 'a silent majority'. It is to be noted that the phrase 'the silent majority' does not make much sense, especially as it usually occurs in the speech of politicians who are engaged precisely in voicing the unvoiced feelings of that silent majority – feelings that usually turn out to be strikingly similar to their own. Yet the phrase has acquired the respectability of the dead metaphor turned cliché because the order of *langue* produces an effect of truth.

The fourth hint is more than implied by the third: it deals with the importance of syntax in metaphor. This goes back to my discussion of the dictionary, the encyclopaedia, and the rhizome in the previous chapter. Most theories analyse metaphor in terms of the dictionary or the encyclopaedia. The most widespread is the semantic conception that states that a metaphor is a double synecdoche, as appears in the following diagram, where Z is the genus common to the two terms A and B involved in the metaphor:

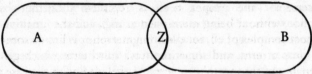

Richard is a lion because courage can be ascribed to both man and beast. Such a theory has no need to pay attention to the words of the metaphorical utterance or to their arrangement. This is why it unduly privileges one syntactic type of metaphor, the 'A is B' model, which is not even the most productive or frequent. Encyclopaedic theories will not improve on this – they will only be a little more refined by appealing to extra-linguistic knowledge.

Against this I wish to argue that metaphor, being part of the remainder, is rhizomatic in form. Metaphor does belong to language, but not to the dictionary – or not primarily to the dictionary. There is a syntax of metaphor, which precedes and governs our attempts at interpreting it in terms of semantic tropes. There is a sense in which the early Chomsky's hostility to meaning is justified. Syntax indifferently provides a number of slots, to be filled by various parts of speech. The remainder exploits the potentialities this situation offers. If it does not defeat syntax itself, but only exploits the potentialities of meaning it opens up, the result is metaphor. For what is 'colourless green ideas sleep furiously' – a syntactically blameless sentence – if not a series of metaphors? Metaphor occurs when the remainder pretends to abide by the rules of *langue*, the better to exploit them.

It might seem that what I am suggesting is the ancient and trivial theory of metaphor as replacement. In the syntactic structure of the sentence, the expected or 'normal' words are replaced by their metaphorical substitutes. If I appear to be doing this, it is only in order to stress the importance not of replacement, but of the first item of the proposition, 'syntactic structure'. And I must say that, so far, theories of metaphor have been singularly oblivious to this.

The main source is still Christine Brooke-Rose's *A Grammar of Metaphor*, which was published more than thirty years ago. Our knowledge of syntax may have advanced since, but not our knowledge of the syntax of metaphor. Merely perusing the table of contents of her book will convince us that the imperialism of the 'A is B' model must be overcome. 'It is surprising [she says] how little the copula is exploited for metaphor in English poetry.'[4] She duly concentrates on the two main types, which she calls 'simple replacement' ('the proper term is replaced altogether by the metaphor, without being mentioned at all'), and the 'genitive link', 'the most complex of all, for the noun metaphor is linked sometimes to its proper term, and sometimes to a third term which gives the provenance of the metaphoric term.[5] I shall deal with the case of the genitive later. But the replacement type is no mere reduction of the copula, 'A is B', type. Exactly as comparisons are excluded frm Brooke-Rose's corpus 'on the ground that they do not present any syntactic problems',[6] the absence of the A term completely changes not only the form, but also the force of the metaphor – it shifts the focus of attention, for instance, on to the determiner that introduces the B term.

A more recent French survey confirms this.[7] Starting from a corpus of French poets, J. Tamine analyses various syntactic frames in which metaphors appear. If we define metaphor as a relationship between a proper and a metaphorical term,

$$T_p \quad R \quad T_m,$$

the classification of metaphors will be conducted along the following lines. T_p belongs, or does not belong, to the same part of speech as T_m. In the first category, we have three cases: V Adj, N Adj and V N. In the second, whether the terms are both nouns or verbs in the infinitive, there are three possible cases: the relationship can be carried by the copula, an apposition, or the genitive. This gives us the diagram in Figure 4.1.[8] Here are a few examples: (1) 'Exécuter religieusement un décret' (religiously to implement a decree); (2) A warm voice; (3) 'Et mon âme dansait' (and my soul was dancing); (4) The sea is a mirror; (5) The sea, that mirror; (6) The mirror of the sea; (7) 'Être poète, c'est avoir de l'appétit pour un malaise' (being a poet is yearning for spleen). The division into two categories covers the old distinction between *in absentia* and *in praesentia* metaphors, except that the syntactic definition of the relationship avoids having recourse to the concept of substitution for the first category. In (2), the relationship is not between the metaphoric adjective 'warm' and an implicit literal adjective that it replaces, but between the adjective and the noun, which happen to be semantically at odds although syntactically at peace. It is syntax, therefore, that carries the weight of the metaphor. Semantic relationships – this is Tamine's conclusion – only have a negative role: within certain syntactic frames, the semantic relationship between the elements is odd.

Figure 4.1

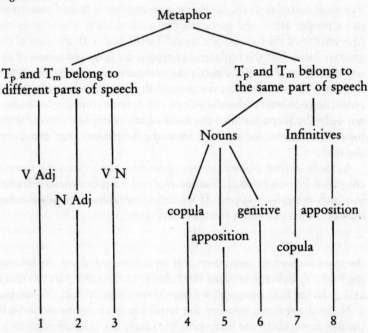

The important phrase is, of course, 'within certain syntactic frames'. If metaphor has something to do with the remainder, it is because it exploits the rules of *langue*, the core of which I have ascribed, in true Chomskyan form, to syntax. My fourth hint, however, is still only a hint. I have shown that there is a syntax of metaphor: I must now develop this insight.

METAPHOR AND THE REMAINDER

I shall attempt to build upon these hints by proposing one main and two subsidiary theses. The *main thesis* is that metaphor is the result of the exploitation by the remainder of the syntactic possibilities offered by *langue*. Metaphor is a locus for the imbrication of *langue* and the remainder. As such, it is one of the main forms of the return of the dismissed remainder within *langue*. The important terms in my thesis are 'exploitation', 'the remainder', and 'syntax'. Exploitation: we have seen that it was one of the main characteristics of the remainder-work. Note, however, that in this case it does not take the form of defeasibility – it is of the essence of metaphor, unlike the sentences analysed in Chapter 1, that it uses only legal moves. There is no question of breaking 'essential' rules, i.e. rules of syntax, only of playing off one level of interpretation against another. On this interpretation, semantic 'rules' are secondary. Their flouting does not involve the same disruption of language as breaking the rules of syntax does – it is never illegal to the same extent. The remainder: it is language that plays, more than the speaker. This is no pragmatic conception of metaphor. We remain within language and explore only the syntactic paths that it offers us. Syntax: the core of metaphor is indeed syntax, and the role of semantics is only negative – we temporarily forget that there might be semantic constraints, and let syntax speak. The result is that our ideas become colourless and green.

Such a conception of metaphor goes back to Husserl – only under another name. In the *Logische Untersuchungen*[9] he makes a distinction between two types of unacceptable sentences: 'This blue crow is green' is a case of *Widersinn*; 'Is green blue crow this' one of *Unsinn*. The difference is that *Unsinn* is no respecter of syntax, whereas in *Widersinn* the 'formal' aspect of language, i.e. syntax, is preserved. What prevents *Widersinn* from being straightforward *Sinn* is that the 'material', the 'ontological' side, i.e. the semantic structure, is under attack. Husserlian *Widersinn* is another name for metaphor. It is obtained when a formal slot is filled up without regard to material coherence. In such a case, the only way to 'preserve meaning', i.e. to interpret the sentence, is to treat it as metaphorical. 'This blue crow is green' is either a contradiction in terms *or* a metaphor. 'This algebraic number is green' is not even a contradiction. Metaphor, therefore, according to Husserl's insight, occurs when the syntactic and the semantic structures do not coincide. And it is true that syntactic structures often provoke such treatment. Thus, case grammar states that, in 'This key opens the door', 'key' is semantically the instrument. But it has been raised to the role of subject, a position typically, but not necessarily, held by the agent, as in 'Tom opened the door with his key'. Hence the possibility of personifying the key. Fantastic texts sometimes originate in grammatical tropes (in *Antigones*, George Steiner develops a conception of myth as embodying the main grammatical structures of the dominant language, in our case Greek[10]). Although personification is not often treated as a subtype of metaphor (see Lakoff and Johnson for the opposite view), the same process occurs with metaphor proper. As Husserl phrased it, 'whenever in the structure there is place for a noun, you can use whichever noun you like.'[11]

On Husserl's concept of *Widersinn*, and on similar ideas in Carnap, Michele Prandi has built a whole *Sémantique du contresens*,[12] exploring the relationship between formal and material structures. Thus, he draws a map of the formal structure of a sentence, showing which solidarities are central (the subject – predicate relationship) and which peripheral (the relationship between the predicative centre and prepositional phrases or local or temporal adjuncts). A syntactic map of *Widersinn* thus emerges. The force of a metaphor will not be the same if it is carried by a syntactically central or peripheral solidarity. Prandi's dual structure, however, is too neat. His 'material' level soars above language, towards the ontological commitments of an encyclopaedia, whereas I wish to remain within language, in the complex imbrication of *langue* and the remainder. This is why I shall have to add two subsidiary theses to the main one.

Before this, however, I shal deal with two examples, for the discussion so far has been a little abstract. This is a slogan for a brand of mustard:

AMORA – le goût de foudre

The taste of lightning: there is a metaphor here, as the author of the paper from which I borrow the slogan has noted.[13] 'The taste of — ' is a syntactic frame in which one can insert any noun. In Husserl's terms, some will make 'normal', ontologically coherent, sense. All we have to do is choose a noun the referent of which can be said to have a taste: a taste of melon, of vinegar, of mustard. Although I must confess I cannot imagine a satisfactory 'normal' substitute for *'foudre'* in *this* context ('a taste of mustard' would be undeniably true, but rather inappropriate as a slogan). Any noun not fulfilling this ontological requirement will be interpreted as a metaphor ('a taste of nostalgia'). In our slogan, this 'taste of lightning' can even receive a fairly straightforward interpretation: the mustard is extra strong. But of course, this is not all – not even the most important aspect. For the syntactic frame device can work both ways: 'a — of lightning' will also produce metaphors. And because of an obvious case of paronomasia, *'le goût de foudre'/'le coup de foudre'* (love at first sight), the second metaphoric possibility must also be taken into account. Between you and such strong mustard, love will be immediate – it is even inscribed in the very name of the brand (an old and venerable one – the name precedes, and has obviously inspired, the slogan): AMOR-A. This exploitation of the structure of *langue*, this Brissetizing of syntax (what the slogan forces us to do is to analyse the string *twice*), is typical of the remainder, and worthy of our rag-bag. I am not claiming that all metaphors work like this – it is obvious that a metaphor is not necessarily associated with paronomasia. What I am claiming is that metaphor is a case of the remainder exploiting syntax.

My second example will be a class of examples – what we may call, broadly speaking, genitive structures. We remember that for Brooke-Rose this is an important type of metaphor. She distinguishes two subtypes of 'genitive link': 'the three-term formula', in which B of C = A, with A either implicit ('the roses of her cheeks') or mentioned ('she is the fountain of mercy'); and 'the two-term formula', 'the B of C' in which B = C ('the fire of love').[14] It is clear that the origin of the distinction lies in the multiple ambiguity of the syntactic link provided by the preposition 'of' or the genitive. Studying the polysemy of genitive constructions in four languages, Fonagy notes no fewer than ten types of semantic relationship between the two nouns involved in the construction, each with a number of subtypes. Here are the main ones: possession, kinship (in the widest sense: cf. 'Lady Chatterley's lover'), part–whole ('Eeyore's tail'), product or cause ('the hen's egg', 'the consequences of his illness'), adverbial complement (*'le dormeur du val'* for *'le dormeur dans le val'*), quality ('darkness of the grave' comes from 'the grave is dark'), superlative ('the king of kings'). Number nine is of particular interest to us: 'in literary texts the two nouns can be the two terms of a poetic simile (metaphor, comparison)'.[15] The English example he gives is 'the Castle of Perseverance', which, he explains, is to be interpreted as 'this castle is the allegory of perseverance'. I

155

would like to argue that, far from being one more item on a list, type number nine consists in exploiting the other types, in playing with the multiple ambiguity that the polysemy of the construction entails. Such is this polysemy that some of Fonagy's types are themselves rag-bags. This is how he defines type number four, which I have not mentioned so far: 'we must reserve a special type for those constructions where N_1 denotes the *essence*, the *form*, the reflection, the function or the number of the object referred to by N_2. This is probably what Lees called the category of "abstractive nominals".'[16] Examples quoted include 'the subject of the book' (essence), 'the shape of the moon' (form), 'the picture of the universe' (reflection), 'in God's name' (sign), 'the Beggar's Opera' (genre), 'the set of empty sets' (whole), 'lack of money' (absence). The subtypes – especially as the examples keep adding new relationships to the rag-bag – are so numerous that Fonagy's classification collapses. This is due to the fact that the syntactic structure of genitives provides only a *formal* structure, in Husserl's sense, to be filled with a vast variety of *material* relationships. Metaphor exploits this syntactic potential to the utmost. In so doing, *Widersinn* is merely imitating *Sinn*. The number of relationships expressed is so vast, and their contents so various, that merely filling the 'N_1 of N_2' or 'N_2's N_1' slots with *any* noun will yield a semantic interpretation. Brooke-Rose's innumerable instances of 'genitive link' metaphors are only cases of this process. Incidentally, we now understand why most critics and philosophers of metaphor are keen on separating metaphors from comparisons. Comparisons, Davidson says, are trivially true (there is always a sense in which A is like B), whereas metaphors are always false (A is emphatically *not* B). The difference, to my mind, is one of syntax: the effect of combined strength and falsity is produced by the syntactic structures (A is B, the A of B) that produce metaphors.

Since most theories of metaphor have been busy computing the possible semantic relationships between the proper and the metaphorical term, in saying that the relevant level is syntax I am swimming against the current. The only content I can give to the idea that the role of semantics in metaphor is negative is that, by way of metaphor, anything goes (again, as we have seen, this is a characteristic of the remainder). In this, I find myself close to conceptions like that of Davidson, who states that the only thing one can say about the semantics of metaphor is that propositions containing metaphors are false, and must be accounted for by

156

pragmatic calculus. I am not happy with the consequence, but I agree with the premiss.

Surrealist poetry has taught us that it *is* the case that, in the matter of metaphor, anything goes. (If this were a historical account of poetic metaphors, the statement would need to be qualified. Poetic metaphors have not always been as free of semantic constraints as they are in the works of the Surrealists. The point is that Surrealist metaphors exploit to the full the latent potentialities that have always been present in the syntactic form of metaphors.) The semantic computation that always, in the end, manages to reduce a metaphor to a double synecdoche is an interpretation after the event. This is why I have chosen *Widersinn*, rather than enforced semantic coherence, as a first step towards understanding metaphor.

Yet it is also clear that, in many cases, semantic computation occurs, and provides a satisfactory solution. An 'apt' metaphor may be declared so after the event, yet its aptness strikes the reader forcefully enough. And it is insulting to suggest that poets select their metaphors at random. If *Widersinn* is the basis of metaphor, and the name of my main thesis, I must qualify it with two subsidiary theses, which it is hoped will tell us what kind of *Widersinn* metaphor is.

The *first subsidiary thesis* concerns the overdetermination of metaphor. I am struck by the fact that many of the more successful poetic metaphors are not merely metaphors, but also cases of pun, paronomasia, alliteration, and all the devices favoured by the remainder-work. The analysis that establishes some kind of semantic relationship between the two terms of a metaphor is often a secondary justification of the real source, which is to be found in the action of the remainder. Thus, J. Soskice analyses the metaphorical phrase 'the writhing script' in terms of models that describe the associative network of the term 'writhing': 'in construing a metaphor like "writhing script", one might associate with "writhing" not only actions similar to writhing such as twisting and squirming, but also entities which are known to writhe, such as snakes or persons in pain.'[17] I do not question the interest of interpreting a certain type of script as serpentine or suggestive of a writer in the grip of pain. Yet I cannot help feeling that we shall be closer to the source of the metaphor if we just cancel the 'h' in 'writhing'. This is what metaphor is about: a material intervention – adding one letter to an innocuous phrase – produces a semantically new combination, which will be duly interpreted, thus literally making (new) sense. In metaphor, the remainder exploits not only syntax, it often over-determines this exploitation by having recourse to its usual devices. Another instance mentioned by Soskice occurs in these lines by W. H. Auden:

> The unmentionable odour of death
> Offends the September night.

In this, says Soskice, Auden 'is not speaking about a smell at all, much less speaking about a smell and meaning something else. He is speaking about the forebodings of war in terms which are appro-priate to odour.'[18] Again, I have no quarrel with the interpretation. All I want to point out is that a genitive construction 'odour of N_2' has been used as the frame for a metaphor, and that the choice of 'death' to fill the frame is also due to 'poetic' reasons, the dissemina-tion of 'o' and 'd' sounds in 'odour of death offends'. I am not claiming, as I did in the previous example, that the remainder-work 'precedes' or 'is the source of' the metaphoric 'thought'. But it will be, I hope, granted that in this case they are indistinguishable: this is what I mean by overdetermination. My last example comes from Keats's sonnet *To a Lady Seen for a few Moments at Vauxhall*:

> Time's sea hath been five years at its slow ebb.

He did write 'slow'. We know why.

My first subsidiary thesis is too strong. If I were to maintain that a metaphor is always overdetermined by explicit recourse to the remainder-work, the weight of evidence would be against me. In many cases the presence of such overdetermination is at best vestigial, at worst null. Yet a similar process – the semantic equivalent of homophony or punning – may be at work. This is an extract from one of Keats's letters to Reynolds, for the benefit of whom he is describing Devonshire:

> Buy a girdle, put a pebble in your mouth, loosen your braces – for I am going among scenery whence I intend to tip you the Damosel Radcliffe. I'll cavern you, and grotto you, and water-fall you, and wood you, and immense-rock you, and tremendous-sound you, and solitude you. I'll make a lodg-ment on your glacis by a row of pines, and storm your covered way with bramble bushes. I'll have at you with hip-and-haw small-shot, and cannonade you with shingles. I'll be witty upon salt fish, and impede your cavalry with clotted-cream.[19]

A metaphor is overdetermined in that it has to follow the paths opened by language. Those may be phonetic, or semantic – opened up by the remainder, or by *langue*. In this passage, we have as fine a case of conversion as we could wish. This, of course, would not normally count as metaphor: a syntactic slot, corresponding to a generic verb of action, with an agent-and-patient case structure, is filled with nouns or noun phrases. We note that, according to Husserl's definition, this could not count as *Widersinn*, but as *Unsinn*, for in cases of *Widersinn* the replacement occurs within the same part of speech. Yet these conversions are easily understandable, for the nouns chosen form a semantic series. The end of the passage, on the other hand, is an instance of what the French call *métaphore filée*: the verbs all evoke the actions of a siege, and some of the nouns are clearly metaphoric. Yet they also form a series, so that we have two co-occurrent series, on which interpretation easily works. In this case, metaphor is semantic conversion: a series of empty syntactic slots is filled with the 'wrong' words – words that nevertheless form a coherent semantic series. The coherence is not one of thought – it is the coherence of words normally co-occurrent in literal contexts. So much so that when one of the series has a gap in it ('I'll be witty upon ...' is not a phrase typical of the description of a siege), the coherence of the other series holds the sentence together (here, '... upon salt-fish'). In *métaphore filée*, each series overdetermines the other. I would like to treat the case of a single metaphor, with no apparent overdetermination by the remainder as a case of incipient *métaphore filée*.

Because such cases are numerous, and serve as the basis for most theories of metaphor, I must introduce my *second subsidiary thesis*: if the overdetermination of a metaphor is not synchronic, it is diachronic. If a metaphor is not supported by homophony or semantic seriality, it will be sustained by intertext or cliché. Here is a famous instance, with no apparent overdetermination – the opening of *Richard III*

> Now is the winter of our discontent
> Made glorious summer by this son of York.

There is no trace of remainder-work in these lines, no playing with the form of language. We have a genitive link, with the usual hesitation as to the proper term: is it 'the winter of our N_2', or 'the N_1 of our discontent', or both? The metaphor seems to cry out for an Aristotelian analysis in terms of proportion (winter is to summer what discontent is to contentment). Only the last term is absent in the context, except that it is almost present in 'glorious', which is also a metaphor. This means that we have the beginning of a series, and that the second line makes the first explicit and overdetermines the famous metaphor. Or again, we might analyse the first metaphor in terms of a double synecdoche:

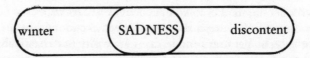

winter   SADNESS   discontent

But there is a problem here, Whatever word I choose to place in the middle as a generic name (any word equivalent to 'sadness' will do), it will either be the literal equivalent of one of the terms (here, 'sadness' and 'discontent') and a metaphor of the other ('winter' is associated with 'sadness' through a metaphor), or it will be so abstract as to be useless as an account of the metaphor. I can escape the circular explanation of the metaphor by another metaphor only if I replace 'sadness' by something like 'unpleasant' or 'negative'. Even these are metaphoric when applied to winter.

There is a reason for this, I think. The metaphor, which as a quotation has become proverbial (so much so that the only way I can revive the cliché is to invert the term and produce the falsely literal 'the discontent of my winter'), was already proverbial in Shakespeare's time. Or so the footnote in my Arden edition tells me, quoting a passage from *Astrophel and Stella*, 'Gone is the winter of my miserie', and various Latin sources. If a metaphor consists in the opening of a new semantic path, starting from a form of 'semantic mistake' or *Widersinn* but using a respectable syntactic pattern, the path, once trodden, remains open, and the metaphor soon becomes established. The Unknown Coiner is at work again: some metaphors catch. It will be claimed afterwards that this is due to the fact that they involve a modicum of truth. I suspect that the process is somewhat arbitrary, and reflects a complex conjuncture, as in the case of coinages – for metaphors are semantic coinages. Why, after all, should a majority be 'silent'? Lakoff and Johnson, who have tackled this problem, produce a convincing explanation in the case of 'orientational' metaphors.[20] One says: 'I feel low' or 'je suis dans le trente-sixième dessous', because bodily prostration is associated with illness and death, whereas an erect posture corresponds to activity and happiness – consequently, we say: 'I am on a high', or 'je suis au septième ciel'. We might therefore account for 'silent majority' in terms of personification. But in all other types, be it 'structural' (a SEASON is a MOOD) or 'ontological' metaphors, the choice of the metaphor is arbitrary, and the only explanation diachronic. Lakoff and Johnson's main structural metaphor is 'ARGUMENT is WAR'. They themselves state that there is no particular reason why we should not rather talk of ARGUMENT in terms of COOPERATIVE WORK OF ART. In many cases the initial choice, like all the dark deeds of the Unknown Coiner, has a large element of arbitrariness in it – which means that it is the product of a historical conjuncture.

From then on, diachrony takes over. Having broken the semantic status quo and won the struggle for its survival, the metaphor develops. It turns proverbial, gives birth to a cliché, produces offspring. One of Lakoff and Johnson's most interesting ideas is that the only metaphors that are alive are the dead ones, as they are the only ones that have been adopted by the community and have survived (when a new word, 'nylon' for instance, has been adopted, we do not speak of a 'dead coinage'). Consequently, they are the only ones that develop. Lakoff and Johnson duly point out that metaphors form systems or families: the HAPPY is UP metaphor is embodied in countless phrases. Perhaps, rather than offspring, I should say offshoot. For metaphors reproduce in the same way as bamboos: through a rhizome. Specialists oppose 'pachymorphous' and 'leptomorphous' rhizomes. The former grow as underground tufts or bunches; the latter grow in a line, giving birth to a new shoot every yard or so. Perhaps we might distinguish between 'pachymorphous' metaphors, which grow in a bunch (the HAPPY is UP rhizome produces a tuft of equivalent metaphors) and 'leptomorphous' metaphors, which grow in a line, each new shoot being an intertextual repetition of the last (this is the case with proverbial metaphors and clichés). The first type is creative – I can always add a new phrase to the bunch; the other constraining – it has the virtues of authority, regularity, and commonsense.

I still do not think that my three theses amount to a theory of metaphor. A sketch of a theory they may be – but not of metaphor. My strategy has been not to praise metaphor, but to bury it – dissolve or dismember might be better words. I have concentrated on the frontiers of metaphors, on what they could be turned into, rather than on what they are. Thus, I have tried to show that, as a category of *lalangue*, metaphor is part of the remainder – indeed, it is overdetermined by homophonic devices, when it is not sustained by semantic series. I have also shown that, as a species of *Unsinn*, metaphor is a kind of semantic coinage, an arbitrary distance taken from common parlance. But this must not give semantics too large a place. I have stated that its role is negative, and that the main part is played by syntax: metaphor is the insertion of (possibly) random items within multiply ambiguous syntactic frames. Lastly, I have shown that there is diachrony in metaphor, either intertextual nostalgia for its ancient past, or anticipation of its potential rhizomatic offshoot. This may not be a 'theory of metaphor', but I believe that drawing a map of frontiers is not an entirely useless task.

I shall not enter – as most treatments of the subject do – into a critique of other theories. What I have said is enough to mark a difference. Against potentially mystic conceptions, I have argued that metaphor has no truck with truth: even when used by the most inventive poet, it keeps an element of arbitrariness about it, the talent of the poet lying in the fact that he lets language speak through him. Against cognitive conceptions of metaphor, I have argued that metaphors are a matter not for concepts, but for language – this is where I part company with Lakoff and Johnson. Against pragmatic theories, of the Davidson–Searle type, I have argued that metaphor is not so much the effect of a subject's intention, to be pragmatically computed, as the work of the Unknown Coiner – the opening up of a path that was already present in language before some speaker ventured upon it. In this, a metaphor is like a pun or a joke. Against semantic theories, of the I. A. Richards or Max Black type, I have argued that the main linguistic level in metaphor is syntax, not semantics.

Since my theses were inspired by an irritation with the constant use of the same simple examples, where Sally is forever an ice-cube and Richard tiresomely a lion, I shall try to analyse a few live metaphors in their context.

TWO POEMS

Sweet is the swamp with its secrets,
Until we meet a snake;
'Tis then we sigh for houses,
And our departure take

At that enthralling gallop
That only childhood knows.
A snake is summer's treason,
And guile is where it goes.[21]

This poem by Emily Dickinson is susceptible of two different readings. A first, literal reading will tell us that the piece is about the chance encounter of a child and a snake, at the bottom of a garden, and the consequent fright and flight of the child. But we soon realize that this child is in fact all children, or anyone's childhood, which suggests a second reading, where the poem tells us about the Fall, and the meeting between our common ancestor and the Snake, giving an inkling of subsequent catastrophe. The meaning of the poem lies in the tension between the two readings. The encounter of child and snake repeats the situation of the Fall, and the loss of childish innocence is the repetition of Man's expulsion from the Garden of Eden. If I may say so, ontogenetic development recapitulates phylogenetic catastrophe. The relationship between the two readings is, in the broadest sense, metaphorical. The first is literal, for this snake is *a* snake; the second figurative or allegoric, for it is also the Snake. We note that the text says 'a snake', thus showing that the literal reading comes first and the metaphoric follows, as a result of interpretation.

Even if I am using the term 'metaphor' metaphorically (I am talking of a poem, not a phrase, and 'allegory' would be more apt), my analysis so far seems to comfort a pragmatic theory of metaphor, of the kind Searle, for instance, has adopted. The word 'snake' has only one meaning, the literal, and the allegorical meaning is the utterer's. The reader reconstructs it through pragmatic calculus. Dickinson tells the story of a child; she intends to evoke the Story of the Fall.

But how does the reader construct the second reading? He deciphers various hints, some prosodic (the poem is written in the metre of Protestant hymns), some lexical ('guile' belongs to the vocabulary of the Bible). Most of all, he understands a few metaphors, in the strict sense. Two of these have strategic importance because, situated as they are in the very middle of the poem, they form a kind of fulcrum on which the passage from the first to the second reading revolves. In the last line of the first stanza, we read 'departure'; in the first line of the last stanza, 'enthralling'. 'Departure' has literal meaning, since the child departs from the scene. It also has the metaphorical meaning associated with the cliché 'our dear departed friends'. 'Enthralling' has its literal contemporary meaning; it also retains its etymological meaning, which is rather easy to recover as the word 'thrall' can still be heard in it. This etymological metaphor tells us that this departure, which condemns the sons of Adam to death, also makes them the thralls of Sin.

The first thing this text proves is that in context, metaphors are less clear-cut than in the discussions of philosophers. 'Departure' is undoubtedly a metaphor, a most venerable one at that, the source of many a pious cliché (the French say: 'partir, c'est mourir un peu'); whereas 'enthralling' is less clearly metaphoric. The child runs, fully absorbed in his panic, which makes his gallop not only swift but also enthralling – literally so, if we take the present participle seriously. It is the recovery of the etymology of the word that makes it metaphoric – which means that my metaphorical second reading interprets the dead metaphor by going back to its forgotten literal meaning. Reviving dead metaphors is one of the strategies favoured by poets.

But the text can also serve to illustrate my thesis. First, it shows that the interpretation of metaphor must follow the paths of language. It is intertext (cliché) and etymology that enable us to construct the second reading, not our intuition of the author's meaning. Second, it makes it clear that metaphors, as part of *lalangue*, are close to puns. Indeed, they are perfect puns, where the two meanings involved belong not only to two homophonous words (as in the Mouse's 'mine is a long and sad tale', to which Alice replies, looking at its tail: 'I can see it is long, but why do you call it sad?'), but to the same word. For, *pace* Davidson, in my two metaphors both meanings are present *at once*, which he claims distinguishes puns from metaphors, where only one meaning is present, the other being pragmatically construed. When we read the poem for the first time the snake is a snake; the second time, it is the Snake. But this chronological distinction between two readings is only a pedagogic fiction. It is the same poem we read twice, and the same words. And the global meaning lies in the co-presence of the two readings. We could paraphrase it as an Aristotelian proportion: the passage from childhood to adulthood, or from innocence to experience is to the individual man what the passage from innocence to knowledge was to the first man. The pun mentioned by Davidson in his essay[22] (he borrows it from Shakespeare) turns out to be an etymological metaphor: 'Our General doth salute you with a kiss' (*Troilus and Cressida*). He claims, quite rightly, that one must give two readings of 'general': the common people, and the leader of the army. Consequently, this is a pun, not a metaphor. What he fails to notice is that the two meanings are etymologically related, through metaphor, to the same word, the general being the leader of the generality of soldiers.

So that, third, the poem also illustrates the overdetermination of metaphor. Both metaphors are overdetermined not so much by homophony (although they are caught in the network of alliteration and assonance that not only gives form to the poem but also contributes to its meaning by opposing the first two stanzas, where 's' and 'z', snaky sounds, abound, to the second stanza, where 't's, 'd's and 'l's abound) as by their history, in the shape of cliché or etymology. As for my main thesis, I shall only remark that the first metaphor is a case of genitive link ('our departure' = 'the child's departure') and the second a simple case of adjectival replacement. The remainder does exploit potentialities offered by syntax. The very simplicity of the syntactic structure, concealing as it does possible ambiguities, 'naturalizes' the metaphor and enables the reader to 'forget' about its syntax.

There is one aspect of my theses that I have not analysed in Dickinson's poem: the role of semantic series. Yet they undoubtedly have a part to play. If I were to define two semantic fields, one broadly called 'pleasant' and the other 'unpleasant' (any similar pair of terms will do), I can arrange the words of the poem into three sets, one for each field, and one for ambiguous or indifferent cases. And I will discover that such taxonomy is not vain. Thus, the first couplet opens on a positive word ('sweet') and ends on a negative word ('snake'), the two intervening words being ambiguous ('swamp' and 'secrets'). Whereas in the last couplet, a lonely positive word ('summer') is surrounded by three negative ones ('snake', 'treason', 'guile'). This adequately charts the semantic evolution of the poem.

I would like to go further, and consider semantic series as generated by the dictionary, that is by language, not by some neutral semantic medium. For this, I shall use a poem by David Gascoyne:

Slate

Behind the higher hill
sky slides away to fringe of crumbling cloud;
out of the gorse-grown slope
the quarry bites its tesselated tiers.

The rain-eroded slate packs loose and flat
in broken sheets and frigid swathes of stone,
like withered petals of a great grey flower.

The quarry is deserted now; within
a scooped-out niche of rubble, dust and silt
a single slate-roofed hut to ruin falls.

A petrified chaos
the quarry is; the slate makes still-born waves,
or crumbling crowds like those
behind the hill, monotonously grey.[23]

The first two stanzas contain a number of metaphors, which can be recognized by the *Widersinn* test: clouds do not crumble, quarries do not bite. These metaphors produce a systematic inversion: whereas the sky is described in terms of stones ('crumbling clouds'), the quarry is described in terms of water ('packs', 'sheets') and life ('bites', 'flower'). The two stanzas play on the opposition between animate and inanimate, and between the elements (the air is petrified, the earth turns to water). If I were to give a pragmatic account of these metaphors, based on my main thesis and forgetting the subsidiary intervention of the remainder, I would state that the author has written a semantically illegal sentence, 'the quarry bites its tesselated tiers', because he meant to evoke the image of a quarry bitten, like an apple, by some Titan – the tiers of slate being tesselated because they bear the mark of the giant's teeth. (How singularly inadequate the paraphrase of a live metaphor always is!)

But the passage from the analysis in terms of *Widersinn*, which is unquestionable, to a pragmatic account of poetic meaning raises questions. This is an early poem by one of the rare English Surrealists. His relationship to what he writes may be presumed to be more complex than mere intention. My contention is that what he meant is beside the point, for he is the kind of poet who lets language speak for itself. And speak for itself it does here. What makes the metaphor, 'the quarry bites', so striking is the existence, in the dictionary, of another sense of the word 'quarry', which will produce the perfectly natural sentence 'the quarry is bitten (by a predator)'. It appears that my thesis about the *Widersinn* quality of metaphor must be taken *together* with the subsidiary thesis on overdetermination. And here comes the semantic series, along the paths of the dictionary. If the evocation of the big bad wolf sounds far-fetched, what about the metaphor in the next line, 'the rain-eroded slate packs loose and flat'? The verb 'pack' has several meanings. Among them, the NED gives the following one: 'to form into a pack, of cards, ice, wolves.' Our wolf is back with us, and the metaphor is beginning to look like a pun.

Perhaps I am exaggerating. Perhaps I am packing more meaning into the poem than it will bear. But that is precisely what a poem is about. Besides, I am not sure that what is often called the 'conduit' metaphor,[24] in spite of the authority of usage, provides an adequate account of the emergence of meaning. Metaphor makes it clear that meaning is not introduced into the sentence (it does not precede it) but emerges from it (it is an effect). Metaphor reveals the process of production of meaning, as a compromise (in the Freudian sense of the term) between the author and his language. Meaning is not poured into language, it is (far)fetched from and by language. My analysis might indeed be pursued in the next line, where we find metaphors on 'sheet' and 'swathe' which look remarkably like puns, for if the two words evoke death (the shroud and the mummy), together with 'frigid' and 'stone', the first also evokes rain (when taken together with 'packs of ice', 'rain-eroded' and 'clouds') and the second recalls a swath of corn and announces 'a great grey flower'. Meaning emerges through dissemination, in semantic series. The text, like a dictionary (not the well-ordered, ideal object of the linguist, but the concrete object in which the language-lover delights in losing his way), is a rhizome.

THE EFFECT OF METAPHOR

Studying metaphors in their natural element, rather than the overworked 'A is B' context, should make me qualify my analysis. My theses do account for the main aspect of the contradiction. They tell us how, in metaphor, language speaks. They tell us where metaphors can be found (in what syntactic contexts) and how they are produced (the initial shock of *Unsinn* is compensated by overdetermination, through homophony, semantic series, intertext, or etymology). But they tell us little about the effect of metaphors, about what counts as a successful metaphor. In other words, they do not tell us how, in metaphor, the poet speaks language. And the poet does speak, at the very moment when he lets himself be spoken by language. He lets himself be guided, the better to guide – a strategy often ascribed, in our male-chauvinist world, to women. Speaking in terms of compromise is not, of course, a way of denying the poet's talent, or making the production of metaphor the result of blind linguistic chance. I do not wish all charms to fly at the mere touch of cold philosophy, nor is it my intention to clip an angel's wings, unweave a rainbow, or deny Philomel her full-throated ease. What I am suggesting is that the creative poet is in the same position as the Unknown Coiner – he obeys (or plays with) the same constraints. Except that, in the case of metaphor, we are dealing with a Known Coiner. Not only in the sense that a name can be affixed to the coinage, but because the process is more controlled, more systematic, more deliberate than in the mere transcription of a clever coinage. Nevertheless, poetic metaphors are not in principle different from jokes: whatever their aptness, it is language that allows them; and yet it takes a world of talent to invent them.

If, therefore, we concentrate on the 'I speak language' aspect of metaphor, on its creativity, we shall still be dealing not with truth (the phrase 'metaphorical truth' is itself metaphorical), but with an 'effect of truth'. *La langue n'est pas fasciste, elle est vraisemblable.* According to Kristeva's well-known theory of verisimilitude,[25] a *vraisemblable* utterance is in the same position as the work of art according to Plato – it is a simulacrum, an imitation of an imitation. For if a true proposition is one that 'imitates' reality, a proposition evincing verisimilitude is one that imitates a true proposition. *Le discours vraisemblable ressemble au discours qui ressemble au réel.* This second-order relationship is what I call an 'effect of truth'. It is not mere illusion, Plato's 'wrong' imitation. It has a reality of its own, albeit one that is restricted to language. The 'aptness' of a metaphor is due not to the fact that it 'resembles' reality (a metaphor is not true) but to the fact that it literally *makes* sense. Left to its own devices, language becomes creative. And if, in neo-Platonist fashion, we interpret the distancing mechanism not as a simple line but as a spiral (see Figure 4.2), we shall be convinced that metaphor is that which is furthest from reality, but also that which returns towards it and is closer to it than any statement of truth.

Figure 4.2

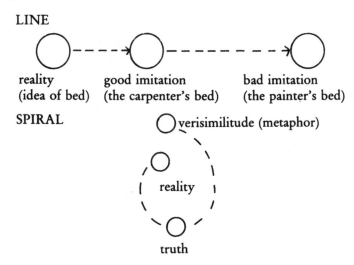

LINE

reality
(idea of bed)

good imitation
(the carpenter's bed)

bad imitation
(the painter's bed)

SPIRAL

verisimilitude (metaphor)

reality

truth

What I am suggesting here is, in my terms, a (garbled) equivalent to a pragmatic theory of metaphor. For Davidson, we remember, distinguishes two levels. On the semantic level, where questions of truth are relevant, a metaphorical phrase is false. On the pragmatic level, it is used to produce an effect. On the syntactic–semantic level, I treat metaphor as a case of *Widersinn*. Because it is overdetermined, because the remainder returns within *langue*, on another level, the poetic level, where the poet makes his compromise and speaks language, it produces an effect of truth. This effect I must now describe. I shall develop a theory of the production/reception of metaphor centred around four characteristics. A quotation from David Cooper's *Metaphor* will provide a useful starting point:

> Merleau-Ponty ... offers a seemingly inconsistent proposal when he writes, of 'authentic' speech, that 'we are *possessed* by it. The end of the speech or text will be the lifting of a spell'. But there is no contradiction here. On the contrary the oscillation between possession by and seizure of is precisely

what many people experience in the face of poetry. On the one hand the reader lets himself be swept along by the words, surrendering himself to the power of the words to conjure up images. But, on the other, he also presses the words into service, using them as pegs on which to hang a chain of fantasies or as spurs to speculations which may have no relation to anything entertained by the poet. And such, it seems to me, is our experience before fresh and interesting metaphors, inside or outside of poems. 'Interpretation' of metaphors can indeed take the form of an oscillation between surrender to the power of the words and a commandeering of them for our own purposes. Hofmannstahl's human dovecots and Nietzsche's female truth are metaphors which take hold of us, yet serve as vehicles which we take over to carry us where we want to go.[26]

It is my contention that the reception of metaphor as described here is the mirror-image of the production of metaphors by the poet; that the reader of poetry 'speaks language' in the same way as the poet does; that there is creativity on both sides of the process.

My first characteristic is *illumination*. A live metaphor is an occasion for a minor, or a mild, epiphany. This is the very embodiment of the 'effect of truth' which I ascribe to metaphor. The syntactic frame 'naturalizes' a semantically alien sentence, turns it into an assertion that, in its unpredictability, conveys an insight. There is a sense in which, when one is confronted with a good metaphor, the strange combination of words is deeply right. We had never thought of it that way, or in that light, but now we see it. And we experience something akin to the release of tension – the jubilation – that according to Freud is the effect of a successful joke. In other words, we have an intuition – as of a truth so far concealed and suddenly revealed – that anticipates on our understanding. We are not necessarily clear as to the content of what we see in a flash – all we know is that the clouds of unknowing have, for a brief moment, dissolved. This illumination is a frequent experience for the user of language. We come across it whenever we realize that an aspect of our linguistic behaviour falls under a regularity that can be formulated by a rule. It is not the same as the feeling of relief that we enjoy when we come to the end of a step-by-step deduction. The difference is neatly captured in Bergson's *La Pensée et le mouvant*,[27] where he opposes two types of clarity. A new idea can be immediately clear if it presents already known elementary ideas ordered in a new way. But then, it is not, of course radically new, rather a mixture of the unexpected and the well-known, like Lakoff and Johnson's systematic metaphors, which grow out of accepted commonplaces. On the other hand, an idea is radically new if it expresses an intuition. According to Bergson, such an idea has two characteristics. It is imposed on us – in other words, it cannot be the object of our conscious search, and never is the result of a discovery. And it is at first obscure, so that its clarity is somewhat contradictory. It is so radically clear because it was unclear at the start. This second type of clarity, the clarity of intuition, is what we experience with the illumination of metaphor. Of course, at the very moment when we are under the impression that we are offered an insight into truth itself, it is by language that we are, as Merleau-Ponty says, 'possessed'. Illumination is the result of syntax, of its exploitation by the remainder. This is what enables us, in David Cooper's words, to 'press the words into service'.

The oscillation must be preserved. If in illumination we 'surrender ourselves to the power of the words', we also 'use them as pegs on which to hang a chain of fantasies.' The surrender is never complete. There is a vast amount of difference between producing or enjoying a metaphor and undergoing a mystical experience. This is due to the second characteristic of metaphor, which compensates for the first, its *exaggeration*. This characteristic is duly recognized and described in Davidson's essay, when he stresses the sheer falsity of metaphor – there is something in a metaphor that comes close to a lie. Of course, this is what allows a pragmatic account of metaphor, for it turns it into an indirect speech act like irony. The poet talks about the blushful Hippocrene 'winking at the brim' with beaded bubbles.[28] But I am not aware that wine 'winks', so the word must be taken metaphorically. This, of course, is facile caricature – but it is difficult to apply a pragmatic calculus to an actual poetic metaphor without making both sound rather silly. Davidson's insight is nevertheless correct: there is something blatantly false, even outrageous, in this winking, with the train of images – some of them potentially ludicrous – it suggests. The outrage is due not to the fact that we have put together two semantic building bricks not normally associated, 'the wine winks', but rather to the new force that the combination acquires when a frontier is crossed. Again, we feel the same exhilaration at the crossing of the border as we do in a good joke. This is one of the reasons why jokes are so often 'naughty'. If it is of the essence that they should cross a linguistic or logical frontier, why not cross the frontier of taboo as well?

I am not suggesting, of course, that Keats's line is effective because the metaphor of winking evokes a chain of grotesque images, in which, for instance, the wine would be stupidly personified. Exaggeration is only the other side of illumination, that is, of aptness. If we look at a dictionary, we shall learn that the verb 'wink', apart from its well-known meanings of 'blink', 'connive at', and 'give a hint by a wink' (the last two of which are already metaphorical – they are the accepted metaphors, the implicit presence of which in our line creates the exaggeration and ludicrousness), also has the meaning 'to gleam or flash intermittently or fitfully', 'to twinkle', a metaphorical development to 'close one's eye', but one that in the context is entirely appropriate (not unexpectedly, the quotation for this meaning in the NED is our passage). And it has the venerable, and now defunct, meaning of 'closing one's eyes *in association with drinking off at a draught*'. In other words, the potential personification is already in the dictionary. It is induced by the metonymic contiguity of words in actual utterances, as in the quotation from Thomas Elyot given in the NED to illustrate this meaning: 'a drynke ... which the Thracians used to drink up at one draughte, wynkyng.' The remainder – work coalesces these words and meanings into a rhetorical gryphon, a metaphor. Keats uses the word both for its aptness, for the beads of wine twinkle as they catch the light, and its exaggeration. Indeed, 'the blushful Hippocrene', that notorious periphrasis for wine, already personifies it, Hippocrene being a fountain whose violet-coloured, 'blushful' waters were usually represented as being endowed with speech. The source of the exaggeration lies not so much in the invention of outlandish images, as in the exploitation of the resources of language – and the source of illumination is exactly the same.

The dictionary, as I have used it to read Keats's line, has turned into a labyrinth. The combined effect of illumination and exaggeration in metaphors is a consequence of the labyrinthine multiplication of paths along which both the poet and his readers freely roam. Reading poetry demands the same *attention flottante*, the same availability for 'free' association as the psychoanalyst is supposed to have while listening to his patient. This characteristic I shall call the *open-endedness* of metaphor. Because the paths that can be followed are so numerous, the resulting interpretation is never assured, never definitive or fixed. This elementary truth has not escaped Searle when he gives his account of dead and live metaphors in a diagram:[29]

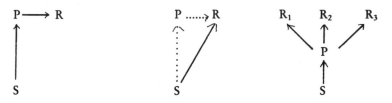

simple metaphor   dead metaphor   open-ended metaphor

'S is P' is the literal utterance, 'S is R' the metaphorical meaning. The dotted lines in the dead metaphor diagram indicate a path that is no longer used. I would like to argue that the model for metaphor is the third one, that the first two are only reductions, the clichéic freezing-up of the third. This is obvious in the case of dead metaphors, as the dotted lines show. Which means that I do not believe in the existence of what Searle calls 'simple metaphor', that notorious indirect speech act, where the path from S to R is both indirect, since it goes through the detour of P, and unique. Even in the case of the Keatsian metaphor of the winking beads of wine, which is as unproblematic, as unlike a riddle or a quibble as one can hope, the paths are many, and the result, if not strictly undecidable, at least richly ambiguous. Which implies, *pace* Searle, that the utterer's meaning is of little importance: the open-endedness of a metaphor's meaning lies in language, not in anyone's mind; it is the effect of the exploitation of the syntax of *langue* by the remainder. Rather than Searle's diagrams, we ought to have a *scale of open-endedness* for metaphors, in three stages. The first stage deals with dead metaphors. The path is fixed and well signposted, and you are requested not to stray into the bushes. There is no open-endedness in this case; there is hardly a metaphor any longer. Richard has been a lion for so long that the metaphorical meaning is now in the dictionary: '*lion* 1. A large carnivorous mammal ... 2. One like a lion either in courage or ravenous cruelty ...' (*Webster's Collegiate Dictionary*, 1941 edition). In the second stage, a dead metaphor is revived, as when I say: 'this cat of mine is a lion.' Here, paths are beginning to diverge, for the dead metaphor comes alive with irony, and the metaphorical lion is also a literal feline, to be compared with the smaller variety. Am I referring to pussy's bravery when chasing a mouse, or to the mane-like quality of her fur? Uncertainty sets in. It will increase and multiply in the third stage, live metaphor, when I blandly state that 'my cat is a sudden shower of rain'. Do not ask me what this fine-sounding metaphor means – I am only the author.

The fourth characteristic, the *indirection* of metaphor, follows from the metaphor of the path. For Searle's diagrams are conceived in terms of paths, always with a fixed direction – they are one-way paths. One is supposed to start from the literal meaning 'S is P', and then proceed to the metaphorical. Because in a dead metaphor one proceeds directly to R, we no longer have a real metaphor, unless we somehow also follow the dotted lines. Against this, I would like to stress that the path of metaphor (a) does not (necessarily) go from the literal to the metaphoric and (b) is not one-directional. The first proposition states that there is no priority of the literal over the metaphoric. The interpretation of a metaphor is not so much a case of progress as of regress. First, the supposed goal is given to us in the flash of illumination – intuition in advance of understanding. Then, and only then, do we work our way backwards in order to understand the metaphor, i.e. to construct the meaning that is revealed in the moment of epiphany. No doubt the sheer ludicrousness, the exaggeration of the revealed meaning, is an incitement to shore it up with explanations. But the construction of a metaphor is always something of a reconstruction. There is no way of constructing meaning step by step, in the orderly fashion of Searle's calculus for indirect speech acts.[30] We cannot proceed, as the King of Hearts advises the White Rabbit, by beginning at the beginning, going on till the end, and then stopping – the end always precedes the beginning. At best, in the case of dead metaphors, when the path is well-trodden, the two terms are given simultaneously, but then the sense of illumination and exaggeration is lost. It is only in such cases that the separation between the literal and the figurative appears natural.

My second proposition goes further. It is not enough to reverse the direction, and say that metaphorical interpretation goes from R to P instead of from P to R. This would only mean that the metaphorical meaning precedes the literal, but the separation would still hold. 'Indirection' means that the process of interpretation, or production, goes both ways indifferently. All the possible meanings of a metaphorical phrase are present at once, without the order they are given in a dictionary, which is normally based on historical principles and treats the 'literal' meaning as primary. This is why I have insisted that metaphors are close to puns. Whether Keats meant it or not, all the meanings of 'wink' are present as potentialities in the line I quoted, so that the distinction between a primary 'literal' meaning and various 'metaphorical' meanings, which I used earlier, is no longer relevant. The reality of this situation clearly appears in the extreme case of anachronism, when it takes philological knowledge to exclude from interpretation more recent meanings that are creeping into the text – sometimes with grotesque effect (every French schoolboy has enjoyed reading the contemporary meaning of the word 'cabinet' into the tragedies of Racine), but sometimes with arresting meaningfulness.

The indirection of metaphor is the consequence and combination of the first three characteristics. Interpretation is multi-directional because true metaphors are open-ended (there is no fixed end to the process of understanding), and because they produce a feeling of both illumination (the goal is given before the beginning) and exaggeration (that goal, which is the right goal, is also deeply wrong). Indirection is in fact what anchors metaphor in the remainder. It explains why metaphors behave like puns, why they are overdetermined, i.e. always prepared to follow the homophonic, semantic or, intertextual paths of the remainder – because there is no fixed computation, be it pragmatic or semantic, for a true metaphor.

METAPHOR AND SENSE

The fact that the account of metaphor just given meanders between various hints and falls short of a full-fledged theory, that it hesitates between a treatment of the reception and of the production of metaphor, is not merely a reflection of the contradiction ('language speaks'; 'I speak language') that I have developed throughout this book. The four characteristics of metaphor point to a theory of meaning, or rather of what Deleuze calls sense.[31]

Since I have expounded this theory elsewhere,[32] the merest lineaments will suffice. Meaning for Deleuze is ascribed to propositions. It is not a simple or single entity, but an effect of the relationships between a proposition and the world, the subject who utters it and the language in which it is stated. The first relationship is one of *designation*. A proposition designates a state of affairs – the intuitive expression of this designation is the ostensive phrase 'this is it'. Designation is logically concerned with truth and falsity, and a proposition is true when it successfully designates. All this is familiar ground, and involves the usual problems. The second relationship is *manifestation*. This is the name Deleuze gives to the relation between a proposition and the subject who utters it. The linguistic realization of manifestation is the first-person pronoun – but one could also mention the rest of the shifters and modality in all its forms. The third relationship is *signification*. It operates between words and general concepts, between the syntactic relations within the sentence and concept implications. It refers to the insertion of a proposition within a demonstration, where it becomes the premiss or conclusion for an argument and links up with other propositions. Its linguistic realization is the word 'therefore'. And it is concerned not with truth and falsity, but with linguistic coherence: propositions that are sometimes termed nonsensical because they are neither true nor false, be they 'Allah is great' or 'the present king of France is bald', in other words propositions that fail to designate, have signification (they can be used as significant premisses in a demonstration). Again, there is nothing here that should unduly trouble the analytic philosopher – except perhaps that 'meaning' no longer exists as a single entity, pulled as it is in three different directions.

But this lost unity of meaning is recaptured when Deleuze adds on a fourth dimension, called 'sense', which has no equivalent in modern theories of meaning. He finds his inspiration for this in the Stoics. The necessity for his fourth relation appears in the fact that the first three are circular, each presupposing the other two. Thus, for instance, there can be no designation without prior manifestation (of the 'I' that designates) or signification (the system of *langue* makes designation possible). Sense is the level that generates, or makes possible, the three relations that define the meaning of a proposition. It is, if not anterior, at least prior to them. And it is a relation of expression: sense is that which the proposition expresses, an incorporeal event (to use Stoic terminology); it is something, *aliquid*, which is neither the terms of the proposition, nor the state of affairs the proposition designates, the beliefs it manifests, the concepts it signifies. It is best conceived through paradox. Deleuze mentions several of these. The first is the paradox of infinite regression. When I state a proposition, I cannot state its sense; in order to do this, I need another proposition, the sense of which in turn is not stated: anyone familiar with the White Knight's song and its many names will have recognized a Carrollian situaton. The second is the paradox of the neutrality or the sterility of sense. Sense is not affected by any of the modes a proposition can take, negation for instance: *contradictoria ad invicem idem significant* (two contradictory propositions have the same sense). The third is the paradox of impossible objects. Propositions without signification, because they are absurd or self-contradictory (for instance, propositions involving square circles or colourless green ideas), are not senseless – we are in the world of Meinong and metaphor.

The interest of Deleuze's concept of sense is that it gives a general theory of meaning as process. Meaning emerges within a structure, where sense plays the genetically most important part. The structure is made up of two series, one signifying, one signified (words and things, or propositions and states of affairs), a paradoxical element (the structuralist's 'empty square'), which moves along the two series, on their frontier, in both directions, making sense but being nonsensical itself; the end result is the emergence of good or common sense (where the direction is fixed) out of nonsense: the operations of designation, manifestation, and signification can then successfully apply.

I believe that this structure is what gives coherence to the four characteristics of metaphor I have described. The illumination of metaphor recapitulates the genesis of sense. Suddenly, something new happens, a proposition 'makes sense' in an original manner – a moment that has been long lost in the passage to 'good' or 'common' sense characteristic of dead metaphors or so-called 'literal' utterances. The exaggeration of metaphor expresses one of the paradoxes of sense just mentioned: the paradox of impossible objects and nonsensical propositions. Before good sense is reached, there is no designation or signification: only sense, which is indifferent to truth, semantic well-formedness, and argumentative coherence. Hence its creativity – it is good sense that goes back to accepted truths, which sense ignores. The indirection of metaphor reflects the bi-directionality of sense. On the level of sense, where assertion and negation have the same value, everything is possible – it is good sense that involves direction (Deleuze puns on the two meanings of the French word *'sens'*, 'sense and 'direction'). Lastly, the open-endedness of metaphor reflects the circulation, or the plasticity, of sense. At this stage, nothing is fixed, no determinate meaning is assigned to the proposition, for that is the function of designation, signification, and manifestation.

In the genesis of every proposition, there is a moment of creation, of potential nonsense, but also of fluidity: the moment of sense, before a (self-)conscious subject takes over, before the world is designated, before *langue* with its fixed units and general rules imposes its structure on language. This moment of sense is obliterated when good sense wins. But it returns, in *délire* or in metaphor. Metaphor, far from being a mere trope, is the essential process of creativity in language, or rather its trace on the linguistic surface. We can now understand the characteristics of the remainder better. The remainder, of which metaphor is a part, is the rhizome traced on the surface of language by the original, never totally obliterated, process of sense. This explains why the remainder always returns, why it is so constitutive as to be primary, why it is compulsively celebrated in all the varieties of remainder-work and items of the rag-bag, why it is linguistic in essence. Sense is concerned neither with the world, for the remainder does not seek to designate; nor with the subject, for there is no pragmatic account of metaphor or the rest of the remainder; nor with *langue*, for there is no fixed order in the remainder.

The remainder, and metaphor its mouthpiece, are so pervasive because they are vital moments in the genesis of propositions. This is why the four characteristics of metaphor can be used to account for other items of the rag-bag. In Chapter 2, I mentioned what the linguistic jargon calls 'exocentric compounds' as an instance of the remainder at work. A ladybird is neither a bird nor a lady. ('Blackbird' is endocentric because a blackbird is a bird.) Here we find the exaggeration of metaphor – a synchronic effect due to the oblivion in which the origin of the word has fallen: this is a strange and striking name for a homely red insect. We also find its indirection – which is the stem, and which the adjunct? – and its open-endedness, for placing the two nouns side by side to form a compound creates potential ambiguity (the lady's bird, the bird is a lady). Lastly, the name itself is an instance of illumination – no doubt due to the fact that an established name has an appearance of inevitability about it. It seems to tell us a mysterious story, an imaginative one, to be captured by an etymological fiction, and this produces an impression of aptness, more so, for instance, than the trivial '*coccinelle*'.

If this last example sounds a little far-fetched, this is because the diachrony of the process interferes with the synchronic effect. How can a name seem to be other than apt once it is established? But the example points to the importance of the activity of naming, traditionally recognized as the essential privilege of the first legislator. Inventing a new metaphor is an instance of naming – except that one never names out of the blue or out of the free exercise of an unconstrained imagination. One names what the remainder, language speaking in its own right, allows one to name. As we have seen, it takes considerable talent to achieve even this: to let language speak is also to make it speak.

I must confess, however, that by proposing an account of metaphor in terms of Deleuzian sense, I have been deeply unfaithful to the master. As clearly appears in his *Anti-Oedipus*,[33] he belongs to the long tradition of hostility to metaphor. *Anti-Oedipus* is rich in extravagant metaphors: the machine, the body without organs, etc. Yet the authors insist that they must be taken literally: the body *is* a machine, the body politic *is* a body. And they most emphatically renounce metaphor and all its ways. They are concerned not with transfer of meaning, but with a change of form, which has material implications. They advocate metamorphosis as an alternative to metaphor. I shall take this as an incitement to go further, to deconstruct the already vacillating opposition between the literal and the metaphoric. The important word in Deleuze and Guattari's critique of metaphor is the word 'material'. The violence of language cannot be limited to the violence of agrammaticality, as the remainder subverts the rules of *langue*. Exploring the material violence of language will take us in two directions: the direction of history, where the opposition is dissolved as the literal becomes metaphoric and vice versa, but also where language is both the locus and the means of historical (political) intervention, and the direction of the social, of the body and the body politic, where the non-autonomy of language will be taken into account.

NOTES

1 A. Grésillon, 'Ambiguïté et double sens', in *Modèles Linguistiques*, 19, Lille, 1988, pp. 9–20.
2 U. Eco, *Semiotics and the Philosophy of Language*, Bloomington, Indiana University Press, 1984, p. 88.
3 D. Davidson, 'What metaphors mean', in *Inquiries into Truth and Interpretation*, Oxford, Clarendon Press, 1984, pp. 245–64.
4 C. Brooke-Rose, *A Grammar of Metaphor*, London, Secker & Warburg, 1958, p. 128.
5 ibid., pp. 24–5.

THE VIOLENCE OF LANGUAGE

6 ibid., p. 14.
7 J. Tamine, 'Métaphore et syntaxe', in *Langages*, 54, Paris, 1979, pp. 65–82.
8 ibid., p. 66.
9 E. Husserl, *Logische Untersuchungen*. II, 1, Halle, Max Niemeyer, 1913.
10 G. Steiner, *Antigones*, Oxford, Oxford University Press, 1984, pp. 132–6.
11 Husserl, op. cit., p. 327.
12 M. Prandi, *Sémantique du contresens*, Paris, Minuit, 1987.
13 M. Douay, 'De la Presse à la pub: l'ambiguïté entre en jeu', in *Modèles linguistiques*, 19, Lille, 1988, pp. 21–31.
14 C. Brooke-Rose, *A Grammar of Metaphor*, op. cit., p. 148.
15 I. Fonagy, 'La Structure sémantique des constructions possessives', in J. Kristeva, J. C. Milner, and N. Ruwet (eds), *Langue, discours, société*, Paris, Seuil, 1975, p. 51.
16 ibid., p. 47.
17 J. M. Soskice, *Metaphor and Religious Language*, Oxford, Clarendon Press, 1985, p. 50.
18 ibid., p. 49.
19 Quoted from Lord Houghton, *The Life and Letters of John Keats*, London, Everyman's Library, 1927, p. 71.
20 G. Lakoff and M. Johnson, *Metaphors We Live by*, Chicago, University of Chicago Press, 1980.
21 E. Dickinson, *Selected Poems and Letters*, New York, Anchor Books, 1959, p. 200.
22 Davidson, op. cit., p. 250.
23 D. Gascoyne, *Collected Poems*, Oxford, Oxford University Press, 1965, p. 3.
24 M. J. Reddy, 'The conduit metaphor – a case of frame conflict in our language about language', in A. Ortorny (ed.), *Metaphor and Thought*, Cambridge, Cambridge University Press, 1979, pp. 284–324.
25 See J. Kristeva, 'La Productivité dite texte', in *Semeiotike*, Paris, Seuil, 1969, pp. 208–45.
26 D. Cooper, *Metaphor*, Oxford, Blackwell, 1986, p. 110.
27 H. Bergson, *La Pensée et le mouvant*, Paris, PUF, 1938, p. 31.
28 Keats, *Ode to a Nightingale*, lines 16–17.
29 J. Searle, 'Metaphor', in Ortorny, op. cit., p. 122.
30 See J. Searle, 'Indirect speech-acts', in *Expression and Meaning*, Cambridge, Cambridge University Press, 1979.
31 G. Deleuze, *Logique du sens*, Paris, Minuit, 1969.
32 See J. J. Lecercle, *Philosophy through the Looking-Glass*, London, Hutchinson, 1985, ch. 3.
33 G. Deleuze and F. Guattari, *L'Anti-Œdipe*, Paris, Minuit, 1972 (English transl., *Anti-Oedipus*, tr. R. Hurley, M. Seem, and H. R. Lane, New York, Viking, 1983).

5

CORRUPTION

Synchrony is one man's crony, and diachrony is another man's crony.

(H. Matthews)

CORRUPTION

'The action of corrupting; the fact of being corrupted; the condition of being corrupt; corrupt matter; a corrupt example or form; corrupting agency: in the various physical, moral, and transferred applications of CORRUPT.' This is how the NED sums up the meanings of the word 'corruption'. It then proceeds to detail these meanings, nine in all. From which it transpires that the word applies, in that historical order, to bodies ('decomposition as a consequence of death', first recorded use 1340), souls ('a making or becoming morally corrupt', 1340; 'perversion or destruction of integrity in the discharge of public duties', 1425), and words ('change of language, a text, word, etc. from its correct or original condition to one of incorrectness, deterioration, etc.', 1494). There is food for thought in this metaphoric drift. Not only does it state the fact of language change, which nobody can deny, but it assimilates it to material change, pessimistically understood as dissolution. The examples the NED offers for meaning number nine, word corruption, are predictably prescriptive and catastrophic: 'the continual Corruption of our English tongue' (Swift); 'by phonetic corruption ... not only the form, but the whole nature of language is destroyed' (Max Müller, 1861).

Strong words, but of little historical relevance to the linguist, who records, but does not regret, language change. However, the strong feelings they evince have to be recorded too, for they have

181

ever-renewed synchronic relevance. It appears that languages, like civilizations, know that they are mortal – indeed, historical linguists metaphorically describe the demise of languages in terms of murder or suicide – and that the violent feelings this awareness provokes, reflecting as they do the violence of linguistic change, ruffle the equanimity of the synchronic *état de langue*. Or at least the equanimity of its most vocal supporters, grammarians, writers, or authors of dictionaries. The past and future of a language become the object of synchronic struggles, as arbiters of linguistic taste resist the moral corruption of linguistic change. But here we are drifting from the purely historical – the systemic evolution of language, in which no individual speaker is involved as such, not even as Unknown Coiner – to the social. A linguistic change in progress involves real people, and questions of prestige, conflict, and struggle are raised. Thus, a study of a teenage subculture in Reading in the 1970s describes the appearance of new verbs with non-standard tense markings, as in 'we fucking chins them with bottles', or 'we bunks it over here a lot' (where 'bunk' means 'play truant').[1] What we have here is not only a new vocabulary, but a new syntax in the making. It emerges through violence – the violence done to language, the violence of linguistic corruption; and also the violence of the social conditions that the subculture reflects.

The theme of this chapter is not the opposition between diachrony and synchrony – an opposition obtained, as in the main Saussurean dichotomies, by exclusion – but their clash. If we take our concept of a remainder seriously, that is if we are not content with describing its operations, in the form either of a rag-bag or of a theory, we shall have to go further than a purely descriptive or synchronic account, and provide an explanation for its existence. Such an explanation will have to take into account the relationships between language, history, and the social. *The remainder is the return within language of the contradictions and struggles that make up the social; it is the persistence within language of past contradictions and struggles, and the anticipation of future ones.* There is no such thing as a stable *état de langue*. Synchrony always inherits the past history of the language; it is itself riddled with diachrony; it is submitted to a constant process of change, anticipating its future. The remainder is another name for this instability. In the example of 'corruption' in progress in Reading, we can recognize what I have ahistorically described as operations of remainder-work: conversion and syntactic change through solecism (not a case of simplification by analogy, since it is the marked '-s' form for the present tense that has been somewhat defiantly chosen). What a sociolinguistic point of view enables us to see is the violence involved in the process. This is an example of social struggle with linguistic consequences, not of language changing according to its own systemic lines of flight. If we project this minuscule example onto language as a whole, a bold but not unwarranted step, we shall realize that an *état de langue* is an ideal construct, and that if we want to account for the real state of affairs, we need a new concept of *linguistic conjuncture*, which we shall have to borrow from the Marxists. Delineating this linguistic conjuncture will amount to drawing a map of the current relations of force (*'rapports de force'*) within a language subject to corruption because dependent on its social environment, not to describing a stable object with the analytical tools of structural science.

The theme of this chapter, therefore, is the return of diachrony within synchrony, the corruption that lies at the heart of a linguistic conjuncture, of which the remainder is both the product and the instrument. The product, because the struggle between the remainder and *langue* is a reflection of this intermingling of diachrony and synchrony – 'historicize the remainder!', in a pastiche of Jameson's celebrated maxim ('always historicize!'), is the motto of these pages. The instrument, because the remainder is the part of language that conserves the past, witnesses to its struggles, and carries them on in the present; conversely, the synchronic violence of its clash with *langue* is itself a source of further linguistic change. The theme of this chapter is already the violence of language, in its first acceptation, the violence of instability, the violence of diachrony.

In the first chapter, I evoked Deleuze and Guattari's critique of the four postulates of linguistics. One further postulate seems to be missing from the list, and to be in great need of a critique: the postulate that the study of *langue* is synchronic, to the strict exclusion of diachrony. But it would be unfair to Deleuze and Guattari to accuse them of omission. The question of synchrony is evoked in their discussion of the third postulate, 'that there are constants and universals of language which allow one to describe *langue* as a homogeneous system.'[2] It is clear that the butt of their critique is Chomsky, with his distinction between constants and variables, his insistence on Universal Grammar, his binary phrase-structure trees. The element in which those systemic constants thrive, in which alone they can acquire their homogeneous character, is of course synchrony, or synchronic competence. Against this, predictably enough, Deleuze and Guattari appeal to pragmatics, i.e. against the distinction between competence and performance ('the primary schoolteacher's competence is performance in the eyes of the inspector of schools'), and also, more interestingly for us, to variables and variations. Language is not the systematic ordering of constants, but is made up of singular abstract machines, constructed out of variables. As a result, it is a composite reality that is essentially heterogeneous. In this case, the reference, *contra* Chomsky, is to Labov and his study of variables and 'inherent variation'. A Labovian 'system', far from being defined by its constants and homogeneity, is characterized by immanent, continuous variability – variable units and optional rules. Consequently, its conditions of existence are to be found not in synchrony, but in what Deleuze and Guattari call 'a-synchrony'.

Variation first. In the same day, Deleuze and Guattari claim, the individual speaker keeps changing languages, and yet is reputed always to speak the same language. He speaks differently in the capacity of a father, an employer, a lover, a dreamer. The phonology, the syntax, and the semantics change. Yet his language somehow remains the same. This is because a language is not defined through its invariant units and rules, but as a network of variables – of dialects, idiolects, registers, and styles. The linguist's idealization of these inherent variables into the invariant units of *langue* is a case of gross and unwarranted exclusion. Witness the uneasy use by linguists of the question mark at the beginning of some of their examples (?'I don't like it none'), as a sign that the utterance in question is attested in some but not all dialects of a language, and is therefore dubious. The rationale for admitting some of those examples and not others is hardly ever explicit, which simply means that the linguist has his cake and eats it, i.e. notices the existence of variables when it suits his demonstration and ignores it otherwise. Against this, Labov conceives of linguistic systems as systems of variables, so that the question of the exclusion of unorthodox variations need not arise. This is how T. Bynon sums up his method:

As a theoretical framework within which the patterns of variation could be stated, Labov postulated for the whole community a single phonological system characterized by a certain number of variable units. Each segment of the phonological system which was found to be subject to variant

CORRUPTION

realizations was considered to form a *phonological variable* and its different realizations were made the object of inquiry. Thus an '(r)-variable' was set up to represent the variation in the pronunciation of words like *car*, *four*, *board*, and an (eh)-variable for that in *bad*, *dance*, *half*. It was then the task of the survey to determine the rule which governed the variation pattern in each case.[3]

The phrases 'single phonological system' and 'determine the rule' must not suggest that we are still within unadulterated synchrony. If it is conceivable to study a system of variables within an *état de langue*, the very fact of variation – the fact that the units are variables, not constants – introduces diachronic change. The rule that accounts for a phonological variation within the system will point to traditions of speech, or changes in speech through imitation of more prestigious models, which are themselves the signs of an aspiration to social change. The synchronic rule governing the variation of 'r' in the speech of New Yorkers soon turns out to be a reflection of historical change. Instead of a purely linguistic, purely synchronic rule, we have a rule that is a function of the age, class, and style of the speaker – in which history and society leave their mark, as appears in the second half of Labov's formulation of his 'New York "r"'-rule:

$$(r) \rightarrow n[r] / \underline{\qquad} \left\{ \begin{array}{c} C \\ \# \end{array} \right\} ; n[r] = f(class, style, age)^4$$

The first half of this has a reassuring Chomskyan aspect; the second looks more dangerous. For it introduces variables that turn the synchronic rule into a rather messy affair. And linguistic rules *are* messy anyway. In the immortal words of Sapir, 'grammar leaks'. In discussing the concept of frontiers in the first chapter, I insisted on the essential fuzziness of rules in language. My account of metaphor was largely based on the semantic vagueness of syntactic structures – structures expressed by rules that are essentially defeasible. At all levels of linguistic structure, we encounter fuzziness and leakage.

In Chapter 1, I suggested a synchronic explanation, in terms of abstraction. Any rule, any delineation of a frontier is an abstraction of the infinite diversity of phenomena. But abstraction implies exclusion: the rule necessarily leaves out a remainder, the size of which depends on its degree of generality. Now I can go further

185

than this in my explanation. Fuzziness is not only due to the reductive action of the linguist; it is constitutive, because it is caused by the intermingling of diachrony and synchrony, the subversion of the synchronic cosmos by diachronic change. What Labov does is to enable us to understand why rules have to be leaky: the second half of his rule introduces factors (age, class, style) that give the lie to the idea that language is an autonomous structure. Indeed, this is why Deleuze and Guattari deal with synchrony in their third postulate. Linguistic change does not operate through disruption and destruction, a revolutionized cosmos giving rise to a new one. It operates through the coexistence and continuity of different types of usage: molecular subversion rather than molar catastrophe. Deleuze and Guattari point out that an utterance like 'I swear to it', which has all the marks of syntactic and semantic stability, is in fact profoundly unstable. The words may remain the same, but in the mouth of a child, a lover, or a witness at a trial, it is not the same utterance. And it is not enough to dismiss this by calling it 'pragmatic' variation. The words are merely the vehicle for a continuum of semantic transformations. Idiolects and dialects subvert the *langue* of which they are supposed to be realizations. The subversion lies in the fact that there is no such thing as *langue* proper (in other words, no *langue* without a remainder that subverts it), but a continuum of dialects, in a situation of 'relation of force' to one another.

The second term in Deleuze and Guattari's analysis of synchrony is *a-synchrony*. Diachrony is too narrowly associated with chronological change. One can easily conceive diachrony – for even generative grammars have their historical counterparts – as the passage from one *état de langue* to another by rule-creation, suppression, or simplification. This has the advantage of keeping the two axes separate, like a matrix for Cartesian coordinates. But this is not the kind of situation that, according to Deleuze and Guattari, obtains in language, where the standard version of the language and its dialects, where the public idiom and the various slangs and secret tongues, where synchrony and diachrony are inextricably mixed. A-synchrony is the name for this variable and continuous state of language. Style is the name for the speaker's appropriation of language. Not of course an individual, but a collective process, for Deleuze and Guattari ascribe style not to individual authors, but to arrangements of utterance: style is a language within a language, competing with other languages that are the same language. Such a

CORRUPTION

state of stylistic variability is best exemplified, for instance, by the
'agrammaticality' of e. e. Cummings's poems. Except that agrammaticality is the wrong word for the strategy that exploits the
potentialities of meaning that language allows the speaker. This
'agrammaticality' questions the constant character of 'correct' forms
and rules, it deterritorializes them, pushes them towards a state of
continuous variation. The study of such variability is what Deleuze
and Guattari call 'internal pragmatics'.

I find Deleuze and Guattari's analysis convincing, but the term
'pragmatics' is unfortunate. Not only because it is an obvious
misprision of what the Anglo-Saxons mean by it, but because it
seems to isolate the phenomenon in a marginal corner – in the
sphere of language use, as opposed to language structure. (It is
interesting to note that Chomskyan linguists have nothing but kind
words for pragmatics – because this enables them to dismiss the
questions it addresses as not concerning the structure of language,
which leaves them in full possession of the field.) Against this, I
wish to maintain that the struggle between synchrony and diachrony,
like the struggle between *langue* and the remainder, occurs within
language (as distinct from mere use or performance). That the
structure of language is erected on the unstable basis of contradiction and strife. The recourse to pragmatics and the dilution of a
specific critique of synchrony within the third postulate of linguistic
homogeneity also has the disadvantage of letting us forget the role
that history plays in the process. If the remainder is both the
reflection and the instrument of change, it is because language is a
profoundly historical entity, and the critique must be historicized.
A-synchrony still contains the word 'synchrony'. It still is a sort of
negative synchrony. Diachrony will not do either as we have seen.
What we need to analyse is not so much linguistic change as such –
this is not a chapter on historical linguistics – as its effect within the
present conjuncture as the representation, in the form of repetition
and anticipation, of diachrony within synchrony. In the words of
D. Attridge, the historicity of language, this unholy mixture of
synchrony and diachrony, is to be analysed in terms of feedback:

It could be called a problem of *feedback*: the rigid insulation
of synchrony from diachrony is threatened by a short circuit
whereby history is reinscribed in the present – not as a series
of 'real events' (which, having passed can no longer intrude)
but as the only way in which history *can* intervene in the
present as a theory or story of the past.[5]

187

ETYMOLOGY

Attridge's essay deals with the question of etymology. If our theme is indeed history 'as a theory or story of the past', the synchronic representation of diachrony, the obvious candidate for such stories is etymology. Etymology it is that claims to tell us the true story of words, the history that can be recovered from their present state by going back to their origin. But there is an immediate problem. As a subject, etymology no longer has pride of place. It has been abandoned as a region unworthy of the linguist's interest. Modern textbooks of historical linguistics devote hardly more than a page or two to it. The only place where it still has its role is in dictionaries. This, of course, strangely contrasts with its ancient splendour. From the Middle Ages to the early nineteenth century, it was the core of historical linguistics. The paradox is that this pristine glory was annihilated by the appearance, in the course of the nineteenth century, of more reliable 'scientific' etymological techniques. The subject seems to have committed suicide by turning serious. This, I think, is due to two related factors. The first is that the old speculative etymology was often associated with even more speculative research into the origins of language, against which modern linguistics has been erected. Etymology was, quite naturally, the main source of evidence and heuristic device for those fanciful theories. As a result, it is now literally a residue, left to marginal or slightly dubious linguists, like P. Guiraud in France or Eric Partridge in Britain. (I confess to considerable affection for these figures.) Modern linguists are interested in structures, not words – this was the case even before they dismissed diachrony for synchrony. The death toll of etymology was sounded, long before Saussure, by the Neo-Grammarians. The second factor is that the old speculative etymology – this is what makes it fascinating to the student of the remainder – was in fact, even when propounded by Church Fathers and enlightened *literati*, a version of folk-etymology. As such, of course, it has never died, and still haunts, if not the discourse of linguists, at least the daily practice of speakers. And folk-etymology is, as we have seen, synchronic etymology, or diachrony-within-synchrony. What replaced it was scientific, i.e. diachronic etymology. By which I mean that the separation between the two axes was already implicit in the theories of the Neo-Grammarians. It was quite fitting that their best disciple should have been the one to formulate it. After this, there was no longer any possibility for

188

'*apes*' (Latin for 'bee') to be interpreted as 'having no legs', *a-pes*, or 'having been born without them' (this is one of Isidore's most notorious etymologies). Again, one cannot help feeling a little nostalgic for those ingenious times.

There is good reason for this nostalgia: the compulsion towards folk-etymology is still with us. It is not only a symptom or a characteristic of the remainder, it is the embodiment of its historicity. The imaginative urge is indeed still present, as appears in the case of Heidegger. Rather than dismissing speculative or folk-etymology as unscientific (it does not matter in the least whether those etymologies are 'true' – unless one is inordinately attached to a rather simple concept of truth), perhaps we should celebrate its creativeness. What a good etymology must be is not so much true as striking, or evocative. Therein its aptness resides. This is the paradox of etymology: it is never so faithful to its own etymology as when it is at its most fictitious or fanciful. Etymology so understood is a kind of folk-metaphor, producing the same contradictory feelings of illumination and exaggeration. It is the inscription of imagination within language.

This conception of etymology is clearly expressed in the essay by D. Attridge already quoted. He makes the following essential points:

- Etymology is story, not science, and it derives its force, its power to change language, from this:

  What are etymologies if not stories? What is the model for the history of the word if not the biographical narrative? ... It is from their success as stories with good plots and ingenious word-play that folk etymologies (and for that matter learned etymologies) derive their power to change the language, not from their accuracy.

- Etymology has its synchronic counterpart in word-play; in other words it is the historicized aspect of the remainder:

  Its rhetorical partner, from which it is sometimes indistinguishable, is the *calembour* or *paronomasia*, the play on words. In both devices the same process occurs: two similar-sounding but distinct signifiers are brought together, and the surface relationship between them is invested with meaning through the inventiveness and rhetorical skill of the writer. If that meaning is in the form of a postulated connection between present and past, what we have is etymology; if it is in the form of a postulated connection within the present, the result is word-play.

- Etymology, because it has force, because it intervenes within the present state of the language, is an instrument in the ideological struggle – not only a reflection of past struggle in language, but a weapon in present struggles, in and through language and an anticipation of future ones:

   etymology *can* be used to confirm a dominant ideology, to deny the possibility of purposeful change, to reinforce the myth of objective and transcendental truth; but it can also be used to unsettle ideology, to uncover opportunities for change, to undermine absolutes and authority – and to do so without setting up an alternative and equally challenge-able truth-claim.[6]

One can use these points, I think, to develop a defence of (false) etymology – a nostalgic celebration of its past and undeserved glory, an account of its modernity, that is, of its interest for the student of the remainder, a description of which it often, in anticipation, provides.

The defence will start with a reading of a hostile view, which nevertheless has its secret failings. For Jean Paulhan's *La Preuve par l'étymologie*,[7] is, at first sight, rather harsh on its object. One of its paragraphs is entitled 'the vanity of etymology', and the core of the argument is that recourse to etymology muddles the clarity of thought. Language is meant to be the expression of thought: those who indulge in etymology spoil the game. The perversion proceeds in three stages: (1) A similarity of sound is noted in several words; the more recherché and archaic some of these words are, the greater the force of the discovered similarity. Thus, in true Isidorian style, we will link *cadaver* and *caro data vermis*. There is food for thought in this. Indeed, (2) the rejected meaning (for at first we are only concerned with sounds) comes back with a vengeance: from similarity of sound we argue to partial identity of meaning. An English instance of this would be the false derivation of 'outrage' from 'rage', which is typical of folk-etymology. (3) The common seman-tic factor, once discovered by such a *coup de force*, is taken to be the origin of the set of words. Thus, *'per-'* (whatever its meaning), in *'perfection' 'perpétuel', 'peroxyde', 'perroquet'*. The result is that, instead of using our words, we become their plaything. The master has been enslaved. On such occasions, Paulhan says, 'il nous arrive, loin d'exprimer notre pensée, de penser notre langage' (far from expressing our thoughts, i.e. speaking our language, we 'think our language', i.e. we let ourselves be spoken by it). This is why a false etymology is usually more successful than a 'true' one: it is more potent, it allows language, that is the remainder, to be master.

But the text on etymology is published with an appendix, in the form of a letter to Maurice Nadeau, in which Paulhan defends his conception of literature as 'language writ large' ('la littérature n'est que du langage grossi'). Literature is the kind of language-game where the workings of language are made explicit and come to the foreground, for instance in the guise of rhetorical tropes. A work of literature is essentially 'a linguistic machine, or if you prefer monument'. Etymology (which is known and practised by rhetoricians as *figura etymologica*) is one of these indispensable tropes that are given a prominent role in literature. As one can see, Paulhan hesitates between on the one hand a recognition of the remainder as that Other of language from which literature draws its specificity (in 'language writ large', we sense the remainder emerging from its timid retirement), in which case etymology, in so far as it is playful and fictive, is a perfectly legitimate practice, and on the other hand a rejection of a remainder-riddled etymology as a hindrance to the subject's mastery of his language. The needs of the thinker are not those of the poet – in showing this, Paulhan is pointing towards our main contradiction: must language be modest and not be heard – or must it obtrude and speak us?

By celebrating the fictions of (folk) etymology, by showing that their mode of operation is that of the remainder, we are faithful to Brisset and his etymological device. It is therefore quite fitting that our celebration should invoke the pre-Brissetic figure of Isidore of Seville, who lived in the sixth century, and whose influence over the culture of the Middle Ages can hardly be overestimated. Yet, his *Etymologies* (or *Origins*) has little to do with a treatise on etymology in the modern sense. It is more of a compendium of contemporary knowledge, an encyclopaedia, a book about the world, not words. Words are the monuments on which our history and our origin are inscribed, and etymology the device that enables us to decipher the inscriptions. Except that it is not a device in the sense of Brisset and Wolfson. There is a certain amount of common sense in the bishop of Seville. The etymologizing through remotivation for which he is famous, and which anticipates Brisset, is by no means the only form of etymology he advocates. In his definition of etymology,[8] Isidore lists not only the Brissetic etymologies from cause ('rex' from 'rectum agere'), origin ('homo' from 'humus'), and opposites ('lucus a non lucendo'), but also etymologies from grammatical derivation ('prudentia' from 'prudens'), place-names (a subtype of eponyms), and foreign languages (the franglais of modern accounts would fall in this category). He even shares the modesty of the modern etymologist by admitting that in some cases the form of the word is so corrupted and its origin so barbaric and obscure that we can make nothing of it. Nor is he strictly committed to a Cratylean position. One expects the rationale for his remotivating etymologies to be that an analysis of this kind recovers the truth of Adamic naming, that it establishes a natural link between noun and referent. And indeed such is his concern – not the endless analysis of words, but knowledge of the world, as inscribed in words. His etymologia must be taken, etymologically, as veriloquium, spelling out the truth about the world.

This seems to be a far cry from Brisset. But it is not. After all, in the midst of his delusions, Brisset does believe he is telling the truth about the world, about man, God, and the cosmos. The main characteristic of all logophiliacs is that, whereas they mistakenly believe in the truth of their revelation about the universe, their devices unfold narratives that describe parts of language that the official truths of science ignore. So is it with Isidore, whose teachings really concern folk-etymology and therefore the remainder. At first, the link between res and vocabulum is fairly straightforward. A state of affairs (res), for instance the fact that a river grows as it flows (flumen fluendo crevit), is the motivation or origo of a name (nomen), which is formed through a kind of abbreviated notation (nota: 'flu-' in 'flumen' is borrowed from 'fluere'). This nota becomes the semantic core of the name, which thereby acquires meaning (vis). Or the same journey can be made the other way round, following the path of rediscovery rather than creation. This is where etymologia comes in: through an argument derived from the nota (interpretatio or notatio), the abbreviated sign is developed into a definition of the original state of affairs, which was the origo vocabuli. Such is the commentary that J. Engels[9] gives of Isidore's definition of etymology: 'Etymologia est origo vocabulorum, cum vis verbi vel nominis per interpretationem colligitur' ('the origin of naming is to be found in an etymology when the meaning of a verb or noun is reached through an interpretation' – I am following Engels's translation). The result is presented by Engels thus:

192

NEPOS = nomen, vocabulum
QUI EX FILIO NATUS EST = vis nomini
QUASI NATUS POST = nota
PRIMUM ENIM FILIUS NASCITUR, DEINDE NEPOS
= origo-veriloquium

This is a commentary on the following etymology: 'Nepos est, qui ex filio natus est. Dictus autem nepos quasi natus post. Primum enim filius nascitur, deinde nepos.'[10] But it will soon be apparent that we have remained within language; that the remainder is at work; that Brisset is not far. For the fulcrum of the argument is the abbreviated sign, the *nota*. And it is strictly linguistic. *N(ATUS)EPOS(T)* – this looks like an intralingual equivalent of one of Wolfson's attempts. In fact we will soon notice an incipient Brissetizing in Isidore. Etymological analysis tends to proliferate, so that a single word comes to have more than one origin. Thus, the already quoted *'apes'* has a second etymology. Not lack of feet, but

A(DLIGANT SE) PE(DIBU)S, or A (=SINE) PE(DIBU)S[11]

Or again, the description of the breast (Isidore, XI, I), which is supposed to be an account, not merely of the word, but of the organ, useful to doctors for instance, is a fine instance of Brissetic creativity. For *mamillae* are so called because they look like *malae*, apples. As for the breast itself, *ubera*, it has two origins: 'Ubera dicta, vel quia lacte uberta, vel quia uvida, humore scilicet lactis in more uvarum plena. Lac vim nominis colore trahit, quod sit albus liquor leucos enim Graece album dicunt: cujus natura ex sanguine commutatur.'[12] What is fascinating in this text is the mixture of Brissetic etymology and scientific theory. For *ubera* comes either from *'lacte UBERtA'*, i.e. 'abounding in milk', or from *'UvidA'* (a kind of Saussurean *mannequin*), that is full of milk as a grape is full of juice. In turn, milk *(lac)* derives its name from the name of the colour white in Greek *(leukos)*. And in the same sentence that gives the etymology of 'milk', after the merest pause marked by a colon, Isidore states the theory that milk is transmuted blood (*ex sanguine commutatur*). So that Curtius may be right to interpret *'vis'* in Isidore's definition as meaning not merely 'meaning' but also 'force'.[13] As clearly appears in the etymology of the body organs, there is no solution of continuity between words and the world. The strict separation from which I started is in fact an *a posteriori* rationalization. For Isidore, *etymologia* is *at the same time* about words and the world – as it is for Brisset. So that the illusions about the world and the truths about words that I earlier opposed are, in fact, two sides of the same coin. Behind both, there lies a recognition of the materiality of language, of its link with the human body, of the force of words. The paths of the remainder, which Isidore follows with zest, do not only circularly lead to other words. They certainly do this, for the ways of the rhizome are well-nigh infinite. But they also – which is the main lesson of Deleuze and Guattari's *Anti-Oedipus*[14] – reach up to the materiality of bodies and their actions. Words not only name parts of the body, they mingle with them. No wonder then that, if we read Attridge's third point again, etymologies should have ideological use – they obviously have political force. As we saw, the etymology of *rex* was *rectum agere*. Horne Tooke must have approved, if not of the contents, at least of the method.

Etymology is not only false history or fictitious science, it is also synchronic history – language being appealed to as a monument to the authority of history. The appeal can be either conservative in the broadest sense (language testifies to the hoary purity of origins, and to the impurity of the contemporary state of affairs, both in its present corrupt state and in the traces of antique glory that etymology can find in it) or anticipatory and revolutionary (language change, the present linguistic struggle, the evidence of past struggle embodied in etymologies point to the necessity of going on with the struggle and changing society). At its most innocuous and apolitical, folk-etymology embodies this kind of appeal. It projects mythical history onto synchronic order, and it threatens this order by bringing about its own change. Thus, it offers an image of the instability of *langue* and of its constant process of reordering. For re-analysis is one of the main sources of language change. This is true of words, of course, especially if they are borrowed from other languages. Linguists know that in Swahili a traffic-island is called a *kiplefiti*, from 'keep left'. They also know that the plural of the word is '*viplefiti*', the '*ki-*' of the singular having been re-analysed as a Swahili prefix. In the same vein, the word 'mudguard', borrowed as '*madigadi*', has been re-analysed as containing the plural marker '*ma-*', thus giving birth to the singular form '*digadi*'.[15] It is also true of syntax, although on a longer time-scale. Thus, the present paradigms of the verb 'be' in Polish and Persian are the products of a process of restructuring or re-analysis, in which the third-person forms, which stem directly from the Indo-European, have been adopted as models for the normalized first- and second-person forms. Aitchison mentions a similar process with the passive in Maori.[16]

Such re-analysis – and here the game becomes less innocuous, for the process carries its load of painful affect – is frequent in Wolfson. His translations imply not only a kind of folk-etymology, across languages (when, for instance, the article 'the' becomes the Hebrew words *'eth'* and *'he'*), but also seemingly endless reformulation, the cause of which is phonetic dissemination, the compulsive need to capture, i.e. to repeat, the phonemes of the hated English word. Thus, he gets rid of 'early' by transforming the word into the following French equivalents:

EARLY   → *suR Le champ*
               de bonne heuRe
               matinaLement
               diLigemment
               dévoRer L'espace
               à La paRoLe

The last instance is particularly dubious as a 'translation'. The reason for its presence is of course that it provides a *mise en abyme* of the whole process, and contains more occurrences of the consonants in 'early' than any other. We are on Semitic ground – vowels obviously do not count. Wolfson's translation, of course, is not etymology. There is neither semantic nor morphological filiation, only phonetic similarity, although, interestingly enough, one of the equivalents, not quoted here because only very tentatively mentioned, is the German prefix *'Ur-'*. But this is precisely what Paulhan accuses false etymology of doing: it constructs semantic links out of chance phonetic similarity. The result is some kind of violence done to language – a symptom, as we shall see more and more clearly, of the imbrication of *langue* and the remainder. If Wolfson's translation is false etymology, folk-etymology is false translation or interpretation. This compulsive activity, which is at work in the logophiliac and the etymologist alike, illustrates the pain, sometimes physical, caused by the indeterminacy of instability of meaning. The sad truth is that the words of our daily life do not keep meaning fixed. It constantly varies, it is never at rest, it eludes the speaker. Hence the fantasized necessity of introducing order into this chaos, of fixing meaning, either by translating or interpreting, or by uncovering the rocky foundations of its origins. This is the source of the etymologist's urge. The irony is that in order to recover etymological origins, he must follow the paths of the remainder, which is precisely what prevents the fixity of meaning. The etymologist falls victim to the same contradiction as the mental patient.

This failed attempt at clarification through etymology will, however, yield unexpected results. Following the paths of the remainder enables one to act on language and with language. As we have seen, it is not because an etymology is false that it is not potent or powerful. The work of John Horne Tooke is a literal realization of this logophiliac principle. As a contribution to the science of language, his etymologies deserve nothing short of oblivion, or the limbo of academic research. As etymologies, or as theories about the origin and structure of language, they are plainly erroneous – but only if one accepts the official narrative of progress, which attributes good or bad marks to pre-Saussurean linguists by measuring their achievement against the yardstick of the master's opus.

If we forget the official narrative for one moment, Horne Tooke will turn out to be a most interesting linguist, who developed another, perhaps equally important, narrative about the political aspect of language. There is a duality in Horne Tooke that his commentators have hardly ever brought into a unified account.[17] Historians know him as a radical agitator in the troubled last decades of the eighteenth century, as the friend of Wilkes and of reform, if not revolution. Linguists on the other hand know only the author of the *Diversions of Purley* (1798–1805). The interesting question is, of course: how could he be both? And it is a relevant question. The *Diversions* were written in gaol, after Horne Tooke had been sentenced to a year's imprisonment for his support of the American revolution. Even if he states that he pursued his etymological research for more than thirty years (indeed, the second volume appeared seven years after the first, and he is said to have destroyed the manuscript of the third shortly before he died in 1812), the redaction of the *Diversions* seems to have been a parenthesis in a political career, the climaxes of which were his two trials – in the second, Horne Tooke, like Hardy and Thelwall, was indicted for treason as one of the leaders of the London Corresponding Society and, like the other two, acquitted. It is true that in those days political radicals were often linguists of a sort. Cobbett and Hazlitt both wrote grammars inspired by Horne Tooke's theories. The conjuncture was apparently favourable, but the conjunction still needs investigating.

The link between language and politics is obvious in at least one area – political discourse. I shall have occasion to discuss the question of slogans and political metaphors. In the case of Horne Tooke, however, the link is more indirect – through legal discourse. There is indeed a natural affinity between law and the politics of language, especially in the shape of political etymology. First, the temporality of law is slower than that of language. Thus, legal discourse was perhaps the last field in which the French language held its own against English, with the result that a point was reached when the laws of the land were written in a language that hardly anyone could understand. In turn, this tension between linguistic means of production and relations of production produced legislative action, for instance in the shape of that linguistic monster, the Statute of Pleadings of 1362, which was written in French, and required English to be the language of the courts and Latin the language of legal records.[18] Second, because of its innately conservative aspect, which it shares with religious discourse, legal discourse is the home ground of archaism and jargon, hence of translation, interpretation, and etymology as the search for true origins or verbal precedents. Third, of course, the courts of law are a natural place for verbal struggle – a place where one's life may depend on the choice of one's words. Horne Tooke, who had studied law and often conducted his own defence, was well aware of this. This is how he explains the origin of his interest in language:

> the substance ... of all that I have to communicate on the subject of language, has been among the loose papers in my closet now upwards of thirty years; and would probably have remained there some years longer, and have been finally consigned with myself to oblivion if I had not been made the miserable victim of – Two Prepositions and a Conjunction.[19]

Horne Tooke attributes the judgement given against him to a false interpretation, in a technical discussion about the legal concept of 'averment', of the conjunction 'that'. In one of the precedents quoted against him, the judge construed the words 'She knowing *that* Crooke had been indicted for forgery, did so and so' as not necessarily constituting an averment of fact, i.e. as not entailing the factual truth of 'Crooke had been indicted for forgery.' Horne Tooke, on the other hand, maintained that the sentence was equivalent to the two following sentences: 'Crooke had been indicted for forgery' and 'She knowing *that*, did so and so.' The conjunction in question, of which Horne Tooke was made the miserable victim, was not a conjunction at all, but a concealed demonstrative pronoun. This has far-reaching consequences, for a whole theory of language hinges on it. It has a legal–political origin, and legal–political effects.

The core of Horne Tooke's view about the politics of language can be summed up in the following two propositions: (1) Etymology is a means of capturing the historicity of language, that is, of reaching back to the purity of the origin of meaning. (2) Conversely, the present confused state of language is taken advantage of by the oppressors in their struggle to maintain their domination. Capturing the historicity of language is also a way of clarifying the issue, of reappropriating, on behalf of the oppressed, the pristine meanings the oppressors are concealing from them. There is a theory of origins in Horne Tooke – a theory not of the origin of language proper, but of language in its original state. Nouns and verbs are the two original parts of speech; the others are obtained by the twin operations of abbreviation and corruption. The distinction shows that the history of language is not merely a story of dereliction. Abbreviation is a positive, nay an intelligent device, enabling man to convey his ideas 'with dispatch'. But it does tend to obscure the original meaning of the word, and eventually will be contaminated by its negative double, corruption. One senses a hesitation here. Prepositions and conjunctions, the potentially noxious character of which has been demonstrated in the case of 'that', are virtual instances of both operations, as Olivia Smith has noted:

> All parts of speech except nouns and verbs are called 'abbreviations', signs of nouns or verbs that indicate their new function by their altered form and syntax. Technically speaking, these words are corrupt in that they are worn down and altered by frequent use, the remnants and ruins of other words. Tooke's calling the abbreviated forms corruptions does not imply, however, that he yearned for a pure language. Far from it. Tooke praises the abbreviations highly for making as much difference to language as the wheel did to transportation.[20]

Rather, perhaps, he wanted to clarify words back to their lost purity, and *at the same time* to celebrate their use as progressive instruments for liberation. This contradiction is central to the politics of language. On the one hand it is true that on the corruption of language the oppressors have erected their metaphysical power: 'the participles and adjectives, not understood as such, have caused a metaphysical jargon, and a false morality, which can only be dissipated by etymology.'[21] But on the other hand, as the end of the quotation makes it clear, etymology will dispel the metaphysical mist, and the internal forces of abbreviation will make language useful for reform. The recourse to etymology expresses Horne Tooke's explicit aim, which is mythical: to clarify linguistic issues, to reach back to original truth. Thus, the etymology of 'right' is the Latin *'rect-um'*, or *'regitum'*, the past participle of *regere*. On the basis of this, Horne Tooke claims that 'when a man demands his Rights, he asks only that which is *ordered* he shall have.'[22] (We can compare with Isidore on the etymology of *rex* as *rectum agere*: etymology is indeed not indifferent to the historical conjuncture.) But the implicit aim of Horne Tooke's etymologies, also to be read in his praise of abbreviations, is to suggest that the essential characteristic of words is not their *truth*, but their *force*, the *'vis'* of Isidore's definition. Language is an instrument not for communication, but for action, and Horne Tooke's theory reflects and celebrates this capacity for intervention, on the radical or materialist side. Olivia Smith quotes Horne Tooke as stating that 'mankind in general are not sufficiently aware that words without meaning, or of equivocal meaning, are the everlasting engines of fraud and injustice: and that the *grimgibber* of Westminster Hall is a more fertile, and more formidable, source of imposture than the *abracadabra* of magicians.'[23] And she adds: 'By reforming ideas about language, Tooke intended to clarify the meaning of discrete words and to contribute to the reformation of social relations.' We shall not be surprised, therefore, to learn that Horne Tooke held a relativist conception of truth ('there is no such thing as eternal, immutable, everlasting truth; unless mankind, such as they are *at present*, be also eternal, immutable and everlasting. Two persons may contradict each other, and yet both speak truth'[24]) – in other words, a historical and agonistic conception of truth. Horne Tooke's theory of language is indeed political.

There are two kinds of revolutionists, the Adamic and the Promethean, as there are two meanings of the word 'revolution'. The former want the wheel of history to go full circle, back to the ancient rights of which free-born citizens have been deprived. Their field of battle is the law, and their attitude to language is etymological. The latter look forward to turning the order of society topsy-turvy. The field of their struggle is politics rather than the courts of law, for they appeal not to ancient rights but to new ones. Their attitude to language is metaphorical: they invent slogans, give polemical names, look forward to the liberated language of the future. Actual reformists or revolutionaries are a little of both, but there is no doubt that Horne Tooke's bent was strongly Adamic, which accounts for his political limitations – he was essentially a reformist, and his support of the French revolution was contained within strict limits. Nevertheless, it would be unjust to him to limit the politically revolutionary character of his linguistic theories to a matter of contents, as Olivia Smith does when she claims that he was progressive, for instance in not despising oral English, the language of the common people. They involve more than this, for they concern the structure of language. For Horne Tooke, there is something in language that is fundamentally historical, which causes its political–historical instability. This, for which he has attempted, in the terms of his period, to provide an account, I have called the remainder.

Horne Tooke, that honorary logophiliac, takes etymology out of the sphere of truth and falsity. As a result, it becomes not only a narrative, but a political narrative, an intervention as well as a story – which reveals its dual nature. As clearly appears in *figura etymologica*, etymology is an excrescence of the remainder, the rhizome sprouting new historical shoots, thus multiplying the paths along which meaning circulates – the practice of literate or of folk-etymology, and the fact that the whole of a language is potentially a pretext for folk-etymology, give the remainder its depth. If linguists are so often tempted to account for language along the metaphor of a living organism, it is because this historical depth in words, syntactic structures, and discourses is what makes language alive, or rather makes us want to talk about it not as a piece of computer software in the mind-brain but as a living organism. The second feature of etymology is that it marks a frontier of language – one of those limits where language tangentially reaches towards the extra-linguistic, and eventually mixes with the external world. The narrative of etymology, as potted history, is both a reflection of the previous history of the community of speakers and an instrument for action in the present. Etymology is the diachronic equivalent of poetic metaphor – a creative act of misprision. An act, not a statement endowed with truth or falsity. Once again, focusing on the remainder questions our established conceptions of truth.

LINGUISTIC CONJUNCTURE

Etymology is profoundly synchronic – as we have seen, synchrony is what folk-etymology is about. Synchrony is profoundly diachronic – the remainder is unavoidable and it embodies diachrony-within-synchrony. This raises questions as to the specific temporality of language. The separation between synchrony and diachrony, as represented in the structural concept of *état de langue*, no longer holds. I shall account for this strange temporal mixture by having recourse to the Marxian concept of conjuncture.

As usual, we have a predecessor in the field. Althusser's 'The Object of Capital'[25] contains a critique of the Saussurean concepts, based on their dependence on the Hegelian conception of time. The 'object of Capital' that Althusser analyses in Marx's text is the social whole, its structure and temporality. This last, he claims, is usually conceived in terms of Hegelian time, which has two main characteristics. First, it is homogeneous and continuous, the regular process in the course of which the Idea unfolds its various moments, which correspond to so many historical periods. Second, it is contemporaneous: the elements of the social structure are situated within the same homogeneous time, which means that their development is simultaneous. Thus, it is always possible to single out a privileged moment, the present of analysis, to make a progress report on the development of the global structure, in which every single element will fall into its place, linked as it is with all the others by relationships of contemporaneity. Such a progress report Althusser calls a *'coupe d'essence'*, an essential section. The present is an experimental interruption in the continuous development of the whole, which discloses its internal structure. A good image of this would be a sawn-off tree trunk, where the yearly rings unfold the narrative of the tree's growth and enable us to tell its age.

This picture, Althusser claims, is far too smooth. He conceives the social whole not as teleologically determined by the unfolding of the Idea, but as an 'organic hierarchised whole'. Society is no longer homogeneous. It is a complex hierarchy of subparts and levels, between which diverse relationships obtain. This is in turn due to the fact that there is no longer a unique temporality for the whole, no continuous contemporaneous time. On the contrary, we have a differential temporality – unto each level its own time according to its own rhythm – and a globally discontinuous and heterogeneous picture. This provides a solution to the well-known Marxist quandary of survivals (how is it possible for elements of defunct modes of production to survive when a new mode has triumphed?) and provides a principled account of the relatively autonomous development of various levels of the whole, notably in the superstructure. If we adopt this analysis, of course, no essential section is possible. The present moment will yield not a disclosure of order but a rather messy conjuncture.

In the course of this analysis Althusser produces a critique of the concepts of synchrony and diachrony. His point is that they are the main form that the Hegelian conception of time takes in our culture:

> The distinction is based on a conception of historical time as continuous and homogeneous and contemporaneous with itself. The synchronic is contemporaneity itself, the co-presence of the essence with its determinations, the present being readable as a structure in an 'essential section' because the present is the very existence of the essential structure. The synchronic therefore presupposes the ideological conception of a continuous–homogeneous time. It follows that the diachronic is merely the development of this present in the sequence of a temporal continuity in which the 'events' to which 'history' in the strict sense can be reduced ... are merely successive contingent presents in the time continuum. Like the synchronic, which is the primary concept, the diachronic therefore presupposes both of the very two characteristics I have isolated in the Hegelian conception of time: an ideological conception of historical time.[26]

The picture of linguistic temporality that this conception implies is that of a series of synchronic *états de langue* stacked up into a diachronic pile. The contemporaneity of all the elements of the structure in the present ensures that the essential section that yields an *état de langue* provides a systematic picture of the language. In other words, one can derive *langue* from *état de langue*. Whereas the homogeneous continuity of diachronic development ensures that change, as the passage from one *état de langue* to another, is regular. Structural change yields yet another structure.

This is an ideological view of time, and therefore an ideological view of language. It is the view of the linguist of *langue*. It can be held only as long as the remainder remains excluded. Althusser, however, goes further, and tries to recover the concepts of synchrony and diachrony on another level. The real content of the ideological concept of synchrony is not, he claims, the temporal presence of the real object, but the eternal structure of an object of knowledge. As a result, diachrony is no longer reduced to the recording of the sequence of events (*l'événementiel*): its real content is a process, the development of conceptual forms.

I have serious reservations about such a move, which seems to me to renounce the Hegelian present only to lose its way in Spinozist eternity (this is explicit in Althusser: 'synchrony is eternity in Spinoza's sense') – if indeed we are leaving Hegel at all, for the phrase 'the development of forms', which Althusser uses, sounds singularly Hegelian to me. The problem is that Althusser seems to be opening the window for the teleology he has expelled through the front door. The social whole, for instance, may be 'hierarchised', it is still 'organic' – as we have seen, the metaphor of organism is a constant temptation to the student of language, a temptation that nevertheless must be resisted. Even if we accept that Althusser's move is not a return to arrant idealism, that is, even if we take into account his well-known distinction, on which he is obviously drawing here, between 'real object' and 'object of thought', it is not certain that our conception of language, as diachrony-within-synchrony, will be clarified. Kicking the synchronic *coupe d'essence* upstairs into the realm of knowledge, thus leaving a space for the deployment of conjuncture in the realm of reality, is no solution. It leaves the linguistics of *langue* intact, for Chomsky's universal grammar is an excellent instance of such an object of knowledge. We must go beyond the distinction (in its two forms: ideological v. scientific; knowledge v. reality), which does not necessarily involve a falling back into unprincipled empiricism. For the remainder is a concept that deconstructs these oppositions. If *langue* is an object of knowledge, its inseparable remainder is emphatically not a properly constituted scientific object. It returns, it haunts, and yet it is no mere residue, no secondary offshoot, no dross surrounding the golden nugget of *langue*. Its constant return, this unholy mixture of the incompatible and yet inseparable, prevents us from viewing language *sub specie eternitatis*. Rather, we have a messy and arbitrary semi-chaos, with fuzzy contours. No Spinozist eternity of synchrony, no development of forms in language: conjuncture and nothing else.

However, we could perhaps interpret what I have called systemic change as a case of 'development of forms' in language. Sometimes linguistic change is due to the internal pressure of the system, and seems to develop, so to speak, under its own steam. Analogical change and rule simplification could be instances of this, when the motive of change seems to be the internal principle of economy. But there is never analogy without concomitant anomaly; and it is difficult to find a case of systemic change in which extra-linguistic intervention, in the guise of the imitation of prestigious models, canons of taste, or social–political upheaval, can be ruled out.

Since this is rather abstract, let us take an example. Arbiters of taste in English grammar, of the Fowler and Fowler persuasion, have dubbed a rather common solecism the 'unattached participle' solecism.[27] An example of this would be: 'when writing, the paper must be chosen with care', where the implicit subject of the participle is not co-referent with the subject of the main clause, as a result of which the participle is 'unattached'. This is a kind of 'mistake' that is frequent in spoken English. Perhaps the system is changing according to its own pressure, for the unattached participle is an obvious means of syntactic economy and simplification: it (unduly) generalizes the syntactic rule that allows us to erase the subject of a participle clause when it is co-referent with the subject of the main clause. But when you look at the history of the phenomenon closely, you realize that the course of things cannot be described in such smooth terms, in terms of the development of a syntactic form. First, it would seem that this turn of phrase has been a feature of spoken English for a long time, so that it is difficult convincingly to argue that it is a syntactic *development*. Second, in the eighteenth century, it was also standard practice in written English. The picture now becomes clearer. An extra-linguistic intervention, in the guise of a laying down of rules in defence of 'grammatical correctness', which originally appeared in manuals of conversation or usage such as the Fowlers' and its predecessors, has attempted to stamp out a common practice, and has succeeded in doing so in educated written English (were I slyly to introduce one on this page, it would not escape the vigilance of the copy-editor). Not so in spoken English, which accounts for its return today in forms of writing that are close to spoken discourse, or in the journalism of the less reputable papers. The economy or analogy of the solecism turns out to be an overdetermining factor added to social factors, on the frontier between the linguistic and the extra-linguistic.

We must, therefore, be faithful to the starting point of Althusser's critique. Diachrony-within-synchrony expresses the heterogeneous discontinuity of linguistic temporality. On a first level, language change is polychronic because it reflects the polychronic changes of the various elements of the structure. Thus, legal discourse has its own temporality, which is not the same as that of commercial, religious, or literary discourse. There is a second-order heterogeneity as systemic pressure overdetermines this external change – by which I mean that it will make it easier or hinder it, accelerate it or slow it down. But, in apparent contradiction to this, language is also the best embodiment of the idealized and ideological 'essential section'. It is indeed the form in which his present is available to the subject – the subject's sense of the present moment lies in the fact that, in the present of performance, the whole of his language, with its potted diachrony, is available as a set of expressive potentialities to the speaker. The present speaker is the only form the essential section can take. If we must retrieve the Saussurean dichotomy from the mire of ideology, it is in those terms that we should do it. Synchrony is the command the speaking subject has of the whole of his language, diachrony the historical depth that this synchronic mastery requires. A text in English will in all probability use various dialects, registers, and styles; it will, consciously or not, refer to various moments of the history of the language and its people, embodied in the lexicon or in syntax – multiplicity and polychrony reign in the simplest text. Yet it is written *in English*, in a temporarily unified language which the subject masters. This contradiction, which is reminiscent of other contradictions, is the centre of the phrase 'diachrony-within-synchrony'. And it is what the Marxian concept of conjuncture allows us to formulate.

We can go back to Althusser, and his definition of conjuncture:

> On the contrary, we must regard these differences in temporal structure as, *and only as*, so many objective indices of the mode of articulation of the different elements or structures in the general structure of the whole. This amounts to saying that if we cannot make an 'essential section' in history, it is only in the specific unity of the complex structure of the whole that we can think the concept of these so-called backwardnesses, forwardnesses, survivals and unevennesses of development which *co-exist* in the structure of the real historical present: the present of the *conjuncture*. To speak of differential types

of historicity therefore has no meaning in reference to a base time in which these backwardnesses might be measured.[28]

I believe that the concept can be imported into the study of language, and that what I have called so far 'the unholy mixture of *langue* and the remainder', or 'diachrony-within-synchrony', has at last found its proper name – linguistic conjuncture. The importation of the concept, always a tricky business, is made possible by the fact that linguistic conjuncture is part of social conjuncture: the linguistic reflects the social and it acts on the other elements that contribute to it. This is in fact the first determination of the concept: it expresses the *non-autonomy of language*. There is no *état de langue* immune from the contamination of the historical conjuncture. The factors that account for a specific linguistic conjuncture are extra-linguistic in the first instance. We might decide to take this thesis to its extreme point, and argue with Marr, against the pseudo-Stalin (as is now well known, he merely lent his name to the pamphlet on linguistics, which was written by a member of the Soviet academy[29]), that language is not an instrument of communication independent of superstructural or infrastructural determinations. The second determination of the concept is the *instability* of the conjuncture. I have already sufficiently insisted on this, which the term 'corruption' is meant to capture. Again, in this, language reflects the historical conjuncture and contributes to its instability. The third determination is the *arbitrary* character of the linguistic conjuncture. There is no question of teleology here, no predictable outcome for the development of language – there is no gradual unfolding of a form. Not only is language, in the words of Judith Milner, 'as it is', but the linguistic conjuncture also defies certain prediction. There is no narrative of progress to be told about language – nor is there a narrative of corruption as dereliction. This is not an irrationalist plea, rather a call for charting the actual struggles whose traces the linguistic conjuncture bears, and if need be entering the lists oneself, but with no certainty of a golden future of language at rest with itself. Remainderless language is a Utopian fantasy; so, one suspects, is classless society. The fourth and last determination concerns the *polychrony* of the linguistic conjuncture. Different elements have different temporalities (not only discourses, but also levels of language: the rhythm of lexical change is notoriously quicker than the pace of syntactic change). So that if the linguistic conjuncture is the only form of the real present of language, this present will contain within itself a projected past and an anticipated future.

I can make only the briefest allusions here. To the Husserlian concept of *sedimentation* first, as used by Jameson in *The Political Unconscious*.[30] Jameson accounts for the uneven development of the elements of a textual structure ('a synchronic unity of structurally contradictory or heterogeneous elements, generic patterns and discourses') in terms of the persistence, though re-appropriation and reshaping, of past generic forms within new ones, in terms of the sedimentation of forms. 'The history of music [he says] provides the most dramatic examples of this process, wherein folk dances are transformed into aristocratic forms like the minuet (as with the pastoral in literature), only then to be reappropriated for new ideological (and nationalizing) purposes in romantic music.' I would argue that generic sedimentation is made possible by linguistic sedimentation – that language is the natural and privileged vehicle of this process, as clearly appears in the case of clichés or dead metaphors that sediment older scientific theories or religious conceptions. Second, I am referring to the Hegelian concept of *anticipation*, as expounded by Kojève[31] (in other words, I would support Kojève's Hegel against the Althusserian bugbear). It is a strange property of language, according to Kojève's Hegel, that it has the capacity to perpetuate error. I look at my wristwatch, see that it is now 10 o'clock sharp, say aloud 'it is 10 o'clock', by which time my utterance is false since it is 30 seconds past 10. If I write the utterance down, the error will be even more apparent, and longer-lasting – with the interesting development, however, that although my written statement is erroneous for most of the day it is bound to be true twice every twenty-four hours. Which induced Lewis Carroll to declare that a watch that did not work at all was preferable to a watch 1 minute fast, because the first indicated the exact time twice a day, the second never. Language, therefore, has two interesting properties – or rather two aspects of the same property. It enables an error to *persist*, and linguistic monsters (metaphors for instance) are always viable, an important difference from biological monsters, which Mother Nature quickly eliminates. And it allows it to persist long enough to become truth; in other words, it *anticipates* truth. Cyrano de Bergerac writes a Utopian fantasy about a journey to the moon. This piece of ludicrous nonsense has become almost trivially true. Language is a repository of ancient errors and a treasury of potential truths. Linguistic conjuncture describes just this mixture.

LINGUISTIC INTERVENTION

A linguistic conjuncture has two major aspects: it is a reflection of past struggles; it is also the locus of intervention in present ones. There is one word common to the two propositions – struggle. I intend to explore this agonistic view of language. In so doing, I am aware that I am going one step towards the position of Marr. Not that I want to revive outdated texts and forgotten polemics. But language is a field in which Marxism has been singularly silent, and Stalin's pamphlet has been a decisive, but on the whole a regrettable, influence. The urgent task, therefore, is to remind ourselves that language is not immune from the class struggle.

That there is political–historical violence enacted not only with words but in them is clear. One gives battle to appropriate the words of one's opponent, to deprive him of his words. The choice of the right slogans, of the right metaphors is often vital. The principle that governs the use of dialogue in Pinter's plays (adapt your linguistic means to your linguistic end, which is to expel the enemy from the verbal battlefield[32]) could be extended to society as a whole. An example will make my meaning clear. A present-day reader of the clandestine press published by the French Communist Party during the Second World War (especially in the days of general insurrection towards the end of the war) may be shocked by its nationalistic or even xenophobic tones (at times only, for at other times the French CP press made a careful distinction between the Nazis and the oppressed German people: antifascism does not necessarily entail xenophobia). One would have expected such a tone in British jingoistic newspapers rather than in the press of an internationalist party. And I do not think my surprise is an instance of political naïvety – for it is all a matter of language struggle. If the French CP, which was engaged in armed struggle against the Germans, called itself 'patriotic' (not a word of which socialists of any description are inordinately fond) and dismissed the enemy as 'krauts' (*les boches*), with such warlike slogans as '*à chacun son boche*', this was, for at least an important part, because the armed struggle was at the same time an ideological and a linguistic struggle, waged on two fronts. The main front was against German propaganda, which portrayed communists as foreign terrorists (cf. the slogan, first used by the Germans, *'communiste pas français'*). The secondary front was against the rival Gaullist Resistance movement, whose forte was the nationalist rhetoric of patriotism and the grandeur of France. In these conditions, one can understand how a party all too easily branded a bunch of Moscow agents felt the need to fight for words, that is, to reappropriate the words of patriotism and nationalism, which were essential for rousing the French masses in what was not a revolutionary but a national struggle. The irony that made an internationalist movement the spearhead of a national struggle has been repeated many times since. From this example, we can draw conclusions as to the importance of linguistic struggles – as appears for instance in the choice of slogans.

In the vast corpus of Lenin's works, one finds a small pamphlet entitled 'On Slogans', written in July 1917 and published by the Kronstadt committee of the Bolshevik party. It is rather surprising that only a few months before the October Revolution Lenin should have devoted some of his time to the question of slogans. Actually, the title is somewhat of a misnomer, for the pamphlet is mostly concerned with the current political events – after the July demonstrations, the Bolsheviks had been outlawed in Petrograd, there were warrants for the arrest of their leaders, and a smear campaign accused Lenin of being a German spy. Indeed, Lenin was in hiding in the outskirts of Petrograd when he wrote the pamphlet. There is more to this, however, than a political leader forced into inaction by circumstances and turning to political reflection. The pamphlet is an intervention in the current political events. Lenin analyses the new situation after the July demonstrations and the alliance of all the political parties in the Provisional Government against the Bolsheviks. He wants to convince his comrades that the historical process has reached a new stage, that peaceful revolution is no longer on the agenda, and that one must prepare for the violent overthrow of the old regime or face destruction. This implies not only a change of line, but a change of slogans, hence the title. The slogan 'all power to the Soviets' is now inadequate, since the Menshevik–Social Revolutionary majority of the Soviets, which Lenin claims represents the petty-bourgeoisie, has decided on an alliance with the bourgeoisie against the proletariat.

So far, there is nothing that particularly concerns language, except the title and the role of slogans in the revolutionary process. But there is a conception of language as intervention and of political action within language implicit in this. In fact, a careful reader will realize that the text hesitates between two conceptions. On the one hand, Lenin seems to hold a traditional view of language, where language is the instrument of truth and helps dispel illusion. 'The slogan calling for the transfer of state power to the Soviets would now sound quixotic or mocking. Objectively it would be deceiving the people; it would be fostering in them the delusion that even *now* it is enough for the Soviets to want to take power, or to pass such a decision, for power to be theirs . . .'[33] One must tell the truth to the masses. A good slogan is one that states the truth – a truth that can be discovered in the political situation, independently of its formulation as a slogan. But, on the other hand, certain passages in the text go beyond this and another view of language emerges. Lenin takes the conception of slogans as reflections of the political situation seriously, almost to excess. In fact, a distinction must be made between passive representation and active reflection, which does not only picture but also intervenes. Language as an instrument of representation has considerable defects. In particular, it is abstract ('the substitution of the abstract for the concrete is one of the greatest and most dangerous sins in a revolution'[34]). This is the consequence of sedimentation: slogans outlive their proper conjuncture, they persist, become general and abstract. As a result, they may retain their truth (the slogan 'all power to the Soviets' retains its general validity, as a long-term goal), but they lose their correctness, that is, their power of intervention in the conjuncture. The emergence of another view of language in Lenin's text is linked to this conceptual shift from truth to correctness. What is important is not that the slogan be true, but that it be correct. This, of course, does not mean that we are discovering performatives – that a slogan, belonging as it does to the imperative mode, is not a proposition and therefore is neither true nor false. Slogans are derived from a general line, which is in turn expressed as constative utterances (for instance, 'the Social Revolutionary party represents a fraction of the petty-bourgeoisie'). Lenin is not discovering speech acts: as a lawyer and political leader he has sound practical knowledge in the field. He is trying to capture the relationship between language and historical events. What the 'correctness' of the slogan expresses is the sheer novelty of the historical event, of the new situation. This is the opening paragraph of the pamphlet: 'Too often has it happened that, when history has taken a sharp turn, even progressive parties have for some time been unable to adapt themselves to the new situation and have repeated slogans which had formerly been correct, but had now lost all meaning – lost it as "suddenly" as the sharp turn in history was sudden.'[35] The purpose of the slogan, therefore, is not to provide a true representation of a conjuncture that is independent of it, but to *name* it – to name the unnamed and so far unnameable. It must make good a failure of language; being essentially persistent, of the nature of a record, a trace, a monument, language is too slow to follow the events, and there is a temporary gap, a silence, during which language ossifies and loses its concreteness, that is, its insertion in the conjuncture, its participation in the world. This the correctness of the slogan must recover. Which means that a slogan is no representation of the conjuncture: it is part of it, it contributes to it, and by naming it makes it complete. This closure is what is expressed by the adverbs 'materially and formally' in the following passage: 'During that period of the revolution now past, the so-called "dual power" existed in the country, which both materially and formally expressed the indefinite and transitional condition of state power.'[36] Note the inverted commas around 'dual power': it is the name, the elliptic slogan, which completes the conjuncture, gives it 'material and formal' existence. There is a surprising aspect to Lenin's pamphlet – he does not suggest any new slogans to replace the now outdated 'all power to the Soviets'. And indeed the text contains a strange contradiction. It is obviously written during the run-up to the October Revolution, which it clearly announces by stating that peaceful revolution is now impossible. Yet the text does not issue a call to action, and even suggests that violent action would be counterproductive. But this is precisely because the conjuncture is not yet closed – because it cannot yet be named. The pamphlet works its way towards this baptism, which still eludes it. Its material effect will be to bring about the realization of the conjuncture (for instance, by mobilizing the masses around the slogans that will eventually emerge). We understand the discrepancy between the title and the contents, since this is a pamphlet on slogans that not only says very little on slogans in general, but fails to provide new ones. What the pamphlet does tell us is that a historical conjuncture is also a linguistic one, and vice versa. The reason why the usual problems of concept importation do not arise in the case of historical and linguistic conjunctures is that we have in fact a single concept.

The science of politics consists in finding the operative words to name the temporarily unnameable, because radically new. And here we find the Promethean revolutionist at his best, practising the

THE VIOLENCE OF LANGUAGE

linguistic intervention of revolutionary naming. For, as in the case of Adam, it is not enough to name: the naming must be right. This is the second sense of 'correctness'. A slogan must respect the temporality of linguistic intervention, it must come neither too soon nor too late, as opposed to the abstracted distance or persistence of representation. This opens up the possibility of incorrect, or irresponsible naming, which fails to complete the conjuncture, prevents its closure, and makes him who utters it powerless, like a failed performative. Lenin was aware of this possibility, which is at the centre of his later pamphlet on leftism. To use the terminology of Deleuze and Guattari, the irresponsibility of metaphor, as mere playing with language, must give way to metamorphosis, where language reaches out to the world and becomes action. A slogan does not merely celebrate a historical event, it is a historical event itself.

But the question of naming persists. We must give a more explicit account of its possibility. I have in fact already suggested an explanation, in terms of the opposition between Adamic and Promethean revolutionists, or between sedimentation and anticipation in language. If naming fails, if it cannot manage to anticipate, it is because repetition has overcome anticipation. Language is not a neutral instrument for naming, any more than for communication. It is heavily sedimented: the remainder, like the unconscious, conserves. Sometimes this conservation helps anticipation, witness the Luddite slogan, 'Long live the levelution!', mentioned in Chapter 2. In fact, no slogan, at the moment when it is attempting to name the radically new, has radically new language at its disposal. A slogan, like all other utterances, must negotiate its way through the paths of the remainder, and, in the best manner of Marxian repetition, the new is a farcical restatement of the old. The task of the political leader is to worm his way through layers of linguistic sedimentation to provide correct anticipation.

The relationship between language and event (language names the event; as such it is part of it, it contributes to it – words, when they penetrate the masses, can change the world) is reciprocal. For events, in turn, change language. By being registered in it, by persisting in it, they modify its equilibrium. As a result, language is weighed down with past conjunctures. Because it is stable, because it conserves, it is condemned to constant instability, as new conjunctures disturb its precarious balance.

I shall illustrate this point with an obvious example, the word 'revolution' (although any other item from Raymond Williams's *Keywords*[37] would have been equally helpful). The history of the word shows that linguistic sedimentation is contaminated by corruption, that the remainder leaves its mark on the process. The original meaning (Latin *'revolvere'*) is that of the revolution of planets or of any rotating object. The phrase 'revolutions per minute' applied to engines still bears this sense in contemporary English. The appearance of a political meaning, in the seventeenth century, was due to a metonymic transfer (a rotating becomes a vertical movement – a revolution is an uprising) made possible by the fact that in both movements the result is the same, for the old world ends up topsy-turvy. But it was also due to political–linguistic struggle for the appropriation of words. Cromwell's 'revolution' was called 'the great rebellion' by his opponents. One struggled to capture the laudative term (revolution) and foist the pejorative one (rebellion) on the enemy. That 'revolution' was indeed a laudative term appears in the phrase 'the Glorious Revolution', which, in the light of later revolutions, is a blatant misnomer. The term acquired its moern connotations with the American and especially the French revolutions. The process starts as a revolt (no mere rebellion, for the authority of the powers that be is no longer recognized), ends up in complete upheaval (revolution is opposed to evolution) obtained through violence (revolution is opposed to reform). It is in the light of these semantic changes that the phrase 'the Glorious Revolution' appears as a misnomer. But there is something more, which partly accounts for the modern British reticence towards revolutions (one no longer calls them 'glorious'). This is due to its association with the term 'revolt' (from Latin *rebellare*) and to the workings of the remainder. From 'revolt', we derive the present participle 'revolting'. But 'revolting' is also an adjective that corresponds to the noun 'revulsion' (from Latin *revellere*). So that the process of corruption, through what historical linguists call 'homophonic collision', produces the following associative chain: revolution – revolt – revolting – revulsion. The fulcrum of this semantic series is the 'pun' on 'revolting', but the false prefix 'rev-', which functions as one of Whorf's phonesthemes, also helps. We understand why we can so easily interpret Frankenstein's monster as an embodiment of the French revolution, why Burke's rhetoric when he inveighs against the revolutionary French so often draws on the metaphor of monstrousness. Metaphors sedimented in language not only give rise to metamorphosis, they

THE VIOLENCE OF LANGUAGE

also give rise to myth. The task of the political leader is to produce the former out of the latter.

CORRUPTION REVISITED: RUSSELL HOBAN'S
RIDDLEY WALKER

If we want to celebrate the positive side of corruption, perhaps the best text to turn to is Russell Hoban's *Riddley Walker*.[38] Here is indeed a new, that is, a corrupted, tongue, much more so than Orwell's Newspeak or Anthony Burgess's fake Russian in *A Clockwork Orange*. This language does not merely obliterate the past, it is not restricted to slogans or catchwords – it is a brand new language, alive and kicking, which means that it is endowed with a rich past. This is what corruption consists in – the survival, and therefore the life, of a dead language.

One could easily dismiss *Riddley Walker* as one of those works of highbrow science fiction or fantasy of which the British are inordinately fond – *The Hobbit* with a linguistic twist. On the surface, the story is as trivial as it is extraordinary. In 1997, the Bomb has finally exploded, and the nuclear holocaust has destroyed civilization as we know it. The survivors have had to rebuild not only their material lives, but their culture, on the ruins of ours. The story takes place in 2347 O.C. ('Which means Our Count', p. 120). It is, as we may expect, grim. Legend has it that Einstein claimed that he did not know what the ultimate weapon of World War III would be, but that for World War IV he felt quite sure it would be the stone axe. In the world of *Riddley Walker* stone axes rule. The Bomb has taken mankind backward, into physical corruption – life is again short and nasty – and cultural backwardness. Even the dogs have gone wild and hunt in packs. On the first page of the novel the hero, Riddley Walker, marks his entry into adulthood, at the age of 12, by killing one of the last surviving boars with his spear: 'On my naming day when I come twelve I gone front spear and kilt a wyld boar he parbly ben the las wyld pig on the Blundel Downs any how there hadnt ben none for a long time befor him nor I aint looking to see none agen' (p. 1).

But I am being unjust to the novel. As the quotation shows (and indeed the very first non-grammatical word in the text is 'naming'), this is a novel about language, the corrupt language of the future, and therefore the corruption that lies at the heart of our language. The first task of the reader is not, as it usually is, to grasp the

214

unfolding of the story and choose the right identifications. He must do all this, but he has a prior task to accomplish: he must learn the language. The language spoken in the novel is undeniably English (there is little linguistic verisimilitude in the time scale: fortunately for us, the English of *Riddley Walker* is much less corrupt than English is likely to have become in 2,000 years), and yet it is distinctly not our English, to the point that it is sometimes hardly intelligible. At least it is so at first, for we do learn the new phonetic, syntactic, and semantic rules, as we would have to learn the rules of one of the more outlandish dialects of English that go by the name of new Englishes.[39] French Canadian films, when shown in France, are often subtitled in metropolitan French for the first half-hour – the time it takes to learn your own language when it becomes other by coming back to you from abroad.

As a result, the first task of the reader is to become a linguist. He must note recurring occurrences of new words, in order to grasp their meanings by constructing semantic contexts; he must analyse new instances of strange syntax or phonetics so as to formulate the rules of phoneme shift or syntactic simplification that characterize the dialect – both synchronic rules, for the dialect of *Riddley Walker* is systematic and coherent, and diachronic ones, for it differs from our English in regular and predictable ways.

But the aim of the game is not the construction of a grammar. The interest lies in the consciousness we acquire of the process of corruption. And we soon realize that the fictional picture of language change that the novel offers is both convincing – in other words, this looks like actual linguistic change and can be described with the help of a textbook of historical linguistics – and familiar, for it looks singularly like a concentrated version of our rag-bag. The fictional picture of diachrony is equivalent to a real description of the remainder and its work, not merely as a matter of convenience, because what the writer has access to is his own synchronic remainder, but, as we have seen, for reasons of principle, because the remainder is the locus for diachrony-within-synchrony, the place of inscription for past and present linguistic conjunctures.

Russell Hoban is highly aware of this. Indeed, when he talks of *Riddley Walker*, he tends to use the Romantic topos of inspiration and possession – the 'language speaks' pole of our central contradiction. The cover of my paperback edition quotes him as stating that *Riddley Walker* 'took five and a half years to write and ended up being written not even in proper English but in a broken-up and worn-down vernacular of it. What happened was that something took hold of me and didn't let go until it got itself onto paper in the way that it wanted to be.' His heroes too are convinced of the magical power of language, and a mythical text, the legend of St Eustace (corrupted to 'the Eusa story'), plays a major part in the daily life of their twilight world. In the words of one of them, 'Words! Theywl move things you know theywl do things. Theywl fetch. Put a name to something and youre beckoning' (p. 118).

At first sight, the dialect of *Riddley Walker* sounds like an exaggerated version of some juvenile urban working-class dialect. We can actually recognize the result of changes that we know are taking place at this very moment. Thus, predictably enough, 'used to' has lost its affix: 'Every 1 else the formers and them what jobbit and foragit or what ever they had the country of the day time. That same country I use to go in' (p. 168). In this passage, Riddley has left the society of men and is travelling with a pack of dogs, mostly at night. He is musing on the altered circumstances of his life. But we understand him well – we have heard the likes of him, or almost, with their restricted vocabulary and garbled syntax. Were it spoken by an actual adolescent, the speech would delight a Tory of the old school, deploring our falling standards of education and advocating a return to corporal punishment and learning by rote. Corrupt affixes (-ed > -it), simplistic spelling ('every 1 else'), the altered syntax of sentential subjects ('every 1 else ... they had') and relative clauses ('them what jobbit' – a very old grammatical 'mistake', this): this is spoken English gone wild.

This passage is typical of the novel. We could have used Hoban's text as a corpus for our rag-bag. Everywhere, whether we approach the text from the point of view of synchrony or diachrony, the remainder is seen to be at work. As the quoted passage shows, there is a certain amount of phonetic corruption in this dialect ('farmers' > 'formers' – the implicit pun is rich in meaning), although it is of course difficult to be sure of the exact sounds of a dialect the only trace of which is a written text. The case is clearer for consonants, and we note a consistent consonant shift, whereby initial or final 'th', that bugbear of foreign learners, becomes 'f'. Thus, we find 'earf' and 'froat' – familiar sounds for the Cockney. But the change is not complete yet, for articles and personal pronouns, protected as they are by the extreme frequency of their use, have so far resisted (cf. 'them' in the passage quoted). More interesting for us is the massive presence of metanalysis, that is of Brissetizing remotivation:

'interference' > 'inner fearents' (p. 43); 'symposium' > 'some poasyum' ('it aint jus poasyum you all ways say *some* poasyum', p. 103); 'an island' > 'a nylan' (p. 117), a classic case of metanalysis; 'millions' > 'millyings', where the remotivation is also a conversion. Sometimes the metanalysis takes the form of folk-etymology, of a kind we have already evoked in Chapter 1: 'Becaws a woman is a *woom*an aint she. Shes the 1 with the woom' (p. 163). This generalized Brissetizing naturally affects place names and proper names, as it does in our own dialect. Names are among the monuments that the dark ages of the past have left to Riddley Walker, and their riddles must be interpreted, as the very name of the hero indicates. Thus, the government is in the hands of a Pry Mincer and his shadow, the Wes Mincer, while a religious dignitary goes by the name of the Ardship of Cambry (also called elsewhere the Hard Bitchup of Cantser Belly, p. 133). And his title announces his fate: 'Which the hardship be come the Ardship you see' (p. 77).

The corruption of Brissetizing has the usual effect. It opens up new paths in the remainder, and is a source of punning, metaphor, and interpretive wit. The distinction between ʊ and /u:/having been more or less lost, 'would' and 'wood' have become homophones: 'From now on when I write down about the tree in the stoan Iwl write *wud* not wood. You see what Im saying its the hart of the wud its the hart of the wanting to be' (p. 160).

Syntax is equally affected. We have to learn new rules, to adapt to new practices. This corrupt dialect Wolfsonizes as much as it Brissetizes. A few passages will be enough: 'When I said that I thot on Fister Crunchman what he said about connecting' (p. 85); 'Wherever that mans face come from it fult me sad' (p. 160); '1ce that Powers luce itwl fetch itwl work itwl move itwl happen every 1 whats in its road' (p. 193). The first passage shows that syntactic rules are eminently defeasible. The sentence is in our terms hardly grammatical and yet it is highly intelligible. We can even find a good reason for the change, for the sentence is a kind of syntactic portmanteau, combining two constructions of the verb 'think' that for us are normal: 'I thought about Fister' and 'I thought about what he said'. And we do combine them ourselves: 'I thought about what Fister said.' What Riddley's dialect does is to topicalize the subject of the subordinate clause, which is agrammatical but coherent. The second passage offers various instances of simplification. The distinction between 'come' and 'came' has disappeared; the verb corresponding to the adjective 'full' is 'to full'; and the construction

217

'it filled me with sadness' has been modified by analogy with 'it made me sad'. A general principle of economy and analogy seems to be at work (not without innumerable exceptions) in this dialect as in others. The third passage shows that the rule of contraction for 'be', 'have', and modal auxiliaries has had its scope extended and has been made obligatory ('1ce that Powers luce' < 'once that power is loose'; 'itwl'). It also shows that the syntax of the verb 'happen' has been modified: it is now transitive. We have no difficulty in grasping its slightly wider range of meaning. In fact, conversion is one of the major rules of this dialect, as it is of our English. When Riddley goes south-east towards Folkestone, this is how he expresses it: 'So we Souf and Eastit then for Fork Stoan' (p. 86).

New words also appear, or words extend their meanings in unexpected ways, which means that the semantics of the language has been corrupted too. This is sometimes more difficult for us to grasp, as a single occurrence may not be sufficient for us to translate into our dialect. Since we cannot point to things and ask confirmation from our native informant, in order to find out what he meant by 'gavaga' we have to wait for the repeated occurrences to form a series of contexts, although our task is on the whole easier than that of Quine's philosophical linguist, since after all the alien dialect is still part of our language. A case in point is the adjective 'blipful' and the noun 'blip'. Before the Bomb, the word must have meant a signal on a computer screen. This original meaning has disappeared (it returns to the hero in an illumination on p. 85) because 'computer' is a magic word for something unintelligible, which has only survived in the obscure set phrase 'the Puter elite'. As a result, 'blip', by metaphor and/or metonymy, has come to mean a sign, and 'blipful' to mean 'significant' (objective sense) or 'aware of signs', therefore 'intelligent' (subjective sense), as appears in the following passages: '"All them other storys tol by mouf they ben put to and took from and changit so much thru the years theyre all bits and blips and all mixt up." I said, "That about the 1st knowing in the story. How they got it looking in the dogs eyes. Be that blip or jus a way of saying or what?"' (p. 20); 'So that dog is dubbl blipful' (p. 24).

So far, I seem to have described a mere linguistic *tour de force*, the source for many a feat of remainder-wit of the kind evoked in Chapter 2. The culmination of this occurs on pages 122–4, where the Pry Mincer gives Riddley a close commentary on the sacred text and founding myth of their society, the Eusa story, written in an archaic language that needs to be deciphered. The novel includes its own Rosetta stone. The legend originally came as a commentary on a series of frescoes on the life of St Eustace, and this it is that the Mincer comments: '"*Wooded landscape with many small hamlets.*" Well thats littl pigs innit then theres a *variety* which thats like a pack or a herd and *creatures* thats creachers parbly dogs . . . "*Meanders to the open sea.*" Mazy ways to a open see meaning a look see is what I take that to mean . . . "*St Eustace is seen on his knees before his quarry.*" Which a *quarry* is a kynd of digging' (p. 122). Some of these 'etymologies' are meant to produce a smile, some, like 'quarry', will remind us of more serious business. But again, it would be unfair to the text to leave it at that. Beneath the rather facile or predictable science fiction tale, there is an entirely serious and profound reflection on the link between language corruption and myth. For the interesting question is: why does the reader have such a strong feeling that this fictional language is not only coherent but alive (unlike the reconstituted Indo-European in which Schleicher wrote his celebrated fable – very much unlike the feeble jargon of the run of the mill science fiction tale)? The answer to this, I think, is that it manages what other fictional languages fail to achieve – to convey a sense of the past, of its intervention, its weighing down a 'worn-out' dialect, of the violence of the relationship, as the present speakers try to shape their lives by coming to terms with their linguistic origins, in an endless attempt at unravelling the riddles of their past through deciphering their own language. What the tale portrays is the part that language, as the main guardian of the memories of the nation (an unreliable guardian, intent on cheating his wards of their inheritance), plays in historical change, that is, in the corruption of history and the creation of myth. The subject of the tale is the emergence of a creation myth. This is what the Eusa story – perhaps the most important 'character' in the novel – conveys: a religious myth corrupted out of old religious myth revived (the medieval legend of St Eustace) and new scientific myth garbled (the narrative of scientific progress, of atomic physics, and of the computer elite).

Far from being the medium of a science fiction tale, with its fake quest and facile moral lesson ('the only power is no power'), language is the subject of the tale. It does indeed speak – and it tells a tale of violence. The violence of language itself, for the hero is a language specialist, the son of a 'connexion man', the local shaman, destined to succeed his father and give his tribe the 'reveals' they need to guide action, and to end up as a travelling showman who replaces the customary Eusa story with straightforward Punch and Judy – these shows are the main religious ceremonies in this culture, where deciphering plays the central role. The violence of society, for there is social division and strife in Inland, between the foragers, who live off the remains of the pre-holocaust world, and therefore look back, and the farmers who have started building a new world and look forward. Riddley is a forager, and his inner world is riddled with the linguistic past, with the need to understand, and the unconscious object of his quest is to become his own linguistic master, no longer to be obsessively spoken by the old language – the language of power and catastrophe (this is the meaning of his abandonment, a Luther-like figure, of the Eusa story for the ludic lay myth of Punch and Judy). The two types of violence are clearly linked, as appears in the structure of the state apparatus in Inland – it is hardly an apparatus of physical power at all (the Mincers have a guard of 'hevvys' with them), but rather an ideological apparatus. The role of the Pry Mincer in this government is to tour the country as a travelling Eusa showman and to conduct linguistic ceremonies. Politics in Inland not only takes place through the medium of language, it also has language for its main object. Power lies in words, more specifically in etymology. The Horne Tookes now rule, except that their rule is a religious one, intent on magically recapturing past scientific power through the vestigial power of words. So that political activity is an endless Talmudic commentary on linguistic fragments: nursery rhymes, corrupt versions of religious hymns, riddles. The society of Inland can never be truly reborn, for it is ceaselessly re-enacting the death that gave birth to it. It is dying of the violence of the past, the violence of the language it has received as a poisonous gift from irresponsible ancestors. As we know, the etymology of 'gift' is 'poison'.

FLOWERS

In *The Lord of the Harvest*, a novel of Suffolk country life by the Victorian novelist E. Betham Edwards,[40] we come across this description:

> The garden possessed some fine old apple trees, a row of veteran gooseberry bushes, potato and pumpkin beds, flowers adorning the front path. There flourished 'Welcome home

husband tho' never so drunk,' as, nobody knows why, country folks always called the yellow stonecrop, 'granny's nightcap' or monks' hood, sweet Williams, picotees in abundance, with lavender and rosemary for sweetening bed linen, a few pot herbs, and rue to drive away flies.'

If, delighted by the wit of the name, we look into an English flora, we shall find the following entry for the yellow stonecrop:

Yellow stonecrop. Sedum reflexum L. 67, H. 21. Local names. CREEPING JENNY, Heref; GINGER (cf. *Sedum acre*), Kent; INDIAN FOG, Ire; INDIAN MOSS, Donegal; LOVE-IN-A-CHAIN, Cumb: LOVE LINKS, Scot; PRICK-MADAM, Cumb.[41]

There is something striking in the names of plants – each has at least three. A scientific Latin name, marking its place in the Linnaean order; a host of colourful local names, full of allusions to local customs, country life, and antiquated beliefs (thus, the Cumbrian name of 'prick-madam' may hint at the fact that the plant was believed at one time to be an aphrodisiac); and a common or garden name, accessible to all speakers, into which the other two can be translated. I would like to treat this as an image of the relations between *langue*, the remainder, and history. The Linnaean classification is a good illustration of the order of *langue*: it is a semiotic system in which each unit is given a unique place, and univocal meaning. Confusion is impossible, and people who know the same plant under different names will come to an agreement on its Linnaean name. On the other hand the multiplicity of local names provides an excellent picture of the remainder and its rhizomatic deployment. For the naming of plants is one of the regions where the poetic creativity of a language, its gift for folk-metaphor, is most apparent. And it is also one of the regions where the links between a language, and the community that speaks it, with its history, become clear. There is a story in each of these names, and a reminder of history in the guise of customs, traditions, local lore. Most of these names, besides, are good instances of corruption, that is of the remainder's diachronic work. 'Prick-madam', my flora tells me, is a corruption of the French *'trique-madame'* – the interesting point is that in the process of mis-translation into English, the erotic innuendo has been preserved. Lastly, the fact that agreement can be reached on a neutral third name, neither too abstract nor too

idiosyncratic, is an image of the compromise that language is always
striving after – between *langue* and the remainder, between 'I speak
language' and 'language speaks'.

NOTES

1 Quoted in J. Aitchison, *Language Change: Progress or Decay?* London,
 Fontana, 1981, p. 93.
2 G. Deleuze and F. Guattari, *A Thousand Plateaux*, London, Athlone,
 1987.
3 T. Bynon, *Historical Linguistics*, Cambridge, Cambridge University
 Press, 1977, p. 200.
4 ibid., p. 207.
5 D. Attridge, *Peculiar Language*, London, Methuen, 1988, p. 116.
6 ibid., pp. 110, 120, 122.
7 J. Paulhan, *La Preuve par l'étymologie*, Paris, Le temps qu'il fait, 1988
 (first published, Paris, Minuit, 1953).
8 J. Engels, 'La Portée de l'étymologie isidorienne', in *Studi Medievali*, 3,
 Spoleto, 1962.
9 ibid., p. 99.
10 ibid., p. 114.
11 ibid., p. 116.
12 Quoted in D. Jacquart and C. Thomasset, *Sexualité et savoir médical au
 Moyen Age*, Paris, PUF, 1985, p. 22 (English transl., *Sexuality and
 Medicine in the Middle Ages*, London, Polity Press, 1988).
13 E. R. Curtius, *European Literature and the Latin Middle Ages*, London,
 Routledge, 1953, p. 497.
14 G. Deleuze and F. Guattari, *Anti-Oedipus*, transl. R. Hurley, M. Seem,
 and H. R. Lane, New York, Viking, 1983.
15 Aitchison, op. cit., p. 121; Bynon, op. cit., p. 231.
16 Bynon, op. cit., p. 101; Aitchison, op. cit., p. 143.
17 O. Smith, *The Politics of Language, 1791–1819*, Oxford Clarendon
 Press, 1984, is the main exception.
18 R. Wardaugh, *Languages in Competition*, Oxford, Blackwell, 1988, p.
 69.
19 J. Horne Tooke, *The Diversions of Purley*, vol. 1, quoted in M. C.
 Yarborough, *John Horne Tooke*, New York, Columbia University
 Press, 1926, p. 115.
20 Smith, op. cit., p. 119.
21 Quoted in Yarborough, op. cit., p. 135.
22 ibid., p. 139.
23 Smith, op. cit., p. 138.
24 Yarborough, op. cit., p. 144.
25 In L. Althusser and E. Balibar, *Reading Capital*, London, New Left
 Books, 1970.
26 ibid., pp. 95–6.
27 H. W. and F. G. Fowler, *The King's English*, Oxford, Clarendon Press,
 2nd edition, 1924.

28 Althusser and Balibar, op. cit., p. 106.
29 J. Stalin, *Marxism and Linguistics*, London, 1951.
30 F. Jameson, *The Political Unconscious*, London, Methuen, 1981, pp. 140–1.
31 A. Kojève, *Introduction à la lecture de Hegel*, Paris, Gallimard, 1948, pp. 462–4.
32 See Chapter 6.
33 Lenin, 'On Slogans', in *Collected Works*, vol. 25, London, Lawrence & Wishart, 1964, p. 185.
34 ibid., p. 189.
35 ibid., p. 183.
36 ibid.
37 R. Williams, *Keywords*, London, Fontana, 1976.
38 R. Hoban, *Riddley Walker*, London, Picador, 1982 (first published, Jonathan Cape, 1980).
39 J. Platt, H. Weber, and M. L. Ho, *The New Englishes*, London, Routledge, 1984.
40 E. Betham Edwards, *The Lord of the Harvest*, Woodbridge, The Boydell Press, 1983, p. 6 (first published 1899).
41 G. Grigson, *The Englishman's Flora*, London, Paladin, 1975, p. 197.

6

THE VIOLENCE OF
LANGUAGE

Mr Graves's way of speaking did not displease Watt. Mr
Graves pronounced his *th* charmingly. Turd and fart, he said,
for third and fourth. Watt liked these venerable Saxon words.

(Samuel Beckett)

THE NON-AUTONOMY OF LANGUAGE

A man and a woman are waiting for a bus at a request stop. He
remains silent, but she keeps talking to him, or rather at him, for she
accuses him, in no uncertain terms, of having made a pass at her.
Her insults, her threats, her attempts at striking an alliance with
other members of the queue founder upon his inscrutable silence.
The more he remains quiet, the more she talks, exposing her frailty,
her need for affection, her anxiety, and anger. When the bus
eventually comes, he boards it, and she remains by the stop, and
immediately attempts to seduce the first man who joins the queue.

In this sketch by Harold Pinter,[1] conversation is not strikingly
cooperative, and every utterance is a speech act, to be interpreted in
terms not of meaning but of effect. (Will the utterance achieve the
woman's goal of shouting her opponent off the verbal battlefield?
Will it on the contrary expose the weakness of her position and
reduce her to silence?) This is language at its most banal, the
language of *scènes de ménage*, which is very much in the world and
part of it.

A linguist will argue that this has nothing to do with the
Saussurean principle of the autonomy of *langue*. A marginal subpart
of linguistics, pragmatics, deals with these margins, on the frontier
where alas language touches on the world and where the purity of
langue is spoilt. Indeed, it is the recognition of this unfortunate

224

non-autonomy of language, of this intermingling of words and things that justifies the abstraction of *langue* from language and the exclusion of the remainder. But our point of view, being the point of view of language as a whole, that is, of the inseparability of *langue* and the remainder, is of necessity different. If the remainder is the inseparable other of *langue*, the world is the inseparable other of language, each acting on and being acted upon by the other. Corruption, as we have seen, is one of the names of this non-autonomy. And the remainder, the part of language that is corrupted and that corrupts, is the frontier between language and the material world. A paradoxical frontier as we shall see.

Our point of view, therefore, is not that of linguistic idealism: this is no conception of a self-enclosed language. The relationship of text and world is one not of absorption (the world is a text, the text is the world), but of paradox, a material mixture of word and world, which yet will allow language to belong to a different order of entities from the bodies that make up the world. This type of paradox is central to Stoic philosophy, and to the reading that Deleuze gives of it (both in *Logique du sens* and in *plateau* no. 4 of *A Thousand Plateaux*). We recall that, according to the pan-somatic monism of the Stoics, everything, including the soul, is a body. But bodies are not the only entities – they are merely the only entities endowed with existence, with being. Besides beings, there are manners of being; besides bodies, there 'are' 'existential nothings' ('*néants d'existence*' is the phrase used by Bréhier[2]), incorporeal entities. This duality cuts across language, where the Stoics distinguish between words, which are bodies, and the incorporeal 'expressible' ('*exprimables*' in Bréhier), the *lekta* that are attributed to them. On the one hand, there are bodies in language, because words have material existence in the form of sounds; on the other hand, there is something incorporeal to it, the *lekton* that is expressed, the utterance as event. The canonic illustration of this situation is the case of the Barbarian and the Greek speakers who hear the same utterance. They are physically affected in the same way by the sounds, but the Greek speaker catches something that the Barbarian misses, the *lekton*. Nor is this to be interpreted simply as the opposition between sound and meaning, form and content. The link between the words and their *lekta* is not one of representation, but of intervention. In *plateau* no. 4, Deleuze and Guattari read the Stoic dichotomy in terms of the distinction that Hjelmslev, the Danish linguist, makes between 'forms of expression' and 'forms of content'. Utterances as arrangements of *lekta*, as 'forms of expression', express forms of contents, that is mixtures of bodies, as the utterance 'the knife cuts the flesh' gives form to the incorporeal transformation of the event denoted by the verb 'cut', and expresses the bodily mixture of knife and flesh. The important point is that the incorporeal transformation, the event, is not a representation of the mixture of bodies, but intervenes on it, to delay or precipitate it. One does not speak *of* things or states of affair, one speaks *in the midst* of states of affair ('à même les états de choses').

Language lies on both sides of the divide. Words take part in material mixtures, their *lekta* intervene on the surface of bodies, as their incorporeal attributes. This is the meaning we must give to the pseudo-paradox of Chrysippus (an obvious paralogism, of the type Aristotle engages in *De Sophisticis Elenchis*): 'If you utter something, that something goes through your mouth; therefore, when you utter "a chariot", a chariot goes through your mouth.'[3] Deleuze quite rightly comments that this is the kind of paradox one expects to find in Zen Buddhism and Victorian nonsense. He goes on to interpret it as a play on surfaces, and their priority over depths – there is indeed, in this piece of false reasoning, a flattening out of logically distinct levels of utterance. In this elevation of a joke to the level of paradox, I sense an intimation of the paradoxical duality of language, of its inseparably material and immaterial nature – the solid materiality of bodies mixing with other bodies to make up the world, the active immateriality of intervention, not abstraction or representation.

Both aspects – whether the knife penetrates the flesh or whether the event of cutting occurs – involve violence. This chapter is concerned with the violence of language – with the literal violence that language exerts in and on the body, and with the immaterial violence of linguistic interventions on states of affair. As has already been made clear, I share Deleuze and Guattari's rejection of the Stalinist vulgate of Marxism within linguistics, which treats language as a neutral 'form of expression', giving abstract form to ideologies, which in turn represent economic contents and the form given them by the structure of economic production. Against this, that is, against an account of language in terms of information and communication, they advocate the use of the category of production to describe language, a category that is to be taken literally, a production of meaning not as an effect of the superstructure, but right at the level of the base. The concept of 'collective arrangement of utterance', which for them has priority over *langue*, expresses this active immaterial materiality. It expresses the precise state of the mixture of bodies within society, within the literally understood 'body politic': their attractions and repulsions, sympathies and antipathies, alloys and penetrations. The instance of such an arrangement that Deleuze and Guattari provide is the feudal arrangement of utterance. It consists of a mixture of bodies (the body of the earth, the body of society, i.e. the overlord and his vassal knights, but also the articulated bodies of knight and horse that charged at Agincourt) and of discourses and utterances expressing them and intervening in them: coats of arms and the discourse of heraldry, ordeals, and feudal oaths, *romans de chevalerie*, etc.

Deleuze and Guattari, who thus reject the Marxist distinction between base and superstructure, go on to criticize the classic Marxist conception of ideology as the product of superstructure. If there is such a thing as violence in language, the term must be taken literally – not the violence of symbol, but the violence of intervention, of an event the immateriality of which does not prevent it from having material effects, effects not of metaphor but of metamorphosis. The example they give is familiar. The political situation in Petrograd in July 1917 is characterized by a certain mixture of institutional bodies – the Soviets and the Provisional Government, as well as the various political parties and groups – and the 'mixture' is hardly metaphorical, for the situation *is* fluid, and one wonders with whom the small independent socialist group led by Trotsky and Lunacharsky will mix (eventually, they joined the Bolsheviks). But it is also characterized by language, what Deleuze and Guattari call the 'incorporeal semiotics of the Bolsheviks', that is, the linguistic work of slogans, which precipitates events, in the temporal as well as the chemical sense of the verb. Slogans, as we have realized, actively intervene in the linguistic–historical conjuncture, they are part of it. Lenin's pamphlet literally is an intervention in the discussion in preparation of the next conference of the Bolshevik Party, an attempt at changing its line, and therefore the course of events.

Although I share Deleuze and Guattari's rejection of the conception of ideology as representation – indeed, this is entirely consistent with a view of language that focuses on the remainder – I do not wish to throw away the baby with the bath water. There is a lot to be salvaged and made use of in Althusser's theory of ideology, at least in its late form, the theory of State Ideological Apparatuses. I confess to being a belated and nostalgic supporter of the theory. There is a lot in such a theory that concerns the violence of language and its materiality. The materiality of apparatuses and institutions, for instance, and the materiality of practices, including linguistic practices, help us to understand the somewhat metaphorical concept of 'immaterial violence': the violence of an insult is due not to the high-pitched quality of the scream that carries it, but to its insertion in an established practice, a chain of utterances and gestures, a series of semi-conventional effects and expectations. This means, for instance, that, when confronted with an insult, the range of my options is limited. I must retaliate or lose face, as appears in the following passage from Beckett's *Murphy*:

> Now it was Wylie's turn, but he could find nothing. No sooner did he realize this, that he would not find anything in time to do himself credit, than he began to look as though he were not looking for anything, nay, as though he were waiting for it to be his turn. Finally, Neary said without pity: 'You to play, Needle.'[4]

The scene describes a conversation, not a competitive game. But, obviously, there is more than meets the eye in the concept of 'turn' used in conversation analysis and ethnomethodology: a whole *practice* is involved, with its rights and duties, one that involves danger, victory or defeat, attack and defence, and therefore a certain amount of violence (which accounts for Neary's lack of 'pity').

Or again, I shall attempt to salvage the Althusserian concept of interpellation of the subject by ideology and/or language, for our contradiction between LS and ISL is aptly expressed at this level by a conception of the shaping power of ideology and of meaning (the subject's meaning) as the object of a Freudian compromise between the speaker's expressive needs and the mastery of ideology/language in the shape of ready-made discourse, cliché and polemical positions. The lady in Pinter's *Request Stop* ultimately exposes her weakness and loses the verbal battle because she cannot negotiate such a compromise – because, in order to express what she believes to be her most private and personal meaning, her indignation at being the victim of attempted seduction, she has recourse to the most worn-out clichés, teling her opponent that her best friend is a plain clothes detective and accusing him of being a wog, a criminal, a pervert, or a country bumpkin up 'for a bit of a lark'. In so doing, she exposes what she does not recognize as *her* meaning, what she certainly does not mean, her own attempt at seduction, her own desperate need for (verbal) relationship, which makes her speak in the first place. The violence of the scene is inseparable from the violence of her desire, of her delirium, and of her frozen-up language. If the Marxist concept of linguistic conjuncture expressed the corrupting impact of diachrony, or rather history, on language, the privileged locus of which is the remainder (that frontier between language and the world), perhaps in order to describe the specific struggles between *langue* and the remainder that form *a* language, English or French, we ought to import another Marxist concept, and speak of a 'linguistic formation'. The concept 'social formation', as we know (a typical formulation would be 'historical materialism is the science of social formations'), seeks to account for the specific mixture of modes of production, some dominant, some mere 'survivals', within a nation state, at a given moment in history. In the same vein, when we speak of 'English', we speak of a multiplicity of dialects, registers, and styles, of the sedimentation of past conjunctures, of the inscription of social antagonisms as discursive antagonisms, of the coexistence and contradiction of various collective arrangements of utterance, of the interpellation of subjects within apparatuses embodied in linguistic practices (schools, the media). My task is to describe the violence that this Babel involves.

THE MATERIAL VIOLENCE OF LANGUAGE: LANGUAGE AND THE BODY

Before it is a practice, language is a body – a body of sounds. There is violence in a scream. As we say in French, a voice can pierce my ear-drums. My conception of the material violence of language dates back to an early reading of the adventures of Tintin, and to a picture of *La Castafiore* singing the part of Marguerite in *Faust*, when the sounds produced by her ample bosom broke various items of glass. Violence here is to be taken at its most literal, as body penetrating body. Such penetration is often met with in cases of delirium or possession – there is, for instance, an eroticism of religious enthusiasm.[5] Thus Wolfson. The sounds of his native English cause him 'pain'. He never actually calls it 'physical' pain, or notes its intensity, but the account he gives of it makes it clear that it has nothing to do with grief or sorrow – pain is the only word that corresponds to what he feels. Perhaps the conjunction of language and pain (and of the material and the immaterial violence of language) appears most clearly at the beginning of his second book,[6] which is devoted to an account of his mother's death from cancer. In the first pages, he explains, or rather expresses, for there is no didactic explicitness in his writing, the reasons for the structure of the book, which is composed of extracts from his mother's medical diaries and lengthy commentaries and accounts of his own life at the time, the main feature of which was his compulsive betting on horses. The subject of the book is pain – the physical pain of cancer, the mental–physical pain of language and its effect on the body, the mental pain of the gigantic cancer that will go on affecting the whole planet until the nuclear holocaust sets everything and everyone at rest. At the time, he tells us, when he started writing his second book, he was in the compulsive habit of screaming the English word 'enema' at the top of his voice. One of the sources of this 'mania' was the persecution of which he believed he was the victim, at the hands of J. B. Pontalis, the French psychoanalyst who published his first book. Pontalis, Wolfson believed, was trying to influence him into assassinating President Pompidou on his visit to New York. As we can see, in this account bodily violence is inextricably mixed with the violence of language, the material violence of the scream, and the immaterial violence of persuasion. And it is also mixed up with the remainder-work, for although, in this his second book. Wolfson no longer seems to Wolfsonize, i.e. no longer seems to practise his translation device, yet he unconsciously does just this, for on the same page as the word 'enema', which being English is printed in italics, there is only one other italicized word, in French this time, 'énième' (he is evoking a bestselling author who has written his *nth* novel), which is a *traducson*, a translation according to sound, not meaning, of 'enema'. But this is the paragraph in which Wolfson generalizes about his practice and reflects on it:

> *Tant pis. Lire, agir, détruire ...! Il faut essayer sans doute de détruire les tumeurs ('Tu meurs!'), surtout les malignes, qui poussent dans les chairs des gens (par chirurgie, irradiation – y compris radioactive! – produits chimiques ...) mais il faut surtout guérir les cancers géants, ceux des 'astres errants' (où seules s'avéreraient effectives, en fin de compte, d'énormes quantités de radioactivité).[7]*

So there is a natural, serial link between reading, writing, action, and destruction. We must be resigned to it: it is 'too bad!' And the destruction in question is both a source of pain and a cure – a painful remedy, like language itself, of which it is an analogon. For language, too, acts and destroys, for better or for worse, in sickness and in health. This is what the Brissetic pun on 'tumour'/'you die' – which Wolfson is not the first to discover (cf. the witty patient mentioned in Chapter 2 – and a pun, as we have seen, is to be found in language, not in the punster's head) – is meant to express. This passage is important to us because of the analogic chain on which it plays: linguistic violence – the violence of physical pain – the violence of world destruction, of apocalypse.

To illustrate the painful material violence of language, we can turn to *Perceval's Narrative*.[8] Perceval is the nineteenth-century schizophrenic rediscovered by Gregory Bateson. He was the son of Spencer Perceval, the prime minister assassinated in 1812 in the House of Commons. He was a former officer and an enthusiastic evangelical, who lapsed into delirium after an experience with the extremist sect of Irvingites at Row in Scotland, where the miracle of Pentecost was held to have present relevance, and the congregation spoke in tongues. After three years in psychiatric asylums, Perceval was cured (if we believe him, no thanks were due to the doctors, and he had to escape from his last asylum) and he published his account of his mental illness in order to support the rights of psychotics and advocate changes in the conventional ways of dealing with them. Bateson is entirely right in hailing in Perceval a forerunner of Freud's psychopathology of everyday life. His lucidity and the depth of his insights are truly amazing. He gives an entirely rational account of the voices in which, like most paranoid schizophrenics, he so firmly believed during his illness and whose commands he religiously obeyed. He explains their appearance in terms of two well-known phenomena of everyday language, the slip of the tongue and the confusion between the metaphoric and the literal. A psychotic is a person who mishears certain utterances in the same way as the absent-minded spoonerist distorts or mispronounces words. And he evinces a strange tendency to take figurative phrases to the letter:

> Thus you will hear one lunatic declare that he is made of iron, and that nothing can break him; another, that he is a china vessel, and that he runs in danger of being destroyed every minute. The meaning of the spirit is, that this man is strong as iron, the other frail as an earthen vessel; but the lunatic takes

the literal sense, and his imagination not being under his own control, he in a manner feels it. In like manner, when I was desired to suffocate myself on my pillow, and that all the world were suffocating for me, etc. etc., I conceive, now, that the spirit referred to the suffocation of my feelings – that I was to suffocate my grief, my indignation, or what not, on the pillow of my conscience.'[9]

We note that language is the source of pain, not directly, as when voices scream inside Perceval's, as they do inside Schreber's head, but through the violence they exert, the linguistic violence of literalness, which threatens to turn into the literal violence of language. The violence of feelings, of indignation, of guilt, once interpreted in the literal terms of language, becomes the painful violence of physical action, for the keepers on many occasions had to prevent Perceval from committing suicide by suffocation, a more active form of the impossible suicide by apnoea, which is the ultimate goal of Murphy's Mr Endon.[10] To emphasize this relation between language and body, Perceval even introduces a physiological theory of madness, the implausibility of which need not concern us. According to Perceval, madness is the result of disorderly breathing. The mind and its states are dependent on the body and its states:

a healthy state of mind is identical with a certain regulated system of respiration, according to the degree of bodily action; ... the exercise of reflection or of conscience, in the control of the passions or affections of the mind, is concomitant with, or effected by a proper control of the respiration – quiet when the mind is quiet, accompanied with sobs and sighs when otherwise. ... The mind and the blood being intimately connected, the health of the body depends also on this healthy regulation of respiration, promoting a proper circulation and purification of the blood; ... consequently, the effecting respiration by mechanical means, without the control of the muscles by thought, is profitable to the health of the body, and also to that of the mental faculties, although they may not be, at least distinctly, occupied by any idea.[11]

There is more to this than an old solution to the mind-and-body problem, or an echo of Oriental techniques of relaxation. For this text occurs as a footnote in the middle of the discussion of madness as *prise au pied de la lettre* of language (this is Perceval's own phrase). In other words, language is the connecting link between body and mind, because only language has the dual form of a body (made up of sounds) and incorporeal *lekta*. It is a frontier, and it contains within itself a frontier between *langue* and the remainder, which is both unceasingly reaffirmed and constantly disappearing. In Perceval's theory of the violence of language and the bodily origin of madness, we perceive the articulation between word and event that Chrysippus's pseudo-paradox sought to express. The voice that makes itself heard in his mind and whose appearance is an event, sometimes with devastating consequences, is but immaterialized sound; in other words, sound that acquires articulation and meaning independently of the subject's volition – a hallucination or a sign, according to the state of mind of the hearer:

> I discovered one day, when I thought I was attending to a voice that was speaking to me, that my mind being suddenly directed to outward objects, – the sound remained but the voice was gone; the sound proceeded from a neighbouring room or from a draft of air through the window or doorway.[12]

The pain that Wolfson and Perceval experience is therefore truly physical pain – its ultimate cause is a sound striking the ear-drum. But, by being articulated, by becoming language, it increases in efficiency and intensity. When he attempts to answer the voices, to use language to reject their incomprehensible or contradictory commands, Perceval experiences 'pain in the nerves of [his] palate and throat'.[13] And this pain-giving language is of course the remainder, the rhizome which has become violent and all-powerful at the expense of the speaker's control. These voices draw on all the tricks of the remainder-work. They speak in verse, they play on the vagueness and reversibility of linguistic segments, they practise compulsive repetition at the expense of meaning, as appears in the following instances of voices actually heard by Perceval:

> The time of the trial of the time of the trial,
> And the trial of the time of the trial of the time,
> And the trial of the time of the time of the trial.

> I would if I could, and I could if I would,
> I will if I can, and I can if I will,
> I could if I would, and I would if I could,
> I can if I will, and I will if I can.[14]

THE VIOLENCE OF LANGUAGE

There is something frightening in this, for the violence of language is concealed under words of honey. An innocent-looking piece of nursery nonsense, a jingle, has become the instrument of acute pain.

It might be objected that my account of the material violence of language has been restricted so far to the relatively marginal case of possession and delirium, and that the relation between language and the body is still indirect, as clearly appears in the case of Wolfson's 'pain'. A direct relationship would be one in which words would kill. Hardly has the magic formula escaped my lips when my foe collapses. This type of fatal language exists only in fairy tales or in the superstitious practices of magic, the reality of which always dissolves in the light of reason. But does it? Official France, rational, urban, and progressive as it is, has always despised the benighted louts who, in the backward West, still believe in witch-craft – puppets pierced with pins, incantations, and similar nonsense. Jeanne Favret-Saada, a philosopher and anthropologist, has tried to understand their universe from within. The results, which she records in her book, *Les Mots, la mort, les sorts*[15] (the subtitle reads: '*la sorcellerie dans le bocage*'), are highly fascinating. It transpires that what she calls '*la crise de sorcellerie*' (the outbreak, or crisis, of witchcraft) is primarily a matter of language and its violence. There is more than paronomasia to connect '*les mots*' with '*la mort*'. In order to understand this, we have to describe the unfolding of the crisis. It always starts when the victim, the bewitched innocent, becomes aware of a series of coincidences. His cattle die, his wife falls ill, his son has a car accident, etc. Like Freudian symptoms, these coincidences are revealed as such after the event, sometimes long afterwards, when someone realizes that the independent events form a coherent series. This someone is not the bewitched victim himself, but a neighbour or a relative, whose annunciation is the real starting-point of the crisis. So that it all begins with words: 'There is something strange in all this, you must be bewitched.' The annun-ciation works like an illicit performative, one with retroactive effect. Before the utterance, the victim was a normal person; immediately after, he has been bewitched for some time. The author of the annunciation often adds: 'You ought to protect yourself. You ought to consult a sorcerer.' Here a distinction must be made between the witch (*le sorcier*) who is the maleficent, but as we shall see absent, cause of the crisis, and the counter-witch, or sorcerer (*le désorceleur*), who possesses the same powers as the witch but uses them only for the good, white magic against black. So the victim consults, and the

234

sorcerer engages the witch in a fight to the death, which ends in the complete defeat of one of the opponents. If the right one wins, the victim is cured, and the curse is lifted.

The anthropologist sums all this up in the form of the following structure. Each man possesses a vital territory – his body, his family, his chattel – which he fills with his vital force. The witch is one who has surplus vital force. He needs to find new territories for it, and consequently invades his neighbour's, thus provoking the crisis. The sorcerer is able to withstand this aggressive thrust and reflect it back, like a protective mirror, towards its source. The situation can be represented by the following diagrams (which I have adapted from Favret-Saada):

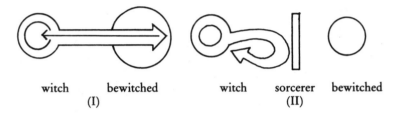

witch	bewitched		witch	sorcerer	bewitched
	(I)			(II)	

There are two concentric circles for the witch: the inner circle marks his territory, the outer his excessive vital force. The bewitched has only one circle, for his vital force does not exceed his territory. Under attack, however, he loses it to the witch, as the left-pointing arrow in the left diagram shows. The loss results in illness, ill-luck, and other symptoms.

This is a fine structure, which is not unfamiliar to the readers of Grimm and Perrault that we all are. The trouble is that, although efficient, that is, although the crisis often has dire effects on the bodies of the parties involved, it is fictitious, for a simple reason: witches do not exist. There is no one of whom we can say, unless in unwarranted and mythical accusation, that he or she is a witch, that he or she has actually cast a spell, or stuck those pins into a puppet – this occurs more often in sensational fiction than in real life, or in the anthropologist's field-work. Those who stick pins into puppets, or cook salt and offal in frying-pans are impostors and amateurs, laughed at by one and all. The structure is now rather unbalanced. Victims there are, sorcerers one can, with a little tenacity, actually meet (in the course of her research, Favret-Saada even became the disciple of one of them), the effects of the crisis are real enough. But witches do not exist. When one tries to check the accusations ('he looked at me in a strange way, and the following week two of my cows stopped giving milk'), they vanish into thin air. There are no witches in reality, but there are witches in speech – people are named as such, sometimes with extreme consequences. There are no witches, but language there is. And it can be deadly.

This is how, in a chapter entitled 'How to do war with words' ('*Quand la parole, c'est la guerre*'), Favret-Saada sums up her findings:

> An outbreak of witchcraft can be described thus: a word, uttered in a moment of crisis by him who will later be pointed at as the witch, is interpreted, after the event, as having had an effect on the body and possessions of the addressee, who will as a result call himself bewitched. The sorcerer [*le désenvoûteur*] will take this word, originally addressed to his client, upon himself, and return it to the sender, i.e. the witch. The claim that 'abnormalities' have occurred is always made after a word has been uttered, a word which will keep insisting until the sorcerer comes as a screen between sender and receiver.[16]

At the origin of the crisis, there is the circulation of affect – hatred, envy, love – in a situation of communication that is both unavoidable and unbearable: a situation of confrontation between an addresser (or aggressor) and an addressee. Psychologists, Favret-Saada reminds us, know that there are situations where even two is a crowd, *où de deux, il y a un de trop* – when one wishes one's nearest and dearest dead, when one is possessively jealous, etc. The situation of communication reproduces the structure of this face-to-face relationship. As a result, the violent affect is inseparable from the words that 'carry' it (here, the conduit metaphor is letting us down). Words are endowed with force, with the performativity of desire. And the struggle is conducted not *through* language, but *in* language. The words of the imagined curse have real effect on bodies; the successful naming of the witch can actually harm him. Favret-Saada tells the story of one Tripier, who, when accused of being a witch and vanquished by the sorcerer, became ill and went to the doctor to ask him to remove part of his intestines, his '*tripes*'. And if this sounds a little far-fetched or metaphoric, Favret-Saada also tells the story of a woman who, again accused of being a witch, died three months later in a psychiatric ward of sheer panic. Words have literal violence, and the crisis of witchcraft is a crisis of words.

THE VIOLENCE OF LANGUAGE

But the *pharmakon* of language also provides the cure. The most moving story that Favret-Saada tells is that of Jean, who claimed to have been bewitched into impotence and alcoholism. It turned out that fifteen years before he had been named as a witch by one of his neighbours. We can understand that, of all the positions in the game, that of the witch is the most difficult to hold, since he is by definition innocent. So that when he becomes aware of his position, he has a choice between three solutions. The first is death (as in the example quoted above): it takes the so-called witch out of the game for good, and it also demonstrates the material force of words – the false accusation actually killed the woman, without even the customary burning at the stake. The second is denial. Sometimes witches claim that it is all nonsense, that they do not believe in witchcraft. Their behaviour, or the state of their health, does not always confirm this. The repressed affect manages to worm its way back and attack the unbeliever's body. The third, which Jean adopted, is fiction, that is, rewriting. The only way to be rid of the noxious words is to translate them, like Wolfson, into a new narrative. The witch becomes bewitched. He produces a fiction, the function of which is to bury the first episode in oblivion, to reconstruct his personal history. This is the witch's family romance, in which he casts himself in the role of the victim. It is also the kind of narrative work that Freud came to recognize in the stories of his hysterical patients.

The position of the witch provides a good illustration of the material violence of language. In the first and the second positions, this materiality is as literal as can be, for words do kill (the case of Tripier shows that it is not merely the affect they 'carry' that is lethal, but their very form). The third position shows that words are both the weapons and the battlefield. The witch's family romance reproduces the structure of the crisis in an inverted form. By becoming bewitched, Jean sends back the lethal words of the sorcerer, as the sorcerer sends back the curse. In all cases, the effect on bodies, in a literal or extended sense (the victim's possessions and territory), is material. The question is: why are the most violent affects and what we hoped would provide an instrument for cooperation, language, so inextricably mixed? I have already suggested an answer when I noted that the structure of communication, involving as it does two participants, reproduces the structure of exchange of the closest and most tense emotional relationships, situations in which two is company with a deadly vengeance. It is time to take not only the materiality, but also the *maternality* of language seriously. Time to ponder on the well-known metaphor, and on the relations between language, family, and sex.

As usual I am not the first to venture on that ground, which is familiar to psychoanalysts. In the course of a psychoanalytic study of plagiarism,[17] Michel Schneider evokes the taboo on writing. Writing is always a risky enterprise, charged with emotional cathexes, because it involves a transgressive, even an incestuous relationship with the writer's mother tongue. 'Beaucoup d'écrivains furent malades de leur mère'.[18] One writes about and against one's mother, one's mother tongue, in order to get rid of the anxiety of influence. Schneider duly notes the well-known symptoms: the pains of gestation and parturition, the *post-publicatum* depression. This involves a theory of the speaker's relation to language, which Schneider sums up in his anti-Chomskyan formula: 'there is no innate language.'[19] The writer's language, his mother tongue, is received not as an instrument for the expression of beliefs and emotions, but through an interdiction, a union that is at the same time a separation (the writer's tongue is always *unheimlich* to him, both strange and homely), repeating the union with and eventual separation from his mother. Not a neutral tool, but a collection of words heavily cathected with desire and hatred, love and guilt; the result of which is yet another formulation of our central contradiction. Style is the result of the separation and struggle between the writer's own language (*sa langue propre*) and the maternal tongue that he tries to appropriate. To appropriate, Schneider adds, is also to destroy. 'Writing is doing violence to one's own language, in sadistic defence against the influence of one's mother – and there is hatred in such a relationship.' Or again, 'You only ever write with words which belong to others, when you recognize that the words are not yours, but do not belong either to those who used them, before or beside you.'[20]

This is why the question of style is central. The concept of style expresses this aspect of the contradiction, between possession by a language neither innate nor transparent, but acquired in tense interpersonal relationship, and appropriation that is destruction and reconstruction into one's own, or proper, tongue. It is normal that such a position should be explicitly anti-Chomskyan, and should on the other hand involve an implicit conception of the remainder, as the maternal side of language, as the locus for the struggle of appropriation and the deployment of style. For Chomsky's philosophical subjectivism – as opposed to the collectivism of Saussure, for instance – leads him into doing away with the notion of *a* language, like English or French, at least if we credit the analysis of one of his philosophical exponents, d'Agostino:

> Chomsky argued that the notion of a language (such as English) is not a legitimate concept of linguistic science because it can be given no coherent definition. In Chomsky's view, the existence of linguistic variation and its social embodiment in dialects presents a crucial problem for those, like Katz, who hold that notions such as 'English' are legitimate concepts of linguistic change.[21]

Against this, of course, I shall maintain either that the proper object of linguistics is *a* language, a specific conjunction of remainder and *langue*, a linguistic formation and linguistic conjunctures, the maternal tongue of a collection of stylists and Unknown Coiners, or that linguistics so defined is not the science of language, but rather a branch of pre-Freudian psychology. Against a conception of language that would in the end restrict it to the subject's intuitions and beliefs about his utterances (d'Agostino takes linguistic subjectivism to this extreme point), I shall maintain that language is both dependent on and independent of the subject, that it is both paternal (*langue* is the representative of the Law) and maternal (the remainder as incest and appropriation).

I have already given an illustration of the maternality of language in Chapter 2, when I evoked Wolfson's relationship with his mother's mother tongue, Yiddish. It is in fact easy to see that his translation device is an implicit declaration of love for his own mother tongue, English. Take, for instance, the mis-translation quoted in Chapter 2 (p. 63), where 'he's a screwball' becomes a mixture of French, German, Hebrew, and Russian. If we consider this as an instance of translation, that is, from the point of view of the translation theory specialist, we shall realize that, in the upward scale of difficulty that goes from borrowing to adaptation,[22] through *calque* (or loan translation), literal translation, transposition, and equivalence, Wolfson restricts his device to the first of these, excluding even *calque*, which imports the structures of another language (one says 'Governor General' in imitation of the French order of words). Only borrowing will do, when the target language is exactly the same as the source language. A notorious impossibility, which means that Wolfson's productions are not translations at all, but a massive symptom of his loving hatred for his mother tongue, which he must escape, and yet refuses to escape. Wolfson's device is an instance of incest with the mother tongue, exactly as his second book reveals that the hostility, even hatred, towards his mother that could be felt on almost every page of *Le Schizo et les langues* was only the obverse side of the deepest love. His second book is his own version of *In Memoriam*, a case history for the Freudian work of mourning.

As a conclusion on the relations between language and the body – which, as we have seen, are characterized by material and immaterial violence – I shall mention a passage from Karen Blixen's *Out of Africa*.[23] It is the story of the shy young Swede, who teaches the narrator how to count in Swahili. Swahili, he tells her, has no number nine. Does this mean that speakers can only count to eight, she asks? Not at all. They have ten, eleven, twelve, and the rest, but not nine. What about nineteen? '"They have not got nineteen either," he said, blushing, but very firm.' It turns out that, according to him, they have all the usual numbers, except those that contain a nine. For the narrator, there is food for thought in this. And it gives her, 'for some reason, great pleasure'. She admires the originality and the courage that must have been necessary to break with the pedantry of the usual series. The Swahili system of numeration must indeed be original, for it is the only one that has two sequential even numbers, eight and ten. And as two has no square root, so three in Swahili has no square number. Such is her interest that when she sees a native boy who has lost the fourth finger on one hand, she thinks that the amputation must have been deliberate, to help the boy with his arithmetic. Alas, when she airs her views, she is disillusioned. Swahili speakers, like everybody else, have a nine. The only problem is that their word for it is strikingly similar to an unmentionable word in Swedish. The whole incident reminds her of the old Danish clergyman who declared that he could not believe that God had created the eighteenth century.

The anecdote, of course, calls to mind certain Freudian concepts. It is the mathematical equivalent of infantile sexual theories. And there is an element of *Verleugnung* about it, for the narrator finds it difficult to abandon her false convictions: 'I have still got the feeling that there exists a native system of numeral characters without the number nine.' I know that Swahili has got a number nine, but all the same . . .: this is the linguistic structure of denial. But the anecdote also has structuralist connotations. For nine in Swahili is the absent number, *la case vide*, the empty square, which organizes, in its very absence, the arithmetic series. As such, it is also a 'point of subjectivity', where the subject finds anchorage in the signifying chain. In other words, the structure of the false system of numeration in Swahili spells out the structure of language, like the circulation of the empty square along the signifying and the signified series, which produces sense – this is Deleuze's theory of sense. But it also demonstrates the relationship between language and the body. For the anecdote would lose all point if sex were not involved, in the guise of the repressed obscene word. And it could never have arisen except as told by a man to a woman. Lastly, it is an instance of the interference of one language with another, of the guilt associated with the mother tongue (the young Swede, the narrator notes, 'blushes'), and of the translingual work of the remainder and its principle of homophony. Words do address bodies directly; they do tell a story of sex and violence. Out of this story, as Brisset sought to show, is meaning born.

THE SOCIAL VIOLENCE OF LANGUAGE

One criticism that has been levelled at Austin's theory of performatives is that he fails to account for the social context of his illocutionary force – he fails to account for its origin (what gives utterances their force) and therefore for its scope (the theory of perlocutionary effect is notoriously underdeveloped). This absence can be read in the form of a symptom when, in his early essay on 'Performative Utterances',[24] he mentions the following situation as an instance of performative failure. An official is on the point of naming a ship the Queen Elizabeth, when a dubious character in Andy Capp headgear gets hold of the champagne bottle, breaks it on the hull and exclaims: 'I name this ship the Generalissimo Stalin.' Such absence is the reason for Deleuze and Guattari's misprision of the concept 'pragmatics'. For them, the term 'force' is to be taken literally. Illocutionary forces find their sources in collective arrangements of utterance; the violence of language, which accounts for utterances having 'force' in the first place, is due to the struggle between the various dialects that make up a linguistic formation, and which the uneasy mixture of *langue* and remainder eventually expresses.

In this context, the concepts of 'major' and 'minor' dialects, which they introduce in their book on Kafka,[25] have particular importance. I have already evoked their critique of the fourth postulate of linguistics in Chapter 1. One cannot limit the study of a language to that of its standard, or major, variety. For not only is a language composed of a multiplicity of dialects, registers, and styles, but even *within* a dialect the major or grammatical aspect is always being subverted by the minor, or remainder-like aspect. This is how we can go from the consideration of a linguistic formation, conceived as an unstable collection of dialects, to the equally unstable conjunction of *langue* and remainder. There is external (interlinguistic), but also internal (intralinguistic) minority. Majority means standards of behaviour, but also power and domination. As such, the majority always leaves out, or excludes, a minority that always returns and threatens to subvert: the necessity of violence lies deep in the structure of language.

I shall give two instances of this. One is borrowed from Deleuze and Guattari, the other is derived from their work. Their attitude to the corpus of Kafka's work is not one of interpretation. They are not looking for archetypes, binary oppositions, or Freudian fantasies. What they are looking at is Kafka's machines, the experiments he engages in, the politics he enacts. What they are analysing is not an individual author, but an arrangement, with its two faces, a collective arrangement of utterance on one side, a mechanical arrangement of desire on the other. The object of a tale like *Metamorphosis*, or of a short story like 'In the Penal Colony', with its famous execution machine, is such an arrangement. Minor literature (the subtitle of Deleuze and Guattari's *Kafka* is 'Towards a Minor Literature') is not concerned with the bourgeois values of eros and the individual. It has three characteristics.

(1) It is deterritorialized. This is Kafka's double-bind, as a Czech Jew. He cannot abstain from writing; he cannot write in German, which is not *his* language; he cannot write in any other language. None of the three languages involved is endowed with a fixed and stable territory.

(2) It is political. There is no question here of families, couples, and individuals. In a work of minor literature, like Kafka's, the family triangle, the old Oedipal story are immediately connected with other structures – bureaucratic, economic, legal, and political. The relationship between father and son goes far beyond the limits of the family and acquires political value.

(3) It is collective. A work of minor literature has no more an

individual author than it has an individual subject. There is no
subject in literature, neither hero nor masterly writer. The letter
K which Kafka so often uses refers not to a character or
narrator, but to a mechanical and collective arrangement.

It is easy to understand that the term 'minor literature' does not
merely refer to a type of literature, the marginal production of
second-rate authors. It refers to the revolutionary conditions of all
literature, to the instability and violence of all language. My second
illustration comes from the work of Thomas Hardy, and notably
Tess of the d'Urbervilles.[26] There is a well-known problem about
Hardy's style. He never went to Oxford and his style smacks of the
self-educated (one would not have far to go to find such patronizing
judgements, Somerset Maugham and Henry James being prime
offenders). This is a typical comment by David Lodge: 'There is the
Hardy who can recreate dialect speech with flawless authenticity,
who shows how closely he is in touch with the life of an agrarian
community through being in touch with its idiom; and there is the
Hardy speaking of "the quality" in orotund syntax and learned
vocabulary, the Hardy who studied *The Times*, Addison and Scott
to improve his style.'[27] What this so-called incoherence points to is
a contradiction within Hardy's style, as the major dialect clashes
with minor ones.

The same linguistic contradiction seems to apply to his character,
Tess. In the third chapter of the novel, we are told that Tess 'spoke
two languages; the dialect at home, more or less; ordinary English
abroad and to persons of quality.'[28] The presence of the phrase 'the
quality' in Lodge's text shows that he is aware of this parallelism
between the linguistic positions of author and character. In a
famous passage of his autobiography (published under the name of
his second wife), Hardy claims to have lived 'a triple existence
unusual for a young man – what he used to call, in looking back, a
life twisted of three strands – the professional life, the scholar's life
and the rustic life.'[29] Three lives, three languages – linguistic
fragmentation is common to Thomas and Tess. The question of
Hardy's style becomes, beyond the usual paternalism, the question
of how he managed to construct an auctorial monophone out of this
dialectal polyphony. And since the result is obviously polyphonic,
or at least contradictory, the question is to assess the mixture of
major and minor that makes up the apparent incoherence of his
style.

The contradiction is not only within the text (Hardy's style in *Tess* is dual); it is also the object of the text. The story of Tess is one of linguistic learning (of the standard dialect) and linguistic repression (of the minor ones) – The English she learns at school versus her own Wessex English. At the beginning of the sixth section, Alec wonders about Tess's progress: 'How is it that you talk so fluently now? Who has taught you such good English?' The reader knows the price she has had to pay for her education – and so does Tess herself, when she answers: 'I have learnt things in my troubles' (p. 301). Tess's tragedy springs from triple oppression: linguistic (her own idiom has been repressed, and she has had to learn how to talk 'properly'), sexual (the language she has to learn is spoken by men, her men – Angel and Alec) and social (the dialect recedes, as the agrarian society of which it is part gives way to industrialization and urbanization: in Hardy's own terms, the railway has reached Dorchester). Tess is a speaker of two incompatible languages, and in the end she dies of this contradiction, exactly as the local dialect dies and is replaced by 'correct' English. In other words, what the contradiction expresses is a linguistic, and therefore also a historical, conjuncture, 'change in the village'. The change is social, for the social structure of the village is in a state of upheaval, and certain strata, as the story of Tess's family demonstrates, are being uprooted and proletarized. But it is also, inextricably, linguistic, as the emotive language of the restricted group ('Tess Durbeyfield at this time of her life was a mere vessel of emotion untinctured by experience. The dialect was on her tongue to some extent, despite the village school', p. 9) gives way to the unified language of the nation-state, which conceals the polyphony of local and social idioms.

This contradiction in the character is central to the novel, where it takes the displaced form of a duality of times and system of values. There are two times in the novel, as there are two languages. The first is the time of myth, of the eternal return of seasons, of May dances and harvest feasts, of the repetition of inevitable acts, seduction and fall, birth and death, which are inscribed in the Book of Destiny. But this folk-time is being encroached upon by the irreversible time of history – a linear advance towards tragic catastrophe and social progress. We have, on the one hand, the time of verisimilitude, of the computable five years that are necessary for the story of Tess to unfold; and, on the other hand, the time of folklore, the year and a day of old ballads, the return of seasons that keep time at a standstill, the change of season having symbolic rather than chronological import. And there are two systems of values, which we shall call Nature and Culture for short and inadequate. (They are embodied in discourses and clichés.) Thus, Angel and Tess are opposed as a man of culture versus a 'daughter of nature', but also as a slave to conventions versus one who trusts her instinct, a man of achievement versus a woman whose moral tendencies are nobler than her acts ('her moral value having to be reckoned not by achievement but by tendency' p. 256). These opposed systems of values, one distinctly Victorian, the other immemorial, produce not so much characters as collective arrangements of utterance.

The intra-narrative opposition between arrangements of utterance has an extra-narrative correlative in the writing of the novel, since, as we have seen, there is no authorial 'suture',[30] no narrative monophone capable of unifying the babble of voices and discourses into an authoritative, because authorial, idiom. There is no vantage point from which the writer is able to represent the linguistic conjuncture as a whole, for he is part of it. But in this domain the failure of suture is of more value than its success, as it lets reality, i.e. the clash between the minor and major dialects, come to the fore, even obtrude. Stylistic incoherence is the aptest way of expressing linguistic violence. There is no doubt that in this linguistic–historical process violence is involved, that the social violence of dissolution and change (the best illustration of which is Tess's widowed mother camping with her family near the tomb of their forefathers in Kingsbere, because she has been made homeless) is redoubled by the linguistic violence of which Tess is the victim: the violence of slogans (we remember the slogan painted on the gate, when she returns home, pregnant but unmarried: 'THY, DAMNATION, SLUMBERETH, NOT. 2. PET. ii. 3', p. 76 – where the intruding commas insist on the collective force of authoritative speech and the authority is duly mentioned in the slogan itself); the pedagogic violence of imposed schooling, as in the passage where Tess is enjoying the folk-practice of peeling lords and ladies, and Angel, with the best of intentions, intervenes: 'Never mind about the lords and ladies. Would you like to take up any course of study – history, for instance?' (p. 122); the violence of naming, which appears in the destiny imposed on Tess by her family name, and in the ironic and disastrous attempt to go back from the countrified Durbeyfield to the historical but also progressive, because urban,

THE VIOLENCE OF LANGUAGE

d'Urberville (in which the urban character is redoubled: '*Urb*' and '*ville*').

That incoherence is the aptest expression of violence clearly appears in what is probably the most famous sentence in *Tess*: '"Justice" was done, and the President of the Immortals, in Aeschylean phrase, had ended his sport with Tess' (p. 387). The use of inverted commas and capital letters, the indication of an explicit allusion (to *Prometheus Bound*, I, 169), show that in this sentence, ascribed to the narrator, more than one voice is speaking. This short sentence speaks the language of law and justice (the legal cliché), of myth and high literature, but also of modern economic life (the phrase 'the President of the Immortals' turns Mt Olympus into the seat of a limited liability company), and of the hunt ('sport'). The narrator's irony joins these various discourses into a single sentence, but does not reduce them to unity. The style is unstable, it is not 'easy' or 'elegant', it is no style. Too many voices speak at the same time. But this is also the only way for the narrator to give vent to his rage at the physical (but also social and linguistic) violence done to Tess in this the execution scene. Hardy's grandeur lies in his ability not to stifle this Babel of voices, not to unify them into a coherent style. In this incongruous mixture, the real speaks – the real of a linguistic conjuncture, of the violence of language. This violence is constitutive of Hardy's style, the defects of which are its symptoms. Far from being 'orotund', Hardy's style is faithful to the violent reality of language. If the novel is based on a contradiction, if it is a myth retelling the age-old opposition between Nature and Culture, folklore and history, *aiôn* and *chronos*, and if this narrative contradiction is a metaphor of the instability and violence of language, Hardy's own stylistic contradiction is the best possible reflection of this. His stylistic gift lies in the fact that he does unleash the violence of language.

In *Tess of the d'Urbervilles*, the heroine is subjected *to* physical violence; she is also subjected *by* linguistic violence. She becomes a subject through language, a process that, as we have seen, is neither easy nor innocuously quiet. So far, I have adopted the point of view of the linguistic formation and collective arrangement of utterance – of the clash between a major and a minor dialect. But I cannot do this without also considering the point of view of the subject, of his interpellation by language. This is where I shall attempt to use the insights of Althusser's theory of ideology. This I shall do by evoking an agonistic view of linguistic exchange, as analysed by the French psychologist, François Flahaut, in terms of 'places'.

246

The standard theory of linguistic exchange is Grice's account of conversation as a cooperative undertaking. Even if our experience of actual conversations, of dialogue in Pinter's plays, and of the dead metaphors that talk of argument in terms of war, does not tally with his account, this is no objection. The cooperative situation described by Grice is an ideal one, as the concept of 'exploitation', of which I have made use, shows. Exactly as it is no objection to Rawls's theory of justice that his 'initial situation', where principles of fairness would of necessity be chosen by rational subjects entering into a social contract, has never obtained, nor is ever likely to obtain. Pointing out the prevalence of actual injustice is no way to refute a theory of justice (at least at first sight). However, it is possible to object to Grice's irenic ideal situation. Thus, we might ask why he chooses ideal *irene* rather than ideal *agôn*. If we abstract and idealize, why not choose the violent aspects of conversation as a starting point? The answer is easy: because Grice's purpose is to save language as an instrument for information and communication. But adopting the point of view of the remainder impels us to raise objections to this, on two counts. First, the student of the remainder is concerned with language as a whole, not with an idealized abstraction. He rejects the whole process of idealization and its concomitant exclusion, be the result *langue* or the postulate of pragmatic cooperation. Second, he also rejects an instrumental conception of language, preferring a view that foregrounds the contradiction between LS and ISL, the uneasy mixture of disorder and order, remainder and *langue*. Linguistic mastery (ISL) is never an initial or ideal datum, but always the result of labour, in all senses of the word, the difficult emergence of communication out of struggle, separation, and misunderstanding. These two objections are two reasons for considering the alternative view of conversation put forward by Flahaut in *La Parole intermédiaire*.[31]

Flahaut starts with a critique of Jakobson's diagram of communication, which allows no room for implicit exchange. His aim is to analyse the implicit meaning in linguistic interaction. In this, he finds himself close to Anglo-Saxon pragmatics, for the notion of illocutionary force involves the production and conveyance of non-explicit meaning. His theses, therefore, are presented as developments of the conceptions of Austin and the French pragmatist Osward Ducrot. In order to go further than they do, Flahaut draws on Althusser's theory of subjectivation as interpellation – as exemplified in the everyday act of hailing. When the policeman blows his whistle, I am always convinced, whether it is the case or not, that *I* am being arrested. The insight he gains from Althusser is that illocutionary force acts not only on the addressee but also on the sender, and that its function in both cases is to ascribe a place within a social system of places. By accomplishing a speech act, by issuing an order for instance, the speaker also tells the hearer (and attempts to force him to accept) who he is for him and what he, the hearer, must recognize the speaker as being for him. In other words, there is implicit demand in a speech act – and every utterance is a speech act in this sense, since even constatives have illocutionary force. To use Lacan's example, saying to a woman 'you are my wife' attempts to impose on her all the duties of that position and claims for the speaker the duties and rights of the symmetrical position – exactly as uttering the words 'I love you' requests that both parties, speaker and hearer alike, occupy certain positions in the interpersonal exchange. Two examples, taken from Flahaut's text, will suffice. A son phones his mother, who lives in the country, to tell her that his business will soon take him close to where she lives, and that he will be able to come and see her. She answers: 'Rather than going to a hotel, come home for the night; it will save you the hotel bill.' The answer is, on the face of it, informative. It is undeniably true that sleeping at home will be cheaper – financially at least, but perhaps not emotionally. For the mother's answer also ascribes her son and herself two symmetrical places: the deserted mother and the selfish son. If a performative involves explicit illocution, insinuation, a familiar language game, involves implicit, but no less efficient, force. The second example comes from Proust, where Mme Verdurin asks Baron de Charlus: 'Would you know a ruined nobleman whom I could employ as a porter?' The answer must be quoted in French, the English language being sadly deficient in past subjunctives: *'Je craindrais que les visiteurs élégants ne s'arrêtassent à la loge'* (I am afraid elegant callers might not go beyond the porter's lodge). Behind the explicit exchange – a straightforward request for information that gets a negative, if indirect, answer – another, implicit, dialogue, the essential part of the exchange, is going on. So much so that we feel that whether Mme Verdurin actually needs a porter is irrelevant – if she did, it would only be a pretext for the expression of her desire, which is a desire for recognition, the desire to ascribe places to herself and to Charlus, or rather to force him to recognize a hierarchy of places in which she, a rich *parvenue*, is superior, by virtue of her fortune, to an impoverished aristocrat.

THE VIOLENCE OF LANGUAGE

THE VIOLENCE OF LANGUAGE

This demand is what Charlus answers, directly this time, by denying it – the common fate of demands of all description. His answer, beyond the explicit words, must be glossed in the following manner: 'You may be rich, but there is something that money cannot buy, the inherited elegance and culture of the aristocrat.' From this point of view, the use of the past subjunctive, a mark of linguistic sophistication, is essential. Here, literally speaking, grammar is power. It assigns a place to speaker and hearer, and turns Mme Verdurin's attempted hierarchy upside down.

These examples are meant to have general value. There is a theory of linguistic exchange involved in this, and a theory of the constitution of subjects by language. 'Each subject [Flahaut claims] accedes to selfhood from and within a system of places which exceeds him by far; there is no word that is not addressed from a place and does not ascribe his correlative place to the hearer'.[32] The word I translate as 'selfhood' is *'identité'*: it has the advantage of being ambiguous between a psychological and a legal meaning ('identity card'). Familial or social language games are not in fact real games, where players contractually accept rules and can symmetrically change places. The place that parents unconsciously assign to the unborn child, for instance by giving it the name of a deceased sibling or a revered grandparent, will partly determine both its identity and its destiny. The same is true of the place the social formation assigns to its members within the relations of production. 'Social and interpersonal relationships make up a "game" which nobody is allowed to opt out of, and in which relations of force [*rapports de force*] are endowed with a violence which constantly overrules the conventions which attempt to contain it'.[33] The reader of novels is familiar with this situation, of which Barthes has given us the theory. When we read the first sentence of a novel, we are addressed by a narrator who must establish his place, the place of the master of the game, and who also must ascribe a place to us, the place of the recipient of imparted knowledge, of the sharer in commonsense values and reasonable ideas, of the object of narrative manipulation. Our 'you' must answer the summons of the narrative 'I'. When we read the first sentence of *Jane Eyre*, 'There was no possibility of taking a walk that day', we are not only hailed by a striking new voice, but given a modicum of background information – these people habitually take a walk – and asked to share a mood, as we realize that the first meaningful word of the novel is 'no'. The heroine–narratrix has taken us in hand. We know our place, and we grant her hers.

249

I intend to illustrate Flahaut's theory of places, and an anti-Grician, agonistic, theory of conversation, by commenting on a page from *Alice's Adventures in Wonderland*. In Chapter 8, the Queen's game of croquet is in full swing. Things, however, are not rosy, as more and more heads are ordered to be cut off. But Alice has a friendly visitor who asks her about the game:

'How do you like the Queen?' said the Cat in a low voice.

'Not at all,' said Alice: 'she's so extremely – ' Just then she noticed that the Queen was close behind her, listening: so she went on ' – likely to win, that it's hardly worth while finishing the game.'

The Queen smiled and passed on.

'Who *are* you talking to?' said the King, coming up to Alice, and looking at the Cat's head with great curiosity.

'It's a friend of mine – a Cheshire Cat,' said Alice: 'allow me to introduce it.'

'I don't like the look of it at all,' said the King: 'however, it may kiss my hand, if it likes.'

'I'd rather not,' the Cat remarked.

'Don't be impertinent,' said the King, 'and don't look at me like that!' He got behind Alice as he spoke.

'A cat may look at a king,' said Alice. 'I've read that in some book, but I don't remember where.'

'Well, it must be removed,' said the King very decidedly; and he called to the Queen, who was passing at the moment, 'My dear! I wish you would have this cat removed!'

The Queen had only one way of settling all difficulties, great or small. 'Off with his head!' she said without even looking round.

'I'll fetch the executioner myself,' said the King eagerly, and he hurried off.[34]

A Grician view of conversation could be developed roughly along the following lines: the aim of the speakers is to exchange information; there must be fair play in the exchange (one takes one's appointed turn, abstains from interrupting, etc.); there must be a will to agree and compromise (one must consider the other's point of view, abstain from issuing threats or indulging in verbal terrorism); and there must be sincerity in the exchange: participants must mean what they say and say what they mean. Our passage exposes this as a myth. Language does not work that way. If idealize we must, why not elaborate agonistic maxims of verbal struggle? You may not say what you mean, or not mean what you say; you may lie; you may fight with tooth and claw, as long as your verbal tactics suit your strategy, which must be to assert yourself at the expense of your opponent, to place him and to place yourself. And this is indeed what happens here.

Alice does not always say what she means. At the beginning of the passage, she starts a sentence ('she is so extremely – ') and ends it in an entirely unexpected manner, because she has realized that the Queen of Hearts is listening. She obviously meant something nasty ('Not at all, she is so extremely vicious'), but what she actually says is neutral. This, of course, is an extremely common language game, the white lie, on which politeness, which is a form of linguistic cooperation that does not conform to Grice's maxims, is based. (But one could easily envisage a pragmatic theory that would include a 'politeness principle'.[35]) What is interesting here is the (mild) violence done to language, i.e. Alice's syntactic skill. The beginning of the sentence requires that it should end on an adjective. But to use an epithet ('she's so extremely Adj') would mean qualifying 'she', that is, passing judgement on the Queen. Which in turn would be dangerous and impolite if sincere, and mendacious if complimentary. For Alice would lower herself if she uttered what she cannot mean: 'she's so extremely nice.' Besides, such an ending would be contradictory with the beginning of her speech: 'Not at all!' Alice has almost blundered, with the result that her head is at risk. But she manages to turn the situation to her advantage, and her insult into a compliment, by a feat of syntactic daring. She manages to turn a personal construction into an impersonal one, by using what Chomskyan linguists call the 'subject raising transformation', which goes (I simplify, and ignore the latest developments of the theory) from 'it is extremely likely that she will win' to 'she is extremely likely to win'. The subjective judgement on the Queen becomes an apparently objective judgement on her performance. The well-bred Victorian miss is a consummate hypocrite. So she must be, if she is to survive in the world of conversation, where survival of the most eloquent is the rule.

There is no denying Alice's skill when, a few lines later, she quotes a proverb: 'A cat may look at a king.' A proverb is a good instance of a case when one utters words, but does not aim at their literal meaning – a sort of extended dead metaphor, which shows that language itself denies the postulate of sincerity. Unless of course we adopt Davidson's analysis of dead metaphors, and decide that the only meaning of the sentence is the metaphorical, or proverbial one: there are things an inferior may do in the presence of his superior. But this ocurrence is the case *par excellence* when it is impossible to hold such a view, for the said inferior and superior are, on this (highly unlikely) occasion, precisely a cat and a king. This is the *best* use of the proverb, for it is the only one in which the literal meaning coincides with the figurative; and it is also the *worst*, for this coincidence precludes the generalization on which the proverb is based. Because it is too apt, the proverb ceases to mean; because it is too true, it becomes false. There is in this an implicit judgement on Grice's view of language – exact literalness, or saying what one means, is no solution.

Alice's cleverness, however, does not only lie in the inapt aptness of her proverb. It lies in the mere fact that she uses a proverb to protect herself, as a move in the verbal battle that is going on between Cat and King, and in which she sides with the Cat, but does not wish to become involved. The proverb allows her to do just that, by withdrawing any responsibility for her utterance under the veil of commonsense. Again, she chooses the advantages of impersonality, and draws on the fact that language, far from always expressing the subject's meaning in a straightforward and transparent manner, allows her to evade responsibility. But in order to understand Alice's position, we must go back to the verbal battle, and to its ultimate aim: gaining ground, forcing the opponent to recognize one's claim to a superior status, or putting him to flight. Such indeed are the contents of the principle of struggle – not the linguistic equivalent of Rawls's contractual cooperation, but the dialectic of master and slave. I fight with words in order to compel my opponent to recognize me and to adopt the image of myself I wish to impose on him.

This is undoubtedly the strategy of the King in this passage. First, he gives the Cat permission to kiss his hand. Naturally, beneath this permission, there lies a concealed order, and the utterance is an indirect speech act. He is actually demanding that the Cat should kiss his hand, i.e. pay allegiance to him, recognize him as a King, whether he likes it or not. This is why he is most put out when the Cat answers 'I'd rather not.' Second, he calls the Cat 'it', rather than 'she', as is customary when you address an unknown pussy, or 'he', as the Queen, who is more frank, because her violence is physical rather than strictly verbal, does a few moments later. In so doing, he refuses to treat him or her as a person. Third, at this stage he does not even address the Cat directly, but only through Alice; not in the second, but in the third person. In other words, he places the Cat in the position of the object of discourse, not of a potential subject: the position of someone who is deprived of the right to talk. This strategy gives him a place, the place of the King, hierarchically superior to a mere cat.

But by talking about the Cat, the King betrays his interest in him – also, as will appear later, his fear of him. He is 'looking at the Cat's head with great curiosity'. This is understandable. The Cat has chosen to let his head, and his head only, appear, and a head without a body is a surprising sight, even for a king. But the very rarity of the spectacle puts the Cat on an equal footing with the King. It is he, the King, who is compelled to demand the Cat's obeisance. And if he demands it, it means first that he is in need of it, and, second, that it may not be forthcoming. As we know, demand is the expression not of need, but of desire, and its unconscious aim is never to be satisfied. So that the Cat fulfils the secret desire of the King, or (which is the same thing) justifies his secret fear, by answering as he does. In so doing, he also undermines the King's hierarchic position, rejects the system of places the King is trying to impose on him, and substitutes his own, where Cat and King are equal (or at least where the Cat remains a free agent whatever happens). We note – a situation reminiscent of Pinter's plays – that the solidity of one's position is in inverse ratio to the amount of speech one utters.

As a result, the King is compelled, first to address the Cat directly, thus elevating him to the level of a second person ('Don't be impertinent'), and, second, to confess his impotence by issuing not orders but interdictions. If I say to someone 'Don't do this!', it implies that he has the capacity or will to do it, and also that it is my belief that he is on the point of doing it or already doing it. Which is the case here, as the Cat has already been 'impertinent' and is looking at the King ('Don't look at me like that!'). These interdictions mark the beginning of the King's retreat. This is confirmed by the further confession of defeat that he makes by gesture, not words: 'He got behind Alice as he spoke.' A rather pathetic king, afraid of a cat, and hiding behind a little girl. As for the Cat, he says nothing – which seems to make him all-powerful, exactly as the King's unceasing prattle makes him weaker.

After Alice, with due caution, has acknowledged impersonal support for the Cat, the King is defeated. He has abandoned his linguistic place, he no longer attempts to fight. When he exclaims 'it must be removed', the passive is used so that the agent can be erased, with the implication that the agent in question is not 'I': it must be removed by some other person, but not him. Who that person is soon becomes clear. The King calls the Queen as a child calls its father, using an ingratiating 'my dear' which proclaims his subservience. This is no king, but a weak prince consort. When he says 'I' again, in his last words, it is only to acknowledge defeat. He regains the position of linguistic subject only by leaving the Cat in possession of the field – and he leaves 'hurriedly'.

This is a violent world. The violence of insinuation and threat, as the opponents try to gain the most favourable position, always threatens to give way to physical violence, as occurs when the King hurries away to look for the executioner. Alice, it must be said, fares rather well in these unfriendly surroundings. She holds her own, gives as good as she gets, displays skill and prudence. The struggle, however, is not finished, for the King comes back. And he is not alone.

> When she got back to the Cheshire Cat, she was surprised to find quite a large crowd collected round it: there was a dispute going on between the executioner, the King, and the Queen, who were all talking at once, while all the rest were quite silent, and looked very uncomfortable.
>
> The moment Alice appeared, she was appealed to by all three to settle the question and they repeated their arguments to her, though, as they all spoke at once, she found it very hard to make out exactly what they said.
>
> The executioner's argument was, that you couldn't cut off a head unless there was a body to cut it from: that he had never had to do such a thing before, and he wasn't going to begin at *his* time of life.
>
> The King's argument was, that anything that had a head could be beheaded, and that you weren't to talk nonsense.
>
> The Queen's argument was that, if something wasn't done about it in less than no time, she'd have everybody executed, all round. (It was this last remark that had made the whole party look so grave and anxious.)
>
> Alice could think of nothing else to say but 'It belongs to the Duchess: you'd better ask *her* about it.'

'She's in prison,' the Queen said to the executioner: 'fetch her here.' And the executioner went off like an arrow.

The Cat's head began fading away the moment he was gone, and, by the time he had come back with the Duchess, it had entirely disappeared: so the King and the executioner ran wildly up and down looking for it, while the rest of the party went back to the game.[36]

Although the fight starts again, it is not the same battle. The Cat has won. He utters not a word – he is in a position of mastery, as Tenniel's sketch of the scene shows, in which the Cat's head towers above rather puny cardboard characters, as the head of God the Father dominates various figures of saints or benefactors in medieval paintings. Besides, the Cat settles the matter for good by disappearing when he decides to, like a withdrawn epiphany, reducing the King to a state of frenzy. In which it appears that, for the King at least, desire was involved in the engagement.

While the Cat is in the position of God, the battle goes on among the mortals. It is no longer waged according to the rules of conversation or politeness, for logic is now the main weapon. And since 'they all spoke at once', this is emphatically no longer a cooperative conversation. This logical controversy, however, is as much of a verbal struggle as the dialogue that preceded it. It must be analysed in terms of places claimed and gained. This is not so much the logic of pure reasoning, as the dialectic, or rather the eristics, of sophistry.

The first two positions, the executioner's and the King's, form a paradox – an absurd one, produced as it is by an impossible object, a head without a cat, but a paradox nevertheless. In order to behead a creature, you have to have a body to separate the head from, otherwise the creature is, so to speak, ready-beheaded; in order to behead a creature, all you need, etymologically speaking, is a head. We must note that the executioner's argument would be sounder, for in a sense the Cat is already beheaded, were not this head so obviously alive. So that we must also sympathize with the King, for in a normal world (in the world of our experience but not in all possible worlds – there is no necessity involved) to behead entails to kill – with beheading, there is no need of any proviso as in the legal formula for hanging, 'you shall hang by the neck until death ensueth'.

However, we must also note that both the King's and the

executioner's arguments involve more than logic. Both use irrelevant propositions, thus showing that their use of logic is purely instrumental, and dependent on their struggle for places. The executioner appeals to precedent (this is the bureaucrat's excuse) and age (the argument becomes subjective, therefore illogical). The King uses verbal terrorism by saying 'don't talk nonsense'. In so doing, he is merely stating his refusal to listen to the other party's argument. Unwittingly, however, he is undermining his own argument. What else but nonsense can you talk in a nonsense tale?

But there is a third position, which has nothing to do with logic, not even at the level of appearances – the Queen's position, which demonstrates that in practice logic is of no importance, that it is only a weapon, among others, in the verbal battle. Not the ground rules for coherent thought and rational argument, but a means of defeating one's opponent. And since it is reduced to the rank of a weapon, it gives way to the ultimate weapon, brute force, might as opposed to rational right. This is what the parenthesis indicates: '(It was this last remark that made the whole party look so grave and anxious)'. There is no solution of continuity between verbal and physical violence. Behind the polite veneer of discussion and logical argument, the truth about conversation is revealed at last. There is violence and desire involved in linguistic practice. I argue from this rather than that position not because it is right but because my desire is involved in it, and my argument is a form of violence imposed on my opponent – if it fails, I may resort to straightforward force.

In this passage, as indeed in the preceding one, Alice does not take a direct part in the struggle. She manages to remain outside the confusion. By which she shows that she has learnt the rules of the game – and, if her adventures can be described in terms of a quest for knowledge, this is the object of her learning. At the end of the tale, when she exclaims 'you are nothing but a pack of cards', the reader will recognize that she has fully mastered the rules of argument *qua* war. In a pastiche of Grice, we can summarize the rules in four maxims, to which I shall abstain from giving the names of Kantian categories:

(1) Conversation conforms to a strategy. The aim is to expel your opponent from the field, i.e. to achieve either his physical departure or his retreat into a state of speechless rage or mute imbecility.
(2) Talking is not as good a tactic as silence. It is often a position of

weakness, and ignoring your opponent's implicit demand is usually a better choice.

(3) But this supposes that the battle has already been won. He who talks *recognizes* the other's position, i.e. becomes his slave. In the first stages, one must talk, in order not to inform, but to assert. Take care of your place, and meaning will take care of itself. Nonsense in this context may make more sense than sense.

(4) Language conveys not information but desire (first of all, the desire to be recognized) and violence (which is necessary in order to achieve recognition).

If I have spent some time in the company of Alice, a company so pleasant that I need not apologize for dawdling, it is because I think the insights into the working of language that we have gained from these passages can be generalized. My path so far has taken me from the straightforward physical violence of the shriek to the indirect, 'immaterial' social violence of insults, orders, insinuations, of performatives in general and utterances endowed with illocutionary force, that is, of *all* utterances. There is violence involved in the linguistic struggle for places, i.e. in the linguistic process of subject-ivation. One becomes a subject by acquiring a linguistic place and imposing it on others.

Perhaps it might be thought that the drift of my argument has taken me a long way from my initial subject, the theory of the remainder. Not at all. The first passage from *Alice* I have analysed, which turned upon the linguistic status of the adjective 'likely', involved the kind of exploitation of the rules of *langue* that we have learnt to recognize as characteristic of the remainder. More profoundly, it is now quite clear that what I have called the work of the remainder, with its obvious parallelism with the Freudian dream-work, joke-work, etc., has something to do with the workings of the unconscious. The remainder is the expression of the workings of the unconscious in so far as the unconscious is 'structured like a language'.

An example will, I hope, help to make this clear. In September 1988, J. M. Le Pen, the leader of the French National Front and a Euro-MP, grossly insulted a liberal cabinet minister called Durafour. Addressing an audience of party faithful, in conditions reminiscent of an older and more sinister type of eloquence, he used straight-forward insults and indulged in dubious jokes on the minister's name. One of them has become famous – he called him '*Durafour crématoire*' ('*four crématoire* is the name for the gas chambers in the Nazi concentration camps). The question was debated in the press – amidst universal condemnation – whether it was a deliberate insult or a slip of the tongue, revealing a deep-seated racism in M. Le Pen. It is immaterial to me whether he was speaking language or being spoken by it. In both cases, the remainder is clearly at work, and it shows that linguistic violence can use the paths of the rhizome – the violence of insult, but also the collective violence of the linguistic conjuncture ('there are things one does not joke about', as the press said – for indeed words crystallize the violence of historical conjunctures), the violence of the unconscious. For the most striking aspect of the insult was its apparent gratuitousness. Not only was the minister in question, to the best of my knowledge, not Jewish (his being a Jew would not of course have made the joke any less odious), but he was not even one of Le Pen's arch-enemies, which might have accounted for the violence of the attack. It was a case not of anger blinding the speaker, but, as the Lacanian psychoanalyst Gerard Miller said, of the Other speaking (in the case of Le Pen, this Other is definitely anti-Semitic),[37] of the remainder, i.e. the unconscious emerging into language, speaking the speaker, whether he wanted it or not.

LANGUAGE, TRUTH, AND FICTION

I know no better illustration of the violence of language than a short story by Jonathan Meades, *Filthy English*.[38] The hero, Roderick Spode, is a linguist, a lexicographer to be more precise, who lives alone with his widowed mother. His field of research is the thousand and one ways of naming a foot in English slang. The reason for his interest in this is personal: when he was a child, his left foot was crushed by falling masonry during a German air-raid that killed his father and sister, and he still has a bad limp. When the story starts, a colleague has just informed him that, in a second-rate novel from the early 1950s, he has come across a new name for a foot, which, by the most extraordinary coincidence, is the same as the hero's family name: 'a spode'. We understand and share the hero's interest in the case, we sympathize with the eagerness, almost amounting to frenzy, with which he conducts his research, looking up specialized dictionaries, writing to fellow lexicographers. His research is vain – nobody has heard of the word, which appears to be a hapax. The only clue is the novel in which it was originally found. Since the author is dead, the hero travels to Southampton, which happens to be his own native town, to interview the widow. She has nothing to tell him, except that her husband was a stickler for detail, and that the character who uses the word 'spode' in the novel was based on a friend, now deceased. The only trail has proved to be a dead end. The hero decides to take advantage of the trip to look at the place of his birth. To his surprise, the house standing at 49 Colony Road is obviously old and cannot have been destroyed during the war. As he is looking at it, the owner comes out and offers to tell him the dark story of the house, which during the war was the scene of a dreadful crime.

The man who lived there at the time, one Spode, was a lunatic. He belonged to a bizarre religious sect whose members believed that Adolf Hitler was the true Messiah. In a fit of frenzy, finding his young daughter insulting a portrait of the great man, he trampled her to death, and had started on his son when he was stopped. During the trial, much was made of the gigantic size of his feet. He was declared *non compos mentis*, and spent forty years in a psychiatric asylum before being released. On the last page of the story, we learn that the hero has killed the owner of the house, in whom he has recognized his father, and is waiting at home for his mother, who is on holiday in Greece, in order to rape her.

But at this point we too have understood, roughly at the same time as Roderick Spode. The hints are in fact spread rather thick. The hero's mother, for instance, has sent him a postcard from Thebes. The hero's name is a quasi-anagram for Oedipus – an anagram that has the advantage that it makes explicit the presence of the root for 'foot', *'pod'*, which is concealed under the nominative form 'Oedipus' (the meaning of which in Greek is 'swollen foot').

It is easy to see why this is a perfect illustration of the violence of language. Violence there is, which affects bodies – the violence of murder and mutilation, rape and incest. But this violence is insepar-able from language; it dwells in language, in the form of the hero's destiny, in which every action is programmed by his name. The hero's name tells the truth of his being, a truth concealed and only discovered after the event, in the repetition of the archaic scene – a truth discovered through linguistic analysis. For truth lies in language, in the dictionary to be precise, since Spode is an author of dictionaries. And the dictionary has links with the human body, since the name that is asking to be added to it is the name of a part of the body – both the object of Roderick Spode's research and the locus of his infirmity. It is also linked to the world in so far as it is historical – this is the function of the mention of Hitler and the war. A signifier is circulating: it comes from outside the story, from our most archaic past, the past of the race and the past of the individual; and its force is exerted on the bodies of the characters.

The force of that circulating signifier, of that name, is also due to its remainder-like properties. For the story, consciously or not, uses devices similar to those of the great logophiliacs, Saussure, Roussel, Brisset, and Wolfson. It is based on an anagram – in a way, it is one of those hymns in which the text is produced by a pre-text that spells out the name of a god or a hero. As in Roussel, this fiction is generated by language, in the form of the remainder. It all sounds like one of Carroll's word-games: how can you go from 'Oedipus' to 'Spode' and back again. As in Wolfson, the object of the story is an exercise in *traducson*: Greek is translated into English, and vice versa. Lastly, as in Brisset, the origin of the story is an etymology that refers to a part of the human body: not the sex, but the foot. And if it were objected that I have described the same phenomenon four times, I would answer that my four delirious linguists shared the same intuition – the intuition of the link (which goes against the Saussurean principle of the arbitrary character of the sign) between language, or rather the remainder, history, and the body. To quote Deleuze, 'words carry with them a story of sex and love.' And the vector is the remainder, for in this story language does speak. If indeed the centre of the story is to be found in the passage from a proper name, Spode, to a common noun, a spode, Jonathan Meades has only made use of what the English language had made ready for him. 'Spode' is indeed a common noun in English, witness the following apocryphal passage: 'I was arranging a display of spode yesterday and I lost my balance; down came the spode crashing on the floor, three hundred pounds worth of it.' True, the word means not 'foot', but a type of china – the important point, however, is that the conversion has already taken place.

The most important lesson to be drawn from Meades' story, however, lies elsewhere – in the explanation it suggests of the origin of violence in language, which is to be found in too close a commerce with truth. Language is so devastatingly violent because it bears the traces of an archaic truth, because it is the locus of its compulsive reconstruction. This ought to make us reconsider our views about the relationships between language and truth, and substitute for them a Roderick Spode concept of truth-in-language, or rather, since I do not claim to have discovered this view, a Freudian concept of truth. I shall propose only the briefest sketch – I have tried to develop this conception in the context of a reading of Godwin's *Caleb Williams*.[39]

To put it roughly, the Saussurean concept of the autonomy of *langue*, or Grice's pragmatics of cooperative conversation, have one ultimate consequence (and, in the case of Grice, probable aim): to purify language, through idealization and exclusion, in order to save it for communication and the utterance of truth. On the other hand, a concept of non-autonomous, impure, remainder-riddled language, a weapon for struggle and a locus for violence, raises questions about the nature of the truth that can be uttered in it (rather than with it).

An answer has already been suggested by my reading of Favret-Saada's account of witchcraft. The whole violent and sometimes deadly process that she calls 'crisis of witchcraft' finds its origin in a fiction, an impossibility, a gross untruth, which nevertheless has the same effect on those who fall within its range as if it were true. It is simply not true that my neighbour is a witch, since witches there are none. But being pointed at, *named* as a witch, will affect him or her – remember the woman who died of fright – as if the accusation had been true. This is a case of an effect without a cause, which retroactively, and falsely, makes up a cause for itself. Of course, backward causality is not on the cards, and it will be objected that there is no need to have recourse to truth to account for the situation, since falsity can have nasty effects too – medieval witch-hunts made thousands of victims, on the basis of false accusations. But if we look at the presumed victim, the bewitched who is 'cured' by this fiction, we realize that truth may be involved after all – not the factual truth of events but the truth of the subject's desire, only attainable indirectly through fiction, and only recoverable through the work of interpretation, the talking cure. In other words, truth-in-language.

This is Freud's concept of truth, which he elaborated when he realized that his hysterical patients, who were all telling him the same awful story of seduction by uncle or father, with consequent trauma, could not all be telling the literal truth. One recalls the Masson controversy.[40] Masson accused Freud of having had cold feet, of taking part in a cover-up and retreating from the political and social implications of his discovery – Viennese bourgeois uncles and fathers *did* rape their nieces and daughters on a grand scale. But in arguing for the literal truth of the patient's story, Masson has theoretical cold feet. He wants to go back to the commonsense conception of an utterance as being straightforwardly true or false. In so doing, he misses Freud's breakthrough. The patients' stories were inextricably false (nobody has actually seduced them) and true (they express the truth of the patients', and perhaps of the fathers' or uncles', desires). Freudian truth is inseparable from fiction and language. A fiction has the effect of truth; language is both the medium and the instrument of the recovery of truth – a truth that has no other existence than in the linguistic work of interpretation that deciphers it.

I shall sum up this conception of truth-in-language in three theses:

(1) Truth is the unuttered content of the archaic scene, of which symptomatic occurrences of repetition are the representatives (*les tenants-lieu*).

(2) Truth is what is reached at the end of the process of interpretation – deduction in true intuition, at the moment of conclusion ('*le moment de conclure*').

(3) Truth is a force that circulates along the linguistic chain as along the subject's symptoms and personal history.

We recognize the first thesis what I have called the Freudian concept of truth as infantile trauma and fantasy. In the third, we recognize the truth that circulates in the crisis of witchcraft. The second thesis refers to a concept of truth defended by the Italian historian Carlo Ginzburg[41] – the non-Galilean concept of truth as intuition derived from hints and traces, the truth of the primitive hunter or of Sherlock Holmes rather than that of the scientist. Because I cannot develop them here, I shall end on a parable, as usual. It will seek to account for truth-in-language as that around which the subject is constructed, and that which it is impossible to utter – two broadly Lacanian propositions. In *Cronaca di un amore*, Antonioni's first film, a (falsely) jealous husband hires a private eye to spy on his wife and look into her past. The detective unearths a rather complicated story. She was in love with a man, who was engaged to another girl. The other girl died in an accident, which may have been murder, after which the lovers separated. But unearthing the old story has an effect. The former lover reappears on the scene. He comes to warn his old flame of the coming of the detective. As a result, they fall in love again and decide to kill her husband. On the night of the attempt, as the lover is waiting to murder him, the husband dies in a car accident. The lovers again separate. The jealous certainty of the husband has turned falsity into truth. A deadly truth, since the husband comes to occupy the third place, which was fatal to the other girl, and duly dies. And this truth is linked to repetition and symptom: in order to be together the lovers need to be separated by the presence of the living; in order to separate, they need the living to die. Jealous certainty is a force, exerted in language, that transforms error into truth and has deadly effect on bodies.

NOTES

1 H. Pinter, 'Request Stop', in *A Slight Ache and Other Plays*, London, Methuen, 1961.
2 E. Bréhier, *La Théorie des incorporels dans l'ancien stoïcisme*, Paris, Vrin, 1987, p. 2 (first published 1908).
3 G. Deleuze, *Logique du sens*, Paris, Minuit, 1969, p. 18.
4 S. Beckett, *Murphy*, London, John Calder, 1963, p. 120 (first published 1938).
5 M. de Certeau, *La Fable mystique*, Paris, Gallimard, 1982, passim.
6 L. Wolfson, *La Mère, musicienne, est morte . . .* , Paris, Navarin, 1984.
7 ibid., pp. 8–9. I cannot translate this into English: I must respect Wolfson's hostility to his native tongue.
8 *Perceval's Narrative*, edited by G. Bateson, New York, William Morrow, 1974.
9 ibid., p. 271.
10 Beckett, *Murphy*, op. cit., p. 105: 'Mr Endon was on parchment and Murphy had his tab: "Mr Endon, Apnoea, or any other available means." Suicide by apnoea has often been tried, notably by the condemned to death. In vain. It is a physiological impossibility.'
11 *Perceval's Narrative*, op. cit., p. 273.
12 ibid., p. 254.
13 ibid., p. 33.
14 ibid., p. 301.
15 J. Favret-Saada, *Les Mots, la mort, les sorts*, Paris, Gallimard, 1977.
16 ibid., p. 25; my translation.
17 M. Schneider, *Voleurs de mots*, Paris, Gallimard, 1985.
18 ibid., p. 284.
19 ibid., p. 285.
20 ibid., p. 286.
21 F. d'Agostino, *Chomsky's System of Ideas*, Oxford, Clarendon Press, 1986, p. 30. The reference to Chomsky is to *Rules and Representations*, Oxford, Blackwell, 1980, p. 118.

22 See J. P. Vinay and J. Darbelnet, *Stylistique comparée du français et de l'anglais*, Paris, Didier, 1958, p. 55.
23 K. Blixen, *Out of Africa*, Harmondsworth, Penguin, 1954, pp. 234–5 (first published 1937).
24 J. L. Austin, 'Performative Utterances', in *Philosophical Papers*, Oxford, Clarendon Press, 1970.
25 G. Deleuze and F. Guattari, *Kafka*, Paris, Minuit, 1975.
26 See J. J. Lecercle, 'The violence of style in Tess of the d'Urbervilles', in L. St John Butler (ed.), *Alternative Hardy*, London, Macmillan, 1989.
27 D. Lodge, 'Tess, nature and the voices of Hardy', in R. P. Draper (ed.), *Hardy, the Tragic Novels*, London, Macmillan, 1975, p. 171.
28 T. Hardy, *Tess of the d'Urbervilles*, London, Everyman's Library, 1984, p. 15.
29 F. E. Hardy, *The Life of Thomas Hardy, 1840–1928*, London, Macmillan, 1962, p. 33.
30 The concept originally comes from J. A. Miller, 'La Suture – Eléments de la logique du signifiant', *Cahiers pour l'Analyse*, Paris, 1966 (English translaton in *Screen*, Winter 1977/8, vol. 18, no. 4, pp. 24–34). An interesting use of the concept is made in E. Laclau and C. Mouffe, *Hegemony and Socialist Strategy*, London, Verso, 1985.
31 F. Flahaut, *La Parole intermédiaire*, Paris, Seuil, 1978.
32 ibid., p. 58.
33 ibid., p. 56.
34 L. Carroll, *The Annotated Alice*, Harmondsworth, Penguin, 1965, pp. 114–15.
35 See for instance G. N. Leech, *Principles of Pragmatics*, London, Longman, 1983.
36 Carroll, op. cit., pp. 115–7.
37 G. Miller, 'L'Infamie-réflexe', *Libération*, 5 September 1988, p. 5.
38 J. Meades, *Filthy English*, London, Paladin, 1986.
39 J. J. Lecercle, 'Vérité et répétition dans Caleb Williams', *Tropismes*, 4, Paris, 1989.
40 J. M. Masson, *The Assault on Truth*, Harmondsworth, Penguin, 1985.
41 C. Ginzburg, 'Spie. Radici di un paradigma indiziario', in *Il segno dei tre*, edited by U. Eco and T. A. Sebeok, Milan, Bompiani, 1983 (English translation published by Radius).

CONCLUSION

In one of her letters to her sister Cassandra, Jane Austen writes the following sentence: 'I am sick of myself & of my bad pens.' To which Chapman, that paragon among editors, adds a note: 'sic; JA did not write *puns*.'[1] Here is the remainder, at its most exhilarating. An unwitting pun on 'pen' is unwittingly duplicated in the note by a (bad) pun on 'sick'. At the very moment when Chapman is asserting that the speaker's control over his language will always be established in the end, the editor's mastery compensating for the edited author's slip of the pun, language (the remainder) reminds us that it, and no one else, is speaking, that whenever we believe that we rule over our words, we are in the grip of an unavoidable but nevertheless delusive illusion. But this is no cause for moaning and a sad face – the experience of meeting with the remainder at work is a profoundly joyful, almost erotic one. If we follow the French philosopher Clément Rosset in his Nietzschean wanderings,[2] we will recognize this as an instance of contact with the real of language. Not the reconstructed reality of the linguist, which is only an example of the grandiloquence of fake mastery, but the exhilaration of language being simply what it is, showing little respect for our need for logical structure and instrumentalization, but telling us, provided we take the trouble to look at what was concealed to us only because it lay right under our very eyes, what we are – that our world is our language.

I have adopted the grandiloquent and hubristic tone of conclusions. I am blowing my own remainder. Language has gone to my head, and prophetic frenzy makes me lay three bold claims to achievement, in the three fields that I have explored: linguistics, literature, and the philosophy of language.

The first claim is that the concept of the remainder wrongfoots

265

the dominant linguistic tradition of this century. Not that I claim to be the only one to have made the attempt. There is nothing new under the sun, not even my main concept. I had already written half the book when I discovered a short essay by F. Nef[3] where the concept was anticipated, or at least its name (*le résidu*) – another instance of language speaking the speaker, or, which is almost the same thing, of the *Zeitgeist* dictating his inventions to the eager theorist (that there is a need for a general theory of residues is demonstrated by the title of the book by the anthropologist Michael Thompson, *Rubbish Theory*).[4] I cannot even claim that my mode of approach is brand new, for it smacks too much of the now classic strategy of deconstruction: the founding dichotomies of linguistics have been inverted so that *parole* dominates *langue*, diachrony returns within synchrony, rule is destabilized by exception; the series of dichotomies is in turn seen as the expression of a central contradiction (between mastery of and possession by language); a supernumerary term, a term of excess, the remainder, is then introduced, which names the unnameable and overturns the paradigm; the dichotomies are only (but necessarily) maintained 'under erasure' (*sous rature*), and the myth of origins of linguistics is demythified. When the intoxication of the Sibyl has subsided, I may settle for a lesser claim: by describing the phenomena that I have called Brissetizing and Wolfsonizing, I think I have drawn our attention to crucial aspects of language that so far had been somewhat overlooked.

If I have been able to attempt the deconstruction of 'objectivist' linguistics (to use Husserl's term in his *Krisis*), it is because my main interest is in literature. The starting point of my research was a certain irritation with the limitations not only of structural linguistics (which was constitutionally unable to go beyond 'legal' sentences, more often than not of a trivial kind, and thus was of little help to the student of literature), but also of structural poetics, in the form of either Russian formalism and its followers or Greimas's semiotics. What I have tried to do is to explore the workings of poetic language in another direction (where a treatment of metaphor plays a central role). A conception of the remainder, of the Brissetizing and Wolfsonizing of language, provides perhaps a better, and certainly a new, approach to the poet's language, to the complexity and paradoxes of his relationship of means of expression that he masters and by which he is mastered. The remainder enables us to understand the workings of 'poetic imagination' better. Again, there is an aspect of swimming against the current in this, for the remainder, being a social–historical entity not a formal one (a code), takes us closer to the traditional concept of 'tradition' (reinterpreted, however, as an intralinguistic object) than to the founding concepts of structural poetics.

The last claim I make concerns the philosophy of language. There, my position has a strong continental flavour, smelling of garlic and full-bodied red wine. The dominant trend in the Anglo-Saxon world, with the notable exception of the followers of Wittgenstein, is a logicist one. The aim of philosophy of language (I caricature, of course) is usually not so much to describe as to purify natural languages – to preserve the possibility of communicative and referential uses, to save language for science. Even when the aim is only to describe, as in the theory of speech acts, another, underlying purpose soon appears – to preserve the possibility of scientific discussion and progress by defending a conception of meaning as intentional and of dialogue as cooperative. The title of Grice's seminal essay, 'Logic and Conversation', manages to weave all these threads together. Habermas's influential theory of communicative action also rests on such premises. Against this, I have tried to argue that linguistic exchange is a locus for relations of power, that far from occurring in a cooperative vacuum it depends on historical and linguistic conjuncture and often involves agonistic strategy and tactics. This, of course, implies a theory of the subject – of subjectification as subjection – that is incompatible with the subject as centre of consciousness and control which cooperation and intentional meaning require. Looking forward, and announcing if not a sequel to this book, at least research in progress, it seems to me that my conception of language ought to develop into a theory of ideology. Althusser's theory of interpellation and state apparatuses, which I have tried to revive, has gone out of fashion because it was never quite able to think the autonomous non-autonomy of language. This, I think, the concept of the remainder enables us to begin to conceive. It is high time we consigned the pseudo-Stalin's effort to the dustbins of history and started elaborating a Marxist conception of language, i.e. that we attempted to understand the collective materiality of language, which cannot simply be a neutral instrument independent of both base and superstructure.

One of Donald Barthelme's short stories is entitled 'Sentence'.[5] It does not, as one might expect, narrate the adventures of a human character. Adventures, some of them erotic, there are, but the reader

THE VIOLENCE OF LANGUAGE

soon realizes that the only hero of the tale is the sentence itself, and that the point of the story is to delay the implementation of the sentence of death that has been passed on it. The story, which lasts for seven pages, is in fact composed of a single sentence. This eponymous sentence does not wish to die, that is to end with a final stop, and uses all the rhetorical tricks that language can provide in order to prolong its temporary stay of execution. This, of course, is an emblem of the main point of this book – it is a superb instance of language being spoken by a speaker but also becoming a speaker itself and speaking the author. The only achievement I would really like to lay claim to is to have explored this aspect of the workings of language – to have provided empirical grounds of justification for Heidegger's famous formula, '*die Sprache spricht*'.

When the last fumes of prophecy have dissipated, only this remains: the infinite enjoyment of language as it unfolds – as it unfolds the reader who is trying to explicate the text. Language is the only Wonderland; what I have been doing is knocking at the garden door.

NOTES

1 J. Austen, *Selected Letters*, edited by R. W. Chapman, Oxford, Oxford University Press, 1985, p. 85, n. 1.
2 C. Rosset, *Le Réel: traité de l'idiotie*, Paris, Minuit, 1977.
3 F. Nef, 'Résidus, déchets et détritus', *Traverses*, 11, 1978, pp. 122–40.
4 M. Thompson, *Rubbish Theory*, Oxford, Oxford University Press, 1979.
5 D. Barthelme, 'Sentence', in *Forty Stories*, London, Secker & Warburg, 1987, pp. 157–63.

INDEX

269

INDEX

Cooper, D. 169, 170, 171
Corot, C. 52
corruption 73, 134–7, *181–8*,
214–20
Courbet, G. 52
Cratylus 31
cummings, e. e. *48–9*, 187
Curtius, E. R. 193

daft definition 68
Damourette and Pichon 22
Darmesteter, A. 57, 59
Davidson, D. 71–2, 146, 147, 156,
162, 164, 169, 171
decay of language 113–14
defeasibility 137
Deleuze, G. 175–8, 225, 226, 260
Deleuze, G. and Guattari, F. 33,
42–51, 52, 132–3, 179, 183–7, 194,
225, 226, 227, 242–3
délire 25, 56, 178
Derrida, J. 38
diachrony/synchrony 183–6
Dickens, C. 67
Dickinson, E. 162–5
dictionary 138–41
dream 128–9
Ducrot, O. 247

Eco, U. 137, 145
Eliot, T. S. 77
Eluard, P. 70, 103
encyclopaedia 138–41
Engels, J. 192
etymology *188–200*, 220
exaggeration 171–2
exception 22, 23
excess 60
exocentric compounds 90, 178
exploitation 122–5
extraposition 15–17, 22

Favret-Saada, J. *234–8*, 261
Flahaut, F. 246–9
folk-etymology 30, 74, 75, 76, 85,
90, 191, 194, 200
Fonagy, I. 47, *155–6*
Fowler, H. W. 83
Fowler, H. W. and Fowler, F. G. 204

Freud, S. 23, 36, 37, 56, 128, 231,
240, 261, 262
frontier 18, 19, 23, *24*, 55, 133
Fuselz, J. H. 76

Gascoyne, D. 166–7
gender 40
Ginzburg, C. 262
Godwin, S. 261
Grésillon, A. 91, 145–6, 147
Grice, H. P. 3, *43*, 122, *247*, 250,
251, 256, 261, 267
Grimm, J. 114, 120, 235
Guiraud, P. 188
Gunn, T. 78

Habermas, J. 267
Hardy, T. 243–6
Harris, R. 27
Hegel, G.W.F. 203, 207
Heidegger, M. 34, 71, *110–15*, 134,
136, 141, 184, 268
Herbert, G. 79
Higgins, A. *123–4*, 133
Hjelmslev, L. 225
Hoban, R. 214–220
homophony 39, 79, 98
Horne Tooke, J. 194, *196–9*, 200,
220
Humboldt, W. von 135, 136
Husserl, E. 153–4, 207, 266

ideology 107, 190, 227–8
illumination 170–1
indirection 174–5
indirect speech 44, 45
Isidore 191–4

Jakobson, R. 12, *130–2*, 144, 247
James, H. 243
Jameson, F. 207
Jennings, P. 66
Jesuitical verse 79
Joyce, J. 91, 93

Kafka, F. 50, 242–3
Kant, E. 106
Katz, J. J. 21
Keats, J. 86, 158, 171, 175